This OPUS edition, published in 1988, is an unabridged and unaltered re-publication of the work originally published by Munroe and Francis, Boston, Massachusetts, 1833.

Library of Congress Cataloging-in-Publication Data

Bourne, H.
  Flores poetici, the florist's manual.

  Originally published: Boston, Ma. : Munroe and Francis, 1833.
  Includes index.
  1. Flowers. 2. Flower gardening. I. Title. II. Title: Florist's
manual.
SB407.H66   1987   635.9   87-31443
ISBN 0-940983-19-2 (alk. paper)

Manufactured in the United States of America on "acid-free" stock.

OPUS Publications, Inc., Post Rd. P.O. Box 269
Guilford, Connecticut 06437

This is copy no. _208_ of 1,000.

America Blossoms

Fashions in flowers were changing just as surely in the horticultural world of 150 years ago as they are today. New introductions were the result of new discoveries, not the intensive breeding that is conducted today. Hermon Bourne's *Flores Poetici: The Florist's Manual* documents that world as it existed in 1833, describing the mix of exotic plants and New England field flowers that were cultivated in contemporary gardens. The seventy-three engravings that were hand painted in watercolors convey the surprise and delight that these flowers provided to their viewers.

OPUS Publications is delighted to collaborate with Old Sturbridge Village to make scarce materials from its Research Library available in facsimile editions. Also included in the "America Blossoms" collection are two titles by Joseph Breck, *The Young Florist, or Conversations about Flowers* (1833) and *The Flower Garden, or Breck's Book of Flowers* (1851).

We suggest you visit Old Sturbridge Village to see many of the flowers illustrated in Bourne growing in re-created period gardens. The Village is more than flower and vegetable gardens, it re-creates many aspects of work, family and community life in early nineteenth century New England through active demonstrations and re-enactments throughout the year. Write to the Village for a free calendar of events.

Old Sturbridge Village
1 Old Sturbridge Village Road
Sturbridge, MA 01566

OPUS Publications, Inc., Post Road Box 269, Guilford, CT 06437

FLORES POETICI.

THE

FLORIST'S MANUAL:

DESIGNED AS

AN INTRODUCTION

TO

VEGETABLE PHYSIOLOGY AND SYSTEMATIC BOTANY,

FOR

CULTIVATORS OF FLOWERS.

WITH

MORE THAN EIGHTY BEAUTIFULLY-COLOURED ENGRAVINGS OF

POETIC FLOWERS.

BY H. BOURNE, A. B.

LATE EDITOR OF THE " LITERARY MAGAZINE."

Καταμαθετε τὰ κρίνα τυ ἀγροῦ πῶς αὐξάνει· οὐ κοπιᾶ, οὐδὲ νῄθει : Λέγω δὲ ὑμῖν, ὅτι οὐδε Σολομὼν ἐν πάσῃ τῇ δόξῃ αὐτοῦ περιεϐάλετο ὡς ἓν τούτων.
Ματθ. 6. 28. 29.

Consider the lilies of the field how they grow ; they toil not, neither do they spin ; and yet I say unto you, that even Solomon in all his glory was not arrayed like one of these.

BOSTON:
PUBLISHED BY MUNROE AND FRANCIS.

NEW-YORK:
CHARLES S. FRANCIS.

1833

PREFACE.

There is a numerous class in this and every community, who are unwilling to devote a long period to the study of botany, that, nevertheless, are desirous of knowing " *something of the subject.*" For such is this work designed.

For the more learned and scientific, works are not wanting. Books on Systematic and Physiological Botany are numerous and well written. To many such is this work necessarily indebted. Obligations to all cannot here be particularly acknowledged. Nuttall, Smith, Torrey, Bigelow, Barton, Thornton, Eaton, Sumner, and numerous others, have been consulted.

The outline of the Sexual Classification at the beginning is deemed sufficiently copious for an Introductory work. The numerous plates of interesting flowers are designed to lead the young beginner pleasantly along. In consulting them, he will become acquainted with the general features of several plants, that may serve as types both of the *Natural* and *Artificial* Classes and Orders. He will be enabled to contrast and generalize. The subject will become less obstructed, and in a degree exemplified. The frequent Analyses of the Classes and Orders, as well as of the Genera and Species, will render familiar this method of investigation. The Physiological part is deemed sufficiently extensive for the general student.

The Linnean System has been followed, not because it is thought there may not have been improvements upon it, but that the young student should first consult it. The Synopsis compared with Nuttall's Tabular View, will exhibit its difference from the modern methods.

It has been aimed to divest the subject of those technicalities, that have too often discouraged new beginners in this pursuit. In an attempt at simplifying, perhaps the style may in some instances have degenerated into a censurable quaintness. It must have been felt, however, by every one who has consulted introductory works on this subject, that their language has been beclouded by an unnecessary use of the dead languages. The study has, therefore, been limited to a few. Those only have been induced to pursue it who are willing to wade through a tedious vocabulary of Greek and Latin terms. Even a tolerable classical scholar would be totally inadequate to a just understanding of " our botanical dialect." He could only arrive at a knowledge of it by much previous study.

The works of Linnæus, it is true, come to us in Latin. For the benefit of the thoroughly scientific, we are happy to find them so. But many have too servilely followed the original, even to copying his very language. Chemistry, Natural Philosophy, and other sciences, are taught in English. Why may not Botany be also ? There has of late been manifested in this country an increasing taste for the cultivation of ornamental plants and fruits. The taste for cultivating flowers seems to pervade all classes. It is a pure taste, and argues well for the state of feeling in our community. It has been well remarked, that, " where flowers are seen in the windows and about the dwellings even of the most humble, the inmates are seldom without some pretensions to refinement and taste." This is a healthy and innocent amusement, and particularly fitted for the occupation of females. The subject of flowers seems to have an intimate connexion with our literature, and particularly with poetry. The most splendid and costly productions of art receive several of their choicest ornaments from floral decoration. The honeysuckle, lily, and rose, are festooned in everlasting marble upon the rich Corinthian capital, whose polished shafts are but imitations of trees, the interlacing branches of which gave model to the light-springing arch of the Gothic edifice, and perhaps to the aërial and peerless dome of the Grecian and Roman temple.

Some of the genera, belonging to the same *Natural Orders,* have been brought together in the following pages. Their affinities are readily seen by comparing them. Those plants, having a common name, and yet belonging to different natural families and different genera, are occasionally presented in the same description, to obviate a confusion that is not unfrequent where different plants are known by the same name.

The specific descriptions will not in all cases be found to answer to the plants figured. The generic ones will in most instances. The vocabulary is not so extensive as might be wished, though perhaps sufficiently so for the work.

B.

Boston, July 1833.

CONTENTS.

INDEX

TO

PARTICULAR FLOWERS, AND INTERPRETATIONS.

ALPHABETICALLY ARRANGED.

GENERAL PREAMBLE

1. THE plants that spring so beautifully out of the face of the earth are almost infinite in variety. In order to avoid confusion, and better to retain in the mind the names of all this multitude of plants, for the number of their varieties amounts to many hundreds of thousands, we have recourse to, and are greatly assisted by, dividing them into classes.

2. These classes are subdivided into smaller classes or orders. These orders again are divided into genera, and these genera into species, and the species into varieties. Linnæus, a distinguished naturalist, a native of Sweden, was the person who took upon himself the trouble most accurately to class all these delightful objects. His classification or division of plants has here been followed. Some other and some more modern divisions have however been invented. More than 50,000 different species of plants have at this time been collected, named, and described.

3. Without the aid of classification, or scientific division and arrangement, it would be impossible for one mind to comprehend or remember all these names. Linnæus divided them into 24 Classes. These classes he divided again into 121 Orders. These orders he again divided into 2000 Genera, and then divided these genera into 30,000 different Species. Of these species there are varieties almost innumerable.

4. By this division and method of classing, we are enabled to remember almost all the names, and many of the individual qualities and peculiarities of these beautiful objects. By attention to Order, we can examine them with much greater pleasure. While we are examining this " artificial system" of Linnæus, we cannot but feel gratified with the ingenuity of his arrangement, and may perhaps derive some assistance to our memories from it.

5. There is nothing in nature without its use, either in the animal, mineral, or vegetable kingdoms. Of Plants, some administer to the wants of man, in affording him *food* ; some in *timber* for his house ; some in *clothing* for him ; some in *medicines* to cure his diseases ; some as *ornaments* to his gardens and fields, and in diffusing fragrance and beauty around his habitation.

6. Some give out, in the sunshine, vital air, called by the chemists *oxygen gas*. This he imbibes into his blood, through the medium of the lungs in breathing, and without it he could not live. Some plants are used for feeding his cattle and other domestic animals. Some afford subsistence to the silk-worm, that spins for him those elegant summer garments, so much worn and admired. In short, without *vegetables* there would be no animals, and man himself would only catch a glimpse of life, and then miserably perish with hunger.

7. Some plants rise to a great height, are of long life, have hard and woody stems and branches, and in cold climates produce buds. These are called *trees*, as the oak and willow. Some are of small size, and are called *shrubs*, as the lilach and thornbush. When they are still smaller than

B

shrubs, and have no young buds, they are called *under-shrubs*. When they grow of a soft, tender substance, with fibres relaxed, and die away in the winter, whether their roots live or not, they are called *herbs*. The differences however between a tree and a shrub, between a shrub and under-shrub, and between an under-shrub and an herb, are with difficulty defined, as in many cases it is doubtful and hard to determine to which of these descriptions plants may belong.

8. Those plants, that are strangers in the countries where they are cultivated, or have been brought from other places, are called *exotics*, from the latin *exoticus*, foreign, outlandlish, or brought from a foreign land. Those plants that are the natural products of the land or country where they grow or are cultivated, are called *indigenous*, or domestic.

9. Such plants as are brought from hot climates require a large share of heat, and are therefore in our country mostly cultivated in the green house, hot house, and by stoves. Those brought from cold countries to warmer ones, generally endure the winters better in the open air, though in some cases they suffer from extreme cold, being protected from it in their native situations, by the early snows which fall and clothe the ground, together with the herbage of those regions.

10. Plants grow in various places. They sometimes grow on plains, or large flat surfaces of uncultivated lands ; sometimes on tilled lands, or lands prepared for tillage or sowing ; sometimes on sown land, in gardens, in trodden places, in hedges, in meadows, in forests and woods, on sands, on hills and mountains, in marshes, on the sea-shore, and on the borders of rivulets and brooks, and around lakes and stagnant waters. In cultivating them, much attention should be paid to these circumstances. *Pinguibus hæc terris habiles, levioribus illæ*, says Virgil.

11. Those plants that grow in high and mountainous districts, or countries, are called *alpine* plants, from the lofty mountains in Europe of this name. These plants are the same over the whole world. They are found of the same kinds on the mountainous and high lands of England, Scotland, Lapland, Siberia, and Greenland. We find them also of the same kinds on the mountains of the Pyrenees, Olympus, Arrarat, and in the Brazils, as well as on the various ranges of the Andes in both Americas. In all these situations, though growing in places so remote, they possess the same essential characteristics.

INTRODUCTION.

1. When we look around on the profusion of beauty, spread over our hills and through our vallies, on the multitude of plants and flowers that 'lavish nature' has so abundantly showered down upon the earth, we feel ourselves confused and lost amid so vast a multiplicity of objects. This, Linnæus, of whom I have already had occasion to speak, felt; and indeed every one felt, who had occasion, before his time, extensively to examine these interesting natural objects, either for instruction, amusement, or use.

2. This distinguished naturalist therefore sat himself at work to obviate this confusion, by adducing method in his researches, and bringing them into classes. He found no better means of accomplishing this, than by selecting and grouping, or arranging together into the same class, all those plants, that had any obvious or striking resemblance to each other.

3. For Linnæus to determine however upon some part of a plant, on which to fix, where those possessing somewhat the same nature might have a common resemblance to them all, was what truly may be supposed to have brought his ingenuity to the test. After a careful examination of the several systems of classification, invented before his day, and after mature deliberation, he at length fixed upon those parts of the *flowers of plants* called the pistils and stamens, which soon will be briefly noticed.

4. These *pistils* and *stamens* exist in the flower of every plant, or rather, when united with the *receptacle*, constitute the essential parts of the flower. The flowers of plants are the parts that are generally esteemed the most beautiful. This part has often, by way of eminence, been styled the *head and face* of plants, because it is supposed to bear the same analogy to the other parts, as the human head and face bear to the body. It is often elevated a little above the plant, on a slender stem or stalk, called the *peduncle*. This, when the flower falls off, gives support to the fruit.

5. The flowers of plants are the most beautiful parts of the vegetable creation. Here, richness of colouring, elegance of proportion, and profusion of fragrance, seem united to delight the eye, and feast the senses. Their various hues and tints far exceed in beauty those of the finest feathers, the most brilliant shells, the most precious stones, and even the most costly diamonds. These beautiful objects have been the delight and wonder of the curious, tasteful, and learned, in all ages. They are spread before us in spring, breathing health and joy around them, and standing as pledges of the fruits of summer and autumn. When their beauty and fragrance have departed, this pledge is redeemed by something more substantially useful to man, *an abundant harvest.*

6. The flower is the organ of fructification in plants, or the instrument by which their fruit is produced. Other uses are, by some, attributed to it. Here, and in the leaves, according to the opinions of many, are elaborated the honey, the wax, the gums, and the odoriferous, volatile and fixed oils. Here, it is certain, that during the 'long, sunny, summer's day,' we find the gay and thoughtless butterfly, and busy, industrious bee, with other

small insects, revelling in sweets, and gathering their choice stores. Some of these little creatures consume them as fast as they are gathered ; while others, more provident, '*haud ignarus futuri*,' as the little bee, return laden with their choice gleanings, to their homes, and securely deposit them, for the use of the distant winter.

7. The essence of a flower consists in the *anthers* and *stigma.* When we examine a flower, as the lily for example, we find it composed of seven distinct parts. Every flower, however, does not possess all these parts.— The parts of fructification of a *perfect* flower, are, 1, the cup or *calyx* ; 2, the *corolla*, foliation or blossom ; 3, the *stamens*, or threads, or chives ; 4, the *pistil*, or pointel ; 5, the *pericarp*, or seed vessel ; 6, the *seed* ; 7, the *receptacle*, or base, on which these parts are seated. The four first-named are properly parts of the flower, and the three last, parts of the fruit.

8. The flowers of the field then, though so infinite in number, and seemingly so diversified, consist of only *seven* different parts. These parts will now be explained. When we look into the centre of the flower of a lily, we observe a small spike or stem, springing up from the middle of the flower. It resembles a small, inverted pestle, in the centre of a little mortar. This is called the *pistil*, or pestle, from the latin word *pistillum*, a pestle, with which we pound in a mortar, because of its resemblance, when growing up within the circle of the blossom or corolla, to a small pestle.

9. The stalks, or threads, that surround the pistil, frequently in circles, are called *stamens*, or sometimes in the plural *stamina*. The meaning of stamina, in latin, is straws or chives. These are so called, because they stand up around this pistil like little straws. On the top, or rather making the top, of the pistil, is a small round, oblong, or oval body, called the *stigma*. This is easily observed. The meaning of the word stigma, in latin, is a stamp, a marking or branding instrument. This part is called the stigma, because, when taken with the *style* of the pistil, or the handle of the pestle, it has a resemblance to a stamp, such as letters are sealed with. The *stigma* was anciently used for branding criminals ; hence our English words, stigma and stigmatize, meaning infamy, and to brand with infamy.

10. A *perfect pistil* is composed of three parts, the *stigma*, the *style* or handle to the stigma, and *germen*, or lower part of the handle or style, where it swells out, and becomes larger, to make room for the small seeds that grow there. The latin word *stilus* means a writing-pen, or little reed, and the word *germen*, in the same language, means a bud, or germ ; hence our english word germinate, meaning to sprout. The *pistil* is then made up of the *stigma*, or stamp, the *style*, or handle of the stamp, and the *germen*, or seed-box, which is but an enlargement of the lower part of the style.

11. The stamens or stamina, that surround the pistil, in our lily, have also on *their* tops small round or oval bodies, which, to distinguish from this on the top of the style of the pistil, are called *anthers*, or sometimes in the plural *anthera*. The threads or handles by which these are attached, are called *filaments*, from the latin word *filis* a thread, because they are frequently fine like threads.

12. The anthers on the top of these filaments, contain a yellow dust or meal, called by botanists *farina*, or *pollen*. The words farina and pollen are of latin origin, and mean fine meal or small dust. This farina may easily be observed, by examining a flower. When this falls, or is blown off upon the stigma or seed-vessel of the flower, it is supposed to render the plant fertile, causing it to produce fruits or seeds.

13. The word *anther* is a greek word, and means a husband. It is so called, because it throws down the meal or farina upon the seed-vessel of the flower, and thereby renders it productive. In the recapitulation of the parts we may then say, that in the centre of a perfect flower, we find the *pistil,* surrounded by the *stamina,* and outside of these, the *corolla,* or blossom, or flower-leaves. These often very beautifully coloured flower-leaves are called the *petals.* Each separate leaf is called a petal. The whole collectively the corolla. The word *corolla* is from the latin, and means a little crown or chaplet. These petals, when united, seem to make a little crown, or chaplet for the top or head of the plant. These seem designed for the protection and nourishment of these central organs, the *stamens* and *pistils.*

14. The blossom or corolla itself is again surrounded, in complete flowers, by a little green envelope, called the *calyx,* or cup of the flower. This seems to be a prolongation of the external covering of the stem. It appears destined to protect and beautify the petals or corolla. The *pericarp,* or seed-vessel, as before observed, is often nothing more than an enlargement of the bottom or lower part of the style.

15. The *receptacle,* or base, is that part of a flower which binds or unites all the other parts of it together into one harmonious whole. Or, it is that part of it, which connects the petals, the pistils, and stamens together. It is called the receptacle or reservoir, because it receives and unites all the different parts of the flower.

16. Externally then, enveloping the beautifully-coloured leaves of the corolla, is the little green cup or calyx. These leaves appear as if growing out of a small green tumbler or cup. This cup is often wanting in flowers. The corolla, which is the interior covering of the flower, is more conspicuous than the calyx, more slender and delicate in its fibre, and more richly coloured. It possesses almost every shade of colour but green. It is *white* in blood-root, *yellow* in buttercup, *orange* in pleurisy-root, *scarlet* in cardinal flowers, *purple* in cranes-bill, and *blue* in spider-wort.

17. When we look within the corolla, or within the circlet of the petals of the lily, and of many other flowers, we observe the stamens or stamina surrounding the pistil. These stamens, or rather their anthers, are never wanting. Their number is very various in different plants. The number of them often determines to which of the Linnæan classes a plant belongs. These, together with the pistils, are essential in the economy of vegetation. They are both equally necessary in the completion of the perfect flower. The number of the pistils, as well as of the stamens, is exceedingly various.

18. As regards the *receptacle,* it is interesting only as the connecting point, in which the other parts are all united. In simple flowers, it is inconspicuous, and cannot be seen with advantage, until the calyx, the petals, and the other organs are removed. The receptacles of compound flowers are much more interesting. If examined after the seeds have been scattered by the winds, the base to which they were attached becomes exposed to our view. The central portion, occupied by tubular, or hollow florets, is called the *disk,* while the margin or edge, where the florets are more frequently strap-shaped, linguate or tongue-shaped, is called the *ray.*

19. The *seven parts of fructification* have now been enumerated and explained. They are immediately connected with, and belong to, the flower. According to the opinions of Linnæus and others, the yellow dust or pollen, that is seen on these little round bodies, on the tops of the filaments, namely, on the *anthers,* falls off upon the stigma or seed vessel, *at the root*

EXPLANATION OF THE CLASSES AND ORDERS.

of the style of the pistil, and causes it to become fruitful. To these round bodies therefore they have given the name anthers or husbands, as before observed. The pistil they have called *gune,* meaning in greek a wife, because it contains the seed-vessels, and matures and brings forth the seeds.

20. We therefore on looking into a flower, according to the preceding notions, observe what they have fancied to resemble husbands and wives. The pistil is the wife, and the stamina or stamens of this same flower, or of different flowers, are the husbands. Sometimes there are in a flower several stamens, and but one or more pistils, and sometimes several pistils with but one or more stamens. So that there may be one wife and many husbands, or one or more husbands and many wives, in the same flower.

21. Since these are the parts of the flower that Linnæus has chosen, on which to found his method of classification and arrangement of the whole *vegetable creation* ; from his considering and naming these parts as husbands and wives, this system has been called THE SEXUAL SYSTEM OF LINNÆUS. Although it is an artificial system, it is a very useful one. Many attempts have been made at a natural arrangement, or natural classification of plants. The object of this arrangement would be to bring plants having a *natural affinity,* into the same *classes* and *orders.* A very happy attempt of this kind may be seen, by consulting the " Natural Orders of Jussieu," in the excellent work on botany, by professor Eaton. Perhaps the attending to the *sexual classification* of Linnæus may be rather dull and tiresome, especially to those who have not learned something of Greek ; yet a brief sketch of it is here inserted for those, who may have the curiosity and patience to examine it.

22. Of all the plants that spring out of the ground, and clothe it with verdure and beauty, Linnæus made 24 classes, as has already been observed. The first 11 of these classes, or one half the whole number of classes lacking one, he distinguished or named merely from the *number of the stamens* or *husbands.* The number of the stamens determines the number of the class. Thus, those flowers, or plants having flowers, possessing 1 stamen, are of the first class. Those having 2 stamens are of the second class. Those having three stamens are of the third class ; and so on, through the 11 first classes. In determining therefore to which of the first eleven classes any plant may belong (should it belong to one of these classes) we have only to *count the stamens of its flower.* Their number will be the number of the class, to which the plant belongs.

23. The Orders also of the first thirteen Classes, are determined by the *number of the pistils* of the flowers. Those flowers having 1 pistil are of the first order. Those flowers having two pistils are of the second order. Those having 3, of the third order, and so on, through the 13 First Classes. Then, to determine the Class, we count the *stamens,* and to determine the Order, we count the *pistils.* The number of the stamens in the 11 first classes determines the number of the Class, and the number of the pistils in the 13 first classes determines the number of the Order.

24. It should be remembered, that, in several of the Classes, *many of the intermediate orders are wanting,* as no plants have yet been discovered having the requisite number of pistils to fill these orders. This will be observed by inspecting the Orders in the Synopsis of the Linnæan Classes at the close of the volume. Thus, in Class IV. for example, having but three orders, there are plants of the Monogynia or one pistil, of the Digynia or two pistils, and of Tetragynia or four pistils, but no plants having *three*

EXPLANATION OF THE CLASSES AND ORDERS.

pistils, or of the order Trigynia, have yet been discovered in this Class. In all these cases we have numbered the order according to the number of pistils. In doing so, we have followed the method of professor Eaton, and some other modern botanists. Dr. Thornton, in his " Exposition of the Linnæan classes and orders," as likewise several others, have followed a different method. The number of the order, in their arrangement, is not as the number of the pistils, but as the number of the orders in the class. Thus, in Class IV. the order Tetragynia would be third order, notwithstanding its flowers have four pistils. They have named it Order 3d, because there are but three known orders in the class, and this Tetragynia is the last of the three. The method we have pursued in numbering the order according to the number of the pistils, leaves room for the insertion of any new or intermediate orders that may be discovered at any future time; whereas the other arrangement, should any new order of plants chance to be discovered, (and many have been discovered since the time of Linnæus), would require an entire new arrangement in regard to numbering the orders.

25. Before giving the names of the Classes, I must beg leave to count in Greek a little, for the benefit of those of my readers, who may not be able to count in Greek for themselves. If they will take the trouble to learn what follows, they will have no difficulty in understanding the Linnæan classes and orders. In this language, μονος *monos*, signifies one; δις *dis* two or twice, τρεις *treis* three, τεσσαρες *tessares* four, πεντε *pente* five, εξ *hex* six, 'επτα *hepta* seven, οκτω *okto* eight, εννεα *ennea* nine, δεκα *deka* ten, δυωδεκα *doodeka* twelve, εικοσι *eikosi* twenty, πολυς *polus* many. It has already been remarked that the word *aner* or *anther* signifies a man, or a husband, and that the word *gune* means wife ; or, in botanical language, that *aner* means the stamen, and *gune* the pistil of a flower.

26. These things being premised, we are now prepared to understand the signification and import of the names of the following classes and orders. We have only to join the numerals above to the words *aner*, meaning stamen, and *gune*, meaning pistil, and we form many of the classes and orders. Thus, Class First is Monandria, from *monos*, one, and *aner*, stamen, because flowers of this class have but one stamen. This Class contains but two Orders. The first order of this class is Monogynia, from *monos*, one, and *gune*, pistil, because plants of this order have flowers with but one pistil. The second order of this class is Digynia, from *dis*, two or twice, and *gune*, pistil, because flowers of this order have two pistils. In this manner, by prefixing the numerals to the words *aner* or *anther*, and *gune*, we form all the following classes and orders.

CLASS I. MONANDRIA.	CLASS II. DIANDRIA.	CLASS III. TRIANDRIA.
Order 1, Monogynia.	Order 1, Monogynia.	Order 1, Monogynia.
2, Digynia.	2, Digynia.	2, Digynia.
	3, Trigynia.	3, Trigynia.

CLASS IV. TETRANDRIA.	CLASS V. PENTANDRIA.	CLASS VI. HEXANDRIA.
Order 1, Monogynia.	Order 1, Monogynia.	Order 1, Monogynia.
2, Digynia.	2, Digynia.	2, Digynia.
4, Tetragynia.	3, Trigynia.	3, Trigynia.
	4, Tetragynia.	4, Tetragynia.
	5, Pentagynia.	6, Hexagynia.
	6, Hexagynia.	7, Polygynia.
	7, Polygynia.	

CLASS VII. HEPTANDRIA.	CLASS VIII. OCTANDRIA.	CLASS IX. ENNEANDRIA.
Order 1, Monogynia.	Order 1, Monogynia.	Order 1, Monogynia.
2, Digynia.	2, Digynia.	2, Digynia.
4, Tetragynia.	3, Trigynia.	6, Hexagynia.
7, Heptagynia.	4, Tetragynia.	

CLASS X. DECANDRIA.	CLASS XI. DODECANDRIA.
Order 1, Monogynia.	Order 1, Monogynia.
2, Digynia.	2, Digynia.
3, Trigynia.	3, Trigynia.
5, Pentagynia.	4, Tetragynia.
10, Decagynia.	5, Pentagynia.
	12, Dodecagynia.

See the Synopsis at the end of the volume.

27. Thus, by counting the stamens and pistils, we can easily determine if a plant belong to any of the *Eleven First Classes*, or Orders of the Thirteen First Classes. The remaining thirteen Classes are equally easy to understand, if it can but be borne in mind, 1st, That flowers are divided by botanists and florists into *male* flowers, *female* flowers, *hermaphrodite* flowers, and *neuter* flowers.

28. 1st. Those flowers that have the pistil, but have no stamens, (for such flowers will often be found,) are called female flowers. 2d. Those flowers that have the stamens, but have no pistil, are called male flowers. 3d. Those flowers that have neither stamens nor pistils, are called neuter flowers. 4th. Those flowers that have both stamens and pistils, are called hermaphrodite flowers, because they partake of the nature of both sexes.

29. If we examine a Sunflower or Dandelion carefully, we observe its blossom composed of several little hollow tubes, or, as botanists express it, of 'tubular florets.' Each of these rolls or tubes, when closely examined, will be found to be a complete flower, containing within its hollow often both stamens and pistils. Yet all these small tubular florets, when united on their 'common receptacle,' or base, have the appearance of a single flower. Each floret or tube, although an entire flower, appears like a single petal, or flower-leaf. Flowers of this description, containing many tubular florets united, or situated on a common receptacle, are called *compound flowers*. They are composed of many simple florets.

30. When there is a single corolla, inclosing the stamens and pistils, situated upon a common receptacle, it is said to be a *simple flower*, as the Lily, Rose, &c. Although many compound flowers appear like simple flowers, when viewed at a distance, they are easily distinguished when closely examined. Simple flowers are much more numerous and common than compound flowers.

31. Hermaphrodite flowers, or such as have both stamens and pistils, are sometimes distinguished into male hermaphrodites and female hermaphrodites. This distinction takes place when, although the parts belonging to each sex are contained in the flower, one of them proves abortive or ineffectual. If the defect be in the stamen, it is a female hermaphrodite. If in the pistil, a male hermaphrodite.

32. Plants, as well as flowers, have also a distinction of sex. Hermaphrodite plants are such as bear flowers upon the same root, that are all

hermaphrodite. *Androgynous* plants are such as, upon the same root, bear both male and female flowers, distinct from each other. These plants are so called from the Greek word *aner*, a man, and *gune*, a woman, or in botanical language, *aner*, stamen, and *gune*, pistil, because these plants bear both staminate and pistillate flowers upon the same root.

33. Male plants are such as bear male flowers only upon the same root. Female plants are such as bear female flowers only upon the same root. Polygamous plants are such, as either on the same or on different roots bear hermaphrodite flowers, and flowers of either or both sexes. These plants seem to be in a state of polygamy. Hence the term *polygamous*, from the Greek word *polus*, many, and *gamia*, marriages. The preceding remarks being understood, we are now prepared to comprehend the definitions of the thirteen remaining classes.

34. It will be proper to remark, before explaining these classes, however, that of the eleven preceding classes already explained, *all the flowers must be hermaphrodite in these classes* ; that is, they must all contain both stamens and pistils. Should the female part be wanting, the plant would belong to some other class, notwithstanding the number of stamens might be such as would otherwise refer it to one of these classes.

35. The understanding and remembering of the thirteen last classes has generally been thought difficult. The explanations that follow are simple and easily understood, provided we understand what has been said in the preceding pages. As no flowers have yet been discovered that have *eleven* stamens, no class has been allotted to that number, and the eleventh class is called *Dodecandria*, from *doodeka*, twelve, and *aner*, stamens. Notwithstanding the term implies that these flowers have twelve stamens, the class is not confined to this number, but includes all such hermaphrodite flowers as are furnished with any number of stamens from twelve to nineteen inclusive. That is, they may have any number of stamens above twelve, and less than nineteen.

36. The 12th Class is called *Icosandria*, from the Greek *eikosi*, twenty, and *aner*, stamen, because flowers of this class have twenty stamens. This title is however to be understood with considerable latitude. For, though it means that the flowers belonging to this class have twenty stamens, they may have a greater number nevertheless. They may have twenty or more. They are therefore not to be known with certainty from the next, or 13th Class, except *by the stamens arising from the calyx or cup*, and not from *the receptacle*.

37. The 13th Class is called *Polyandria*, from the Greek *polus*, many, and *aner*, stamen, because plants of this class have flowers of *many stamens*. The number of their stamens is often very great. This Class however comprehends all those hermaphrodite plants, whose flowers have *more than twenty disunited stamens originating from the receptacle*.

38. The stamens and pistils are sometimes united, or grow together in clumps, at top or at the bottom. This will soon be explained.

39. The 14th Class is called *Didynamia*, from the Greek *dis*, two, and *dunamis*, power or superiority, because plants of this class have flowers of *four stamens*, of which there are *two* longer than the others. In this respect they seem to have a *superiority*, two of them overtopping the other

C

two.   It is from this circumstance we are able to distinguish the 14th Class from the 4th Class.   The 4th Class has four stamens that are equal in length, whereas the 14th Class has four stamens, two of which are longer than the other two.

40.   The 15th Class is called *Tetradynamia*, from the Greek *tessares*, four, and *dunamis*, power or superiority, because plants of this class have flowers with six stamens, four of which are longer than the others.   There seems to be a superiority in length of four of the stamens over the other two. The 6th Class has six stamens, but they are all equal in length, whereas the 15th Class has six stamens, *four of which are longer than the other two.*

41.   The 16th Class is called *Monadelphia*, from *monos*, one, and *adelphos*, brother or brotherhood, because the stamens of the flowers of this class are *all united, at their base*, into one *brotherhood, or family.*   They grow together at their lower extremities into one clump, proceeding from it as from a common parent.   The number of stamina in this class is not limited.   It may be greater or less.   The two following classes have some analogy to this class, as will soon be observed.

42.   The 17th Class is called *Diadelphia*, from the Greek *dis*, two, and *adelphos*, brother or brotherhood, because the stamens of the flowers of this class of plants are united at the *base of their filaments* into *two* brotherhoods or clumps.   They have two clusters of stamens united, as explained in the preceding class.   The number of stamens, in flowers of this class, may be larger or smaller ; the number is not limited.

43.   The 18th Class is called *Polyadelphia*, from the Greek *polus*, many, and *adelphos*, brother or brotherhood, because these flowers belong to the class of plants, where the stamens are united into *many sets*, or brotherhoods.   The 16th Class has the stamina of its flowers united into *one* clump, the 17th, into *two*, and the 18th, into *three* or more clumps or brotherhoods.   These circumstances sufficiently characterize the 16th, 17th, and 18th Classes.

44.   The 19th Class is called *Syngenesia*, from *sun*, with, and *genesis*, generation, or growth, the two words united meaning *congeneration*, or u-nited birth, because the stamens of the flowers of this Class are united *at top* by their anthers into a cylinder.   They are however separate at bottom from one another.   The anthers uniting at the top seem to perform their office together.   Hence the term *syngenesia*, meaning congeneration. This peculiarity sufficiently distinguishes it from all the other classes.

45.   The 20th Class is called *Gynandria*, from the Greek *gune*, wife, or in botanical language, pistil, and *aner*, stamen, because flowers of this Class have *their stamens very curiously growing out of the pistil.*   The male and female parts do not here stand separate, but are united.   The stamens grow upon the pistil or out of it.   Hence the term *gynandria*, or stamen-pistil, or husband-wife Class.

46.   The 21st Class is called *Monoecia*, from the Greek *monos*, one, and *oikos*, house or habitation ; because the plants of this class have flowers that are not hermaphrodite, but androgynous.   That is, the flowers of this class that have the stamens, have no pistils, and the flowers that have pistils have no stamens.   Thus the pistils and stamens seem to have different habitations or houses, growing each in different flowers.   It should be remarked, however, that these separate flowers must all spring from the same root ; that is, they must grow on different stalks of the same root.

47. The 22d Class is called *Dioecia*, from the Greek *dis*, two, and *oïkos*, house or habitation, because plants of this class have flowers that grow, the male on one plant, and the female on another plant. The plants are male and female. These were not the facts with regard to the 21st Class; for although the male flowers grow on one stalk, and the female on another, yet they all spring from the *same root*; that is, both kinds of flowers grow on the same plant. Here they grow on *different plants*. They have two habitations.

48. The 23d Class is called *Polygamia*, from the Greek *polus*, many, *gamos*, nuptials or marriages, because this class produces, either upon the same or different plants, hermaphrodite flowers, and also flowers of one sex only, be it male or female, or flowers of each sex, and the latter receiving impregnation from, or giving it to, the hermaphrodites, as their sex happens to be. Thus there seems to be a state of promiscuous intercourse, or polygamy. Hence the term *polygamous* class. The parts essential to generation, in the hermaphrodite flowers, do not confine themselves to the corresponding parts within the same flower, but become of promiscuous use, receiving impregnation from, or giving it to, one another, as their sex may happen to be.

49. The 24th, and last Linnæan Class, is called *Cryptogamia*, from *kruptos*, concealed, and *gamos*, nuptials; because plants of this class either bear their flowers concealed within the fruit, or have them so small as to be imperceptible. The sexual connexion seems to be concealed or hidden.— This Class has 4 orders, and includes the Ferns, the Mosses, the Flags, and the Mushrooms.

50. The Orders of the thirteen first classes have already been explained. It only remains now to explain the Orders of the remaining eleven classes. On examining the 14th Class, in the Synopsis, we observe it has two orders, the one called *Gymnospermia*, and the other *Angiospermia*. These terms are both from the Greek, the first from *gumnos*, naked, and *sperma*, seed; so called, because plants belonging to it bear naked seeds. They have no pod nor other covering. The second order of this class is named from *angos*, a vessel or covering, and *sperma*, seed; because the seeds of this order are in vessels, or have a covering; they are inclosed in a pericarp or seed-vessel, whereas those of the first order are not.

51. The 15th Class includes two orders, namely, the Order *Siliculosa*, and the Order *Siliquosa*. These two orders are founded on the distinction of the pericarpium or seed-vessel. The term *siliculosa* is of Latin origin, and means a *little pod*. The plants of the first order of this class have their seeds inclosed in a small, short pod; as the Shepherd's-purse, Whitlow-grass, &c. The name of the second order, *siliquosa*, is also from the Latin, and means, *like a bean or pea-pod*, because plants of this order have seeds contained in a long, slender pod, as the Wall-flower, Cabbage, Mustard, &c. The first order has a short pod, and the second order a long one.

52. There are five orders in the 19th Class. Before explaining them, it will be necessary to define what is meant by *polygamy in flowers*. Polygamous plants have already been explained. With respect to flowers, this term is applied to a single flower only. For the flowers of this Class, being compound, a polygamy arises from the intercommunication of the several florets in one and the same flower. Now the polygamy of flowers, in this sense of the word, affords *four* cases, which are the foundations of the four first orders of this class.

53. The first order of this class, is *polygamia equalis*, meaning equal polygamy. Here all the flowers are hermaphrodite. They thus seem to live in a state of polygamy, a kind of equal polygamy. The superfluous polygamy, or *polygamia superflua*, which indicates the 2d order of this class, is when some of the florets are hermaphrodite, and others female only. In this case, as the fructification is perfected in the hermaphrodite flowers, the addition of female flowers seems to be a superfluity.

54. The 3d order is *polygamia frustranea*, meaning polygamy of no use, or vain polygamy. Plants of this order have some of their florets hermaphrodite, and others neuter ; so that the addition of the neuter, in this case, seems of no use whatever. They appear to be of no assistance to the fructification.

55. The 4th order, *polygamia necessaria*, or necessary polygamy, is when some of the florets are male, and the rest female. In this case, there being no hermaphrodite flowers, the polygamy arising from the composition of the florets of different sexes, seems to render it a necessary polygamy, in order to perfect the fructification.

56. The 5th and last order of the 19th Class is called *polygamia segregata*, or separate polygamy. The Latin *segregata* signifies, separated from, severed, or taken out of a flock. The flowers belonging to this order have partial cups, growing out of the common calyx, which surround and divide the florets. They sever or separate them from one another, each little calyx or cup surrounding its own particular floret.

57. The order *Mongamia* signifies, a single marriage, and is opposed to the polygamy of the other orders. In this, although the anthers are united, which is the essential character of the flowers of this class, the flower is simple, and not compounded of many florets, as in the other orders. The term *Trioecia*, applied to the order, in the 23d Class, is from *treis*, three, and *oikos*, habitation ; because the polygamy is on three different plants, one producing male flowers, one female flowers, and another, hermaphrodite or androgynous flowers.

58. The Orders of the other classes, namely, the 16th, 17th, 18th, 20th, 21st, and 22d Classes, are distinguished by the characters of the preceding classes, and assume their names. That is, they do not terminate in *gynia*, as in the orders of the thirteen first classes, for their order is not determined by their number of pistils, but by their number of stamens. They therefore end in *andria*, as Monandria, Diandria, Triandria, &c. They assume the same appellation as the Classes, and are subject to the same exceptions as regards the number of the order—Monandria being the first order, because the flowers have but one stamen, Diandria being the 2d order, because the flowers have two stamens, and so on through all the orders of these classes. Thus the orders of these classes are determined by the *number* of the *stamens*, and not by the number of the *pistils*. It should be remembered, that in determining the orders of the classes, the styles should be numbered at their bottom, or at their origin on the germ. Their subdivisions *above* the germ are not taken into view, in determining the number of the

EXPLANATION OF THE CLASSES AND ORDERS.

order. If the style be wanting (as sometimes happens) and the stigma is set down on the germ, the stigmas are then counted.

59. Thus the artificial Classes of Linnæus are founded, it would seem by a recapitulation, upon 1st, the *number*, 2d, the *position*, 3d, *relative length*, and 4th, *connexion of the stamens*. The first *eleven* by the *number*. The *twelfth* and *thirteenth* by the *number* and *position*. The *fourteenth* and *fifteenth* by the *number* and *relative length*. The *sixteenth*, *seventeenth*, *eighteenth*, *nineteenth*, and *twentieth*, by the *connexion*. The 21st, 22d, and 23d, by *position* of the stamens. The 24th, or last class, is not distinguished by the *stamens*, but is a *natural* class.

60. The Orders of the artificial classes are founded also, 1st, upon the number of styles (or stigmas, when styles are wanting). 2d, the covering or nakedness of seeds. 3d, the relative length of pods. 4th, the comparison between disk and ray florets of compound flowers. 5th, upon the characters of the preceding classes. The orders of the 24th class are distinguished by natural family characters. Then, as a general rule, it may be said,—The Orders of the 13 first classes are determined by the *number* of *pistils* ; the Orders of the 14th and 15th, by the *fruit*, or the circumstances of its nakedness, or being covered, or by the form of its covering ; the Orders of the 16th, 17th, and 18th Classes, by the *number* of the *stamens* (not of the pistils); the Orders of the 19th Class by the *interblending* of the *florets* ; those of the 20th, 21st, and 22d Classes by the *number* of the *stamens* ; those of the 23d Class by the circumstance of the several kinds of flowers being on the same or different plants ; and those of the 24th or last Class, by *natural* characteristics. Or, more generally speaking, we may say, the orders of the 13 first classes are distinguished by the number of the pistils, and the orders of the remaining classes, with the exception of the 19th, 23d, and 24th, by the characteristics of the preceding classes ; the 19, 23, and 24, being distinguished by natural characteristics.

61. This finishes the exposition of the Classes and Orders. This system has received several modifications and alterations by modern botanists, since the days of its author. Whether they have been real improvements or not, is not for me to determine. We do not, necessarily, treasure up all the hard Greek words used in botanical explanations, but only make ourselves so far familiar with the language, as to trace the order and connexion running through the system. By so doing, we shall pursue the study with greater pleasure and profit to ourselves.

EVENING PRIMROSE.

TREE-PRIMROSE, NIGHT-PRIMROSE, SCABISH, DWARF-SCABISH, SUNDROPS, ŒNOTHERA.

CLASS, Octandria, from *octo*, eight; *aner*, stamen.   **ORDER**, Monogynia, from *monos*, one; *gune*, pistil.

Because these flowers have *Eight Stamens*, and *One Pistil*, and are consequently of the *Eighth Class* and *First Order* of Linnæus.

Œnothera fruticosa,	Sundrops.
.. *chrysantha,*	Dwarf Scabish.
.. *biennis,*	Tree Primrose.

Besides these, there are six or seven other species of these flowers, found growing in the Eastern and Middle States of North-America.

THE EMBLEM OF INCONSTANCY.

And one who marked with depth of thought
How the bright day-flowers droop away,
An *Evening Primrose* only brought,
Which opens at the close of day.   *Judgment of the Flowers.*

.... A tuft of *Evening Primroses,*
O'er which the wind might hover till it dozes;
On which it well might take a pleasant sleep,
But that 'tis ever startled by the leap
Of buds into ripe flowers.   *Keats.*

When the *Primrose-Tree* blossom was ready to burst,
In the coolness of the evening hour,
I heard thee, thou busy bee,
As thou wanton'dst o'er its flower.   *Anthology.*

There are several varieties of the Tree-Primrose, found native in this country; one or two varieties in Virginia. The *Œnothera* *biennis*, like the *Tropeolum majus*, or Nasturtion, is phosphorescent, or emits light in the dark. It opens its pale-yellow, delicate blossoms in the evening only. It has hence received the name of the *Evening Primrose*. There is a striking singularity in the opening of this fine flower. The petals, or flower-leaves, are held together by clasps at the end of the calyx or cup. These segments separate at bottom and discover the corolla long before it can sufficiently open to unlock the calyx at the top. When these clasps are unloosed, the petals often open very suddenly. Hence the poet tells us of " the primrose-tree blossom being ready to burst in the coolness of the evening hour." Whoever has noticed the opening of this flower in the evening will feel the perfect truth of the poet's remark, that it seems " the wind might hover o'er it till it dozes, and take a pleasant sleep," were it not " startled by the leap of buds into ripe flowers."

While the writer was conveying to the artist, a distance of only a few rods, the plant from which the above engraving was made, two or three buds, which scarcely appeared as half ripe, unexpectedly expanded into as many beautiful, full-blown flowers. Every variety of this plant, found native in New-England, bears a yellow blossom. It is called *Œnothera*, from the Greek word *oinos*, signifying *wine*, because its dried roots are said to resemble wine in their smell. The *Œnothera biennis*, or Broad-leaved Tree-primrose, usually opens its leaves between six and seven o'clock in the evening. When the corolla acquires sufficient expansive force to unlock the segments of the calyx at top, it expands almost instantaneously to a certain point ; it then makes a stop, taking time to spread ; it may be half an hour from the first bursting of the cup at bottom, to the final expansion of the corolla. In the course of the next day this beautiful flower fades and dies. The uppermost flowers appear first in June ; the stalks keep continually advancing in height, and there is a constant succession of flowers till late in the autumn. There are two species of this genus found native at the Cape of Good Hope. This flower has probably become emblematic of Inconstancy from its sudden and unlooked-for expansion and rapid decay. The *Circæa, Gaura, Epilobium, Œnothera*, and several other *genera*, belong to the same *natural* order. There are eleven *species* of the Evening Primrose.

The stem of the Tree-Primrose, or *Œnothera biennis*, is villose, scabrous ; leaves lance-ovate, flat, toothed ; flowers terminal, sub-spiked, sessile ; stamina shorter than the corol.

POLYANTHUS.

POLEANTHUS, POLYANTHOS, TUBEROSE, PLANTE-A-PLUSIEURS-
FLEURS, PRIMULA-POLYANTHUS, NARCISSUS, TUBE-ROSE.

CLASS, Hexandria, from	ORDER, Monogynia, from
hex, six ; *aner*, stamen.	*monos*, one ; *gune*, pistil.

Because these flowers have *Six Stamens*, and *One Pistil*, and are consequently of the *Sixth Class* and *First Order* of Linnæus.

Narcissus tazetta,	Polyanthos.
.. *pseudo-narcissus,*	Daffodil.
Polyanthes tuberosa,	Tuberose.

Of this *Primrose* plant there are a number of other *Species* with numerous *varieties*, many
of which are found growing in our gardens in New-England.

THE EMBLEM OF PRIDE.

I know a bank whereon the wild thyme blows,
Where oxlips and the nodding violet grows,
Quite over-canopied with lush woodbine,
With sweet musk-roses and with eglantine.   *Shakspeare.*

The poplar there sprouts up its spire,
And shakes its leaves in the sun fantastical,
While round its slender base there rambles,
The sweet-breathed vine,—the pink is there,
There, *Polyanthus* in full cluster'd pride,
In splendid robes of rich unnumber'd dyes,
With scorn from old acquaintance turns aside.   *Matthews.*

Of this rich and fragrant flower, there are at least twenty or thirty
cultivated varieties ; some of them are exceedingly beautiful.   The

Primrose, Oxlip, and Cowslip, all belong to the same *natural* order. These are all of the Primrose family, so named from the Latin, *primus*, first, because they are very early spring flowers. The Polyanthus is found of colours and appearances extremely various. The purple and variegated Polyanthoses are among some of those most admired. The natural order, to which this flower belongs, is called *Preciæ*, from the Latin, *pre*, before, and *cio*, to excite, because of the early appearance of such flowers in Spring. A pleasing instance of the improvement, that art is capable of bestowing on nature, is found in this flower. All its varieties are derived from one original *primrose* stock. These flowers are called *polyanthos*, from the Greek words *polus*, many, and *anthos*, flower, because they bear *many* flowers, or blossoms. In this respect they differ from the *Primula* or Primrose properly so called, because this latter plant bears but one flower on a stalk, whereas the Cowslip, Oxlip, and Polyanthus, bear many. The two first named are very ornamental to our meadows in New-England in early spring, generally having pale yellow blossoms, sometimes bright yellow. The difference of the Polyanthus, produced by its cultivation, in some degree resembles that of an untutored mind compared with one of a person of education. The Polyanthus, in its habits, resembles very much the Cowslip and Primrose. They all come forth at a season, when scarcely any other flowers are to be found, and consequently have been much sought after and generally admired as ornamental flowers. When we look upon these early spring-flowers, after the cold storms of winter have passed away to their home in the north, and the sunny days of spring have come, " with birds in cheerful song," we feel sensations of delight, that later seasons cannot inspire us with.

The *Polyanthus Narcissus* (*N. tazetta*), and the Jonquil (*N. jonquilla*), so called from the Latin *juncus*, signifying a *rush*, because of its rush-like and narrow leaves, are both remarkably fragrant, and bear forcing, or bringing early into flower, in water-glasses, in the ordinary temperature of a dwelling-room. *Narcissus* is the *genus*, of which these and the Polyanthus are *species*. The stamens and pistil of the Daffodil are often found transformed into irregular petals, and the *anthers* destroyed, as in many other double flowers produced by cultivation.

The Polyanthos, or *Narcissus tazetta*, has a spathe many-flowered : nectary bell-form, plicate, truncate, thrice as short as the petals : petals alternately broader : leaves flat.

D

PASSION-FLOWER.

FLEUR-DE-LA-PASSION, GRANADILLA, LA-GRENADILLA, FIORE-DELLA-PASSIONE, PASSIFLORA.

CLASS, Monadelphia, from *mo-nos* one, and *adelphos*, brother.

ORDER, Pentandria, from *pente*, five, *aner*, stamen.

Because these flowers have their *Stamens* growing united by their filaments into one body, and have *Five Stamens*, and consequently are of the *Sixteenth Class* and *Fifth Order* of Linnæus.

Passiflora lutea,	Yellow Passion-flower.
" *cærulea*,	Blue Passion-flower.
" *alata*,	Winged Passion-flower.

According to some, there are thirty-seven species of the Passion-flower. The "Hortus Britannicus" makes sixty-three known species.

THE EMBLEM OF HOPE.

Yon mystic flower, with gold and azure bright,
Whose stem luxuriant speaks a vigorous root,
Unfolds her blossoms to the morn's salute,
That close and die in the embrace of night.
No luscious fruits the cheated taste invite—
Her short-lived blossoms, ere they lead to fruit,
Demand a genial clime, and suns that shoot
Their rays direct with undiminished light.
Thus Hope, the *Passion-flower* of human life,
Whose wild luxuriance mocks the pruner's knife,
Profuse in promise, makes a like display
Of evanescent blooms, that last a day !
To cheer the mortal eye, no more is given,
The fruit is only to be found in heaven.   *Cartwright.*

The Passion-flower affords us an example of a most perfect plant, in all its various parts of stem, leaf, tendrils, involucre, cup, corolla, pistil, and stamens. It is found of several very beautiful varieties, and is a native of America. The petals of one variety are yellow near their origin, a little way from thence curiously pencilled with varying colours, and, at length, near their borders, fringed with a purple blue, streaked with green. The Southern varieties generally bear flowers of a bright red, those of the North yellow or pale blue. This plant is said to owe its name to the early Missionaries, who first discovered it, when traversing South America. Its ten petals were fancied, by them, to represent the ten apostles, besides Judas who betrayed, and Peter who denied, his master. The stamens they compare to a radiance or glory, issuing from the cup of the flower. The small purple threads, at the bottom of the style, to a crown of thorns. The style, to the pillar to which the malefactors were bound, when scourged. The clasper, to the cord ; and the palmate leaf, to the hand. The three divisions at the top of the style, they fancied to represent the three nails ; one of the five stamens being taken for a hammer, the other three remain, to form the cross. The *albastrices*, at the bottom of the corolla, represented the three soldiers, who cast lots ; and the time between the opening and closing of the flower, in its native country, being three days, completes the representation. Thus these superstitious friars made the flower represent the whole history of our Saviour's PASSION, or sufferings, as recorded by the Evangelists. It has hence been called the *Passion Flower*, and been made the emblem of *hope*. The ancient American name is *Mercuria*. It has sometimes been called *Grenadilla,* from the similarity of its fruit to that of the Pomegranate. In Italy it has been called *Fiore della Passione,* Flos Passionis, and Christi passionis Imago. Linnæus changed the name of this genus to *Passiflora*, by combining the words. The *Passiflora quadrangularis* of the West Indies is most magnificent in richness of its flowers. They resemble well-disposed masses of gems, including all the tints of amethyst, ruby, topaz, torquoise, and emerald, sprinkled with jet and pearls. The *Cucurbita, Cucumis, Monardica, Sycios, Melothria,* and *Passiflora,* all belong to the same *natural* order.

———

The Blue Passion-flower, or *Passiflora cœrulea*, has leaves palmate, five-parted, entire : petioles glandular : involucre three-leaved, entire : threads of the crown shorter than the cord.

PANSY.

HEARTS-EASE, LADIES'-DELIGHT, FORGET-ME-NOT, LOVE-IN-IDLENESS, BUTTERFLY-VIOLET, MERIT-NEGLECTED, THREE-FACES-UNDER-A-HOOD, VARIEGATED VIOLET, NONE-SO-PRETTY.

CLASS, Pentandria, from
pente, five, *aner,* stamen.

ORDER, Monogynia, from
monos, one, *gune,* pistil.

Because these flowers have *Five Stamens* and *One Pistil,* and are consequently of the *Fifth Class* and *First Order* of Linnæus.

Viola pubescens,	Yellow Woods Violet.
·· *concolor,*	Green Violet.
·· *bicolor,*	Two-coloured Violet.
·· *striata,*	Striped Violet.
·· *odorata,*	Sweet Violet.

Besides these, there are eighteen or twenty other *species,* with several *varieties,* found growing in the Eastern and Middle States of North-America.

THE EMBLEM OF REMEMBRANCE.

When beechen buds begin to swell,
  And woods the blue-bird's warble know,
The *yellow-violet's* smiling bell
  Peeps from the last year's leaf below.   *Bryant.*

And when this flowret greets her eye,
A prayer is mingled with the sigh,—
While gentle voices from the spot
Seem whispering, *Forget-me-not.*   *The Farewell.*

........Maidens call it *Love-in-idleness.*   *Shakspeare.*

This charming little tricoloured floweret is purple, yellow, and blue, as you observe by the annexed plate. It is called by the

French, the *Pensèe*, or *Pansy*, meaning, in that language, a *thought*, a *remembrance*, a *forget-me-not*. Shakspeare's fine metamorphosis of this little flower,

" Before milk-white, now purple with love's wound ;
" And maidens call it love-in-idleness" . . . . . .

contains an excellent moral, namely, that irregular love has only power " when people are idle," or not well employed. There is certainly no flower, however gaudy and rich, that has been honoured with a greater variety of appellations, at once expressive of tenderness, grace, and delicacy. Indeed the fancy can hardly imagine a more delicate, rich, and tasteful combination of colour, than is to be found united in this flower. Hence there is no flower, not even the Rose excepted, that has been a more universal favourite of every age. From this circumstance we may account for its great variety of names, such as ' *Heart's-ease,*' ' *Flamula,*' or ' *Little flame,*' ' *Flos Jovis,*' or ' *Jove's flower,*' ' *Love-in-Idleness,*' ' *Ladies'-delight,*' ' *Butterfly-violet,*' ' *Winged violet,*' ' *Merit neglected,*' ' *Jump-up-and-kiss-me,*' ' *Herbe-de-la-Trinitè ;*' alluding probably to its three colours ; and ' *Three-faces-under-a-hood ;*' a name, originating probably from the same circumstance. The Latin name of this plant is ' *Viola tricolor,*' *tri-coloured* or three-coloured Violet. The violet is said to have been a peculiar favourite of the Emperor Napoleon, and hence this flower has sometimes been called ' *Napoleon's Flower.*' From being cultivated in gardens and borders, it is sometimes called ' *Garden Violet.*' It is an humble, unpretending plant, that springs up among the earliest flowers of spring, in aggregated masses, or clusters, putting forth its fine little blossoms to the vernal sun. The flower seldom rises but a few inches in height. It grows in cornfields, wastes, and cultivated grounds, flowering all the summer months. The term *violet* is from the Greek word *Ion*, because it was said to have been first found in Ionia, in Greece. Like merit neglected, it is too often passed by unheeded, and although a ' lady's delight,' is often obliged to give place in a bouquet, garland, or wreath, to more gaudy and dazzling flowers. It is a *perennial*, or root that lasts during the cold of winter, and consequently needs very little care, when once introduced into the borders of the walks in our gardens, or around our dwellings.

The stem of the *Pansy* is angular, diffuse, divided : leaves oblong, deeply crenate : stipules lyrate—pinnatifid.

CISTUS.

ROCK-ROSE, FROST-PLANT.

CLASS, Polyandria, from *polus*, many, *aner*, stamen.   **ORDER**, Monogynia, from *monos*, many, *gune*, pistil.

Because these flowers have *Twenty or more disunited Stamens,* and **One Pistil**, and consequently are of the 13*th Class* and 1*st Order* of Linnæus.

Cistus canadensis,	Rock-rose.
" *ramuliflorum,*	Frost-plant.
" *corymbosum*	———

Besides these, there are one or two other *Species* found growing in the Eastern and Middle States of North-America.

THE EMBLEM OF INCONSTANCY.

Dark shrub ! I mark thee morn to morn,
  Thy snow-white flowers renewing,
But long ere evening rent and torn,
On every passing zephyr borne,
  Their leaves the cold earth strewing.

And ere the sun's declining ray,
  O'er lawn and forest bower,
Pours the last glories of the day,
Thy new-born buds have passed away,
  Unshook by wind or shower.   *Anon.*

The Cistus, or Rock-rose, is one of those plants that bear a beautiful, yet short-lived flower. It flowers, and almost immediately casts its petals. It is found growing native in rocky and barren places. It bears a beautiful white, or variegated blossom, which, it is said, often comes forth in the morning, and withers and falls before evening. Scotland, the native land of the Heaths and Ferns, produces this flower in considerable abundance. The Scottish poets have often associated it with their other wild mountain plants. It is frequently mentioned in connexion with the hare-bell and furze. It seems to be related to the Laburnums, and is sometimes confounded with them. From its unstable flower, changing aspect, and rapid decay, it has been made the emblem of *Inconstancy*. It *literally* " blooms at morn, and fades at night." Several varieties grow native in New-England. Professor Eaton informs us, that, during the months of November and December of 1816, he saw several hundreds of these plants at the foot of Pine-rock, near New-Haven, sending out " their curved ice-crystals, about an inch in breadth, from near the roots." These were melted away by day, and renewed every morning, for more than twenty days in succession.

Many beautiful shrubs belong to the genus Cistus, though some of them are herbaceous. In different kinds, the blossoms are white, purple, or yellow. A cup of five leaves, two smaller than the rest, a capsule covered by the cup, and a corolla of five petals, are the characteristics which distinguish this genus.

The species of Cistus, known by the name of *Cistus labdanif- era*, grows native in the Levant. It produces the odoriferous balsam, or resin, known by the name of *Gum labdanum*. This is collected by means of leather thongs. They are rubbed, gently, on the surface of the shrub, that produces it. The Cistus and Hypericum, or John's-wort, belong to the *Rotaceæ*, or wheel-shaped flowers. The *natural* order *Cistus* contains two divisions. The *first* includes the Cistus, or Rock-rose, and Hudsonia ; and the *other* the genus *Viola*, or Violet.

The Rock-rose, or *Cistus canadensis*, is without stipules, erect ; leaves alternate, erect, linear-lanceolate, flat, tomentose beneath, divisions of the calyx broad-ovate-acuminate : capsules shorter than the calyx.

SNOW-DROP.

MILK-FLOWER, SNOW-PIERCER, LITTLE WHITE NARCISSUS,
GALANTHUS, BUCA-NEVE, PERCE-NEIGE, NARCISSOLEUCOIUM.

CLASS, Hexandria, from
hex, six, *aner*, stamen.

ORDER, Monogynia, from
monos, one, *gune*, pistil.

Because these flowers have *Six Stamens* and *One Pistil*, and are consequently of the *Sixth Class* and *First Order* of Linnæus.

Galanthus nivalis,	Snow-drop.
Allium fragrans,	False Snow-drop.
" *senescens*,	False Narcissus.
" *vineale*,	Field Garlick.

There are but one or two species of the *Galanthus* found growing in the Eastern and Middle
States of North-America.

THE EMBLEM OF FRIENDSHIP IN ADVERSITY.

. . . . The Snow-drop foremost,
Breaks through the frozen soil. In calm disdain
Of danger, robed like innocence, steps forth
And dares the threat'ning furies of the north.
Long ere the sap is to the bud conveyed,
Midst icicles in various forms displayed,
The bee had spied the cinque-rayed star which glows
Within the bosom of the pale primrose.
The violet peeped through bush-leaves waving o'er her,
And found the Snow-drop had awoke before her;
And the blush-rose drew back her head of green,
But came not out because her sister queen,
The pale-cheeked lily, in her close pavilion,
Lay still entranced ; while, scatter'd round, a million
Of little flowers on every bank looked forth. . . .   *Eustace.*

This sweet and lovely little flower pierces through the cold
snows and ice of winter. It puts on its meek blossoms while yet

the howling blasts are sweeping over the desolate plains. While all nature seems deformed, and is wrapped in a mantle of snow, this "child of the tempests and nursling of the storms," is seen to peep from the sunny side of hills, and to burst the frozen soil of our glades, woodlands and gardens, shedding joy and delight, as one of the earliest harbingers of spring. Its blossom is of a delicate white, slightly tinged with green. Some of its varieties are nearly of the purest white. In this "robe of innocence," it modestly seems to brave the furies and bid defiance to the threatening dangers of the wintry tempests. Hemmed in with snows on every side, it calmly dares the surly frowns of winter. From the whiteness of its blossom, it has received the name of *Galanthus,* or Milk-flower. The term *galanthos* is a Greek word from *gala,* milk, and *anthos,* flower, because this flower is of the colour of milk. It has also been called by the French *perce-neige,* or Snow-piercer, because it bursts up with its little flower through the snow, piercing it. The term Snow-drop is evidently derived from these circumstances, together with the colour of the flower itself. The beautiful poetess, Mrs. Barbauld, has given us a very fanciful origin of this flower. She tells us, "the breath of Flora, the goddess of flowers, by some transforming power, has changed an icicle into a Snow-drop." One poet tells us, "'tis the wan herald of the floral year." Montgomery calls it "the morning-star of flowers, and welcome messenger of peace." Wordsworth, the "early herald of the infant year, the gentle monitor of coming spring."

As it appears when there is nothing to cheer or enliven, and when every thing looks desolate and dreary, it truly may be said to "awaken joy in the bosom of sadness." This is particularly true in regard to those who are fond of contemplating natural objects. This flower has therefore become the emblem of "Friendship in Adversity." Its corolla is superior, and consists of six white petals; the innermost are the shortest, and are supposed to be the nectary. It appears to great advantage when intermingling its blossoms with those of the Crocus, to which it is nearly related. The *Narcissus, Amaryllis, Polyanthus, Leptanthus,* and *Galanthus,* all belong to the same *natural* tribe of plants.

The Snow-drop, or *Galanthus nivalis,* has leaves linear, keeled, acute, radical : scape one-flowered.

E

MOSS-ROSE.

COMMON RED MOSS-ROSE, ROSA MUSCOSA.

CLASS, Icosandria, from *ikosi,* twenty, *aner,* stamen.   **ORDER,** Polygynia, from *polus,* many, *gune,* pistil.

Because these flowers have *Twenty or more Stamens* inserted on the calyx, or corolla, and *Twenty or more Pistils,* and consequently are of the *Twelfth Class* and *Third Order* of Linnæus.

Rosa muscosa,	Moss-Rose
" *semperflorens,*	Monthly Rose.
" *pendulina,*	Thornless Rose.

Beside these, there are at least twenty or thirty species, with many varieties of the Rose, found growing in the Eastern and Middle States.

THE EMBLEM OF SUPERIOR MERIT.

The angel of the flowers one day
Beneath a *Rose-tree* sleeping lay ;
Awaking from the light repose,
The angel whisper'd to the Rose—
" O fondest object of my care,
Still fairest found where all is fair,
For the sweet shade thou'st given to me,
Ask what thou wilt, 'tis granted thee."
Then said the Rose with deepen'd glow,
" On me another grace bestow."
The spirit paused in silent thought :
What grace was there that flower had not !
'Twas but a moment—o'er the rose
A veil of *moss* the angel throws,
And, robed in nature's simplest weed,
Could there a flower that rose exceed ?   *Monthly Anthology.*

The single yellow Rose from Italy is a rich treasure, for its fragrance and its beauty.   The large double Levantine yellow Rose is a richer, both for its elegance and its fragrance. Its fine odour strongly resembles that of a most delicious pine-apple, which has sometimes caused it to be named the *pine rose.* The Eglantine, or English Sweet-briar rose, more commonly in our country called simply the Sweet-briar, is a very poetic, and much admired species. It adorns and gems our hedges, road-sides, and swamps, in spring, with its beautiful pale-red blossoms, consisting generally of five petals. In this respect it agrees with all the different species of Roses in their native state. The whole genus of this " queen of flowers" agree in a cup of five divisions, a corolla of five petals, and a turban-shaped fleshy berry, formed out of the cup, and terminated by the divisions of it.

The wild Eglantine, a native of our swamps, perfumes the breath of morning with its delicious odour, and the dewy breeze of evening comes loaded with its sweets. It cheers the sight with its gems, spangling the forest glade, and fills the air with the richest aroma that can charm the sense. By the poets it is often associated with the Woodbine and Honeysuckle. Some of its varieties, however, are nearly scentless.

The Musk Rose is beautiful, and the Provins Rose very delicate, and much admired. But the Moss Rose, with its delicate little flowers half concealed in their modest envelope of 'nature's simplest weed, a fold of moss,' is exquisitely lovely. Its retiring and modest habit, half concealing its beauty from the vulgar gaze, has attracted the love and admiration of all in its behalf. When freshly gathered from the stem, and full of dew, it seems scarcely less rich or curious than a 'ruby gem.' It is frequently, in poesy, an associate with the Lily and Violet. These roses are of various tints : the red the most common. The 'sylvan mantle,' or simple covering of moss, that envelopes this charming flower, half concealing its beauty, has rendered it the emblem of *Youth, Love,* and *Retiring Beauty* ; and it has also been esteemed the symbol of *Superior Merit,* perhaps for similar reasons.

The Moss Rose, or *Rosa Muscosa,* has a germ ovate : calyx, peduncles, petioles, and branches hispid, glandular-viscid, (mossy-like) : spines of the branches scattered, straight.

CATCH-FLY.

SILENE, CATCH-FLY, WILD PINK.

CLASS, Decandria, from *deka*, ten, and *aner*, stamen.

ORDER, Trigynia, from *treis*, three ; *gune*, pistil.

Because these flowers have *Ten Stamens* and *Three Pistils*, and are consequently of the *Tenth Class* and *Third Order* of Linnæus.

Silene noctiflora,	Night-flowering Catch-fly.
.. *antirrhina*,	Sleepy Catch-fly.
.. *pennsylvanica*,	Pink Catch-fly.
.. *dichtoma*,	Forked Catch-fly.

There are Sixty-six *Species* of the Silene or Catch-fly, eight or ten of which are found growing in the Eastern and Middle States of North-America.

THE EMBLEM OF ALLUREMENT AND DESTRUCTION.

Unlike SILENE, who declines
The garish noontide's blazing light ;
But when the evening crescent shines,
Gives all her sweetness to the night. *Smith*.

The fell SILENE, and her sisters fair,
Skilled in destruction, spread their viscous snare,
Oh guide from hence your rapid course afar,
If with soft words, sweet blushes, nods and smiles,
The artful Syrens lure you to their toils.

The *Drosera, Dionea, Muscipula*, and *Silene*, might all, without impropriety, be termed Catch-flies. The Dionea Muscipula is indeed called ' *Venus's Fly-trap*.' The Drosera is sometimes known by the name of *Ros Solis*, or Dew-of-the-Sun ; and Sundew. These are all different genera, yet they are all said to be *fly-catchers* : they are sister plants in this respect at least, and are all very pretty little flowers. Many of them are to be found growing about our fields or in our gardens. Some writers make more than 100 species of *Silene*. This number is probably too large. The *Silene Pennsylvanica*, or Pennsylvania Catchfly, grows native about our fields in New-England, and is known by the name of Wild Pink, from its similarity of appearance and habit to some of the pinks. The *Silene Antirrhina* is often known by the name of Snap-dragon Catchfly. A fine variety of the Silene is found in Ohio, with scarlet flowers. The Campion or Lychnis and Silene have a near resemblance to each other. The viscous matter that surrounds the stalks of the flowers of a species of the Catchfly prevents various insects from plundering the honey ; and also keeps them from the *pollen*, which fertilizes the seeds. The Dionea Muscipula, or Venus's Fly-trap, possesses a still more wonderful means of preventing the depredations of insects. The leaves are armed with long teeth, like the antennæ of insects, and lie spread upon the ground around the stem. They are so irritable, that when an insect creeps upon them, they fold up and crush or pierce it to death. It is a white flower, and grows native in the swamps of the Southern states. The Sundew is a plant with a purple, yellow, or white blossom, and very common in marshes. This is furnished with the same means of self-defence. The flower of the Arum Muscivorum has the odour of putrid flesh, which induces the flies to deposit their eggs within the chamber of the flower. The young, hatched from these eggs, are unable to escape from this prison, being prevented by the hairs pointing inwards ; They of course perish. This circumstance has given to this plant the name of Fly-eater. It is presumed that the air evolved by the bodies of these dead insects may subserve the purposes of vegetation to these plants, by affording them nourishment. Leaves are well known to purify air impregnated with carbonic acid from whatever cause. From the circumstance of these plants alluring small insects, and retaining their little prisoners as captives, and destroying them, they have become the emblem of *Art, Allurement, Blandishment, Dissimulation,* and *Destruction.*

The Pink Catch-fly, or *Silene Pennsylvanica*, is viscid-pubescent: lower leaves wedge-form ; upper leaves lanceolate : stems few-flowered at the summit: about three-petals, obtuse, slightly emarginate, sub-crenate.

POPPY.

PAVOT, PAPAVERO, PAPAVER.

CLASS, Polyandria, from *polus*, many ; *aner*, stamen. ORDER, Monogynia, from *monos*, one ; *gune*, pistil.

Because these flowers have *Twenty or more Stamens*, and *One Pistil*, and consequently are of the *Thirteenth Class* and *First Order* of Linnæus.

Papaver rheas,	Wild Poppy.
" *somniferum*,	Opium Poppy.
" *eraticum*,	Corn Poppy.

Besides these, there are several other species exotic, and perhaps one or two native, found grow-ing in the United States.

THE EMBLEM OF FORGETFULNESS.

When jocund summer leads her laughing hours,
And decks her zone with odorific flowers,
'Tis then thy charms attract the vulgar gaze,
And tempt the view with meretricious blaze !
Caught by thy glance, with pleasure they behold
Thy glowing crimson melting into gold.
In vain to nobler minds thy lure is spread,
Thy painted front, thy cup of glowing red :
Beneath thy bloom such noxious vapours lie,
That when obtained and smelt, we loathe and fly ;
Thus pleasure spreads for all her silken joys,
And oft, too late, the painted prospect cloys. *Taylor.*

Of this oblivious and sleep-producing plant there are several varieties. They are found of every variety of colour and shade, from the purest white almost down to the jet black. The juice of the *Papaver somniferum* is the common opium. It is sometimes called *Opium Thebaicum*, from being originally prepared at Thebes. The ancients called it *Manus Dei*, the hand of Deity, because of its extensive use in allaying pain. This plant is a native of the warmer countries of Europe and Asia, where it grows abundantly. Its inspissated juice is used, in large quantities, by the luxurious Asiatics, as a temporary introduction into their fancied Elysium. Thomson, in his ' Castle of Indolence,' represents it as surrounded " with naught but the images of rest,"—" sleep-soothing groves, and flowery beds, that breathe a slumbrous influence from drowsy poppies." Ovid informs us, that " the sombre night gathers sleep from the drowsy breath of the dead-sleeping poppy, and sheds it over the slumbering world." This flower may truly be said to be the *emblem*, as the cause of STUPOR, and FORGETFULNESS. It yields no balm to the passing gale, no " sweets to the sweet." It has no choice buds to adorn the brow of youthful beauty. But a drowsy and oblivious atmosphere surrounds it, and its presence brings only death, or sleep and dreams, the image of death. Yet there is a little *bee*, called the *poppy bee*, that builds, or rather furnishes her house with the leaves or petals of this flower. She makes her appearance, in the spring, in France and some other European countries, just as the wild poppies open their beautifully coloured flowers. She excavates a subterranean habitation, or nest, near some flowery field, and, selecting a flower, cuts from its richly coloured petals, a piece, large enough for her purpose. She then carries it to her habitation, and lines completely its inside with piece after piece, till her little fairy cell is elegantly furnished with this rich tapestry. She makes its lower part, or floor, soft, by the addition of several layers. The Red Poppy has been esteemed the emblem of *Evanescent Pleasure*, the Scarlet of *Forgetfulness* or *Consolation*. The term ' *Papaver*,' from which our English word ' Poppy' is derived, is from ' *Pappa*,' pap, so called because nurses used to mix this plant in children's food to relieve pains and make them sleep.

The *Papaver, Sanguinarea, Nymphæa, Nuphar, Agrimonia*, and several other natural genera, belong to the same *natural* order of plants. The natural order *Papaveraceæ* includes them all.

The Opium Poppy, or *Papaver Somniferum*, has a calyx and capsule glabrous : leaves clasping, gashed, glaucous.

LAUREL.

BAY, BAY-TREE, GREEN BAY-TREE, COMMON SWEET-BAY,
SWEET-SCENTED-LAUREL, BOSE-LAUREL, RAY-LAUREL, LAURUS, LAURIER.

CLASS, Enneandria, from   ORDER, Monogynia, from
ennea, nine; *aner*, stamen.   *monos*, one; *gune*, pistil.
Because these flowers have *Nine* stamens and *One* pistil, and are consequently of the Ninth Class and First Order of Linnæus.

Laurus Camphoratus,	Camphor Tree.
„ *Sassafras*,	Sassafras Tree.
„ *Benzoin*,	Spice Bush, or Fever Tree.

There are thirty-two species of the Laurel, with numerous varieties, several of which are found
growing in the Eastern and Middle States of North America.

THE EMBLEM OF IMMORTALITY.

Amid the plain a splendid LAUREL stood,
The grace and ornament of all the wood.
Her leafy arms with such extent were spread,
So near the clouds was her aspiring head,
That hosts of birds that wing the liquid air,
Perched on the boughs, found nightly lodging there;
And flocks of sheep beneath the shade, from far,
Might hear the rattling hail and wintry war;
From heaven's inclemencies here find a safe retreat,
Enjoy the cool and shun the scorching heat.
A hundred knights might here at ease abide,
And every knight a lady by his side.
The trunk itself such odours did bequeath,
That a Moluccan breeze to these were common breath.   *Dryden.*

The common Sweet-Bay, or *Laurus nobilis,* has been celebrated in all ages. With us it appears as a shrub, but in the south-

ern parts of Europe, and in western Asia, it grows to the size of a majestic tree. It has large evergreen leaves, of a fine texture, with an agreeable smell, and aromatic taste. Strabo tells us, it is found growing plentifully on the banks of the Eurotus, and St. Pierre informs us that it is found abundantly on the borders of the river Pæneus in Thessaly. Hence probably the origin of the fable of the metamorphosis of Daphne, the daughter of that river. The Bay is of very vigorous and hardy growth. It often revives, and regains its verdure, after it has for months appeared lifeless. Hence the practice has been common, in many countries, to throw a sprig of Laurel upon the coffin of the dead at burial, as a symbol of *Immortality*, or as significant of the hope of resuscitation from the grave. The Sweet-scented Laurel, so much celebrated in poetry, was formerly woven into chaplets and crowns, and worn by conquerors and heroes, on their triumphant return from war. Julius Cæsar is said to have worn a crown of Bay, and from him all his successors until the time of Justinian. The poets also, and those who had distinguished themselves in music, were honoured with chaplets of Laurel leaves. The gates of the imperial palaces, and of the courts of the high priests, were wreathed with Laurel. The Greeks bestowed crowns of it upon those who were victorious in their public games. Physicians were fond of wearing it, in honour of Apollo, the god of medicine. Young Doctors wore crowns of Laurel in berry, and students were thence called *bacca laureats*, or bachelors, from the Latin *bacca*, a berry. It was planted before the houses of the sick ; Jupiter wore a crown of it ; Clio, the muse of history, was crowned with it ; the priestess of Delphi wore it, and Apollo wore a chaplet of its leaves. This and the Misletoe are used in England for decorating churches at Christmas. It is deemed the meed of virtue and merit, the symbol of the desert of praise and immortality, and its honours are claimed by the poet and hero, as a just inheritance. The term *laurel* is from the Latin *laus*, signifying praise or glory. The Mountain Laurel is the emblem of *Ambition*, and the Rose Laurel, of which the above plate represents a variety, that of *Virtue*. The *natural* order MAGNO-LIÆ embraces the two genera *Liriodendron*, and *Magnolia*. The genus *Laurus* belongs to another order, the order KAURI.

The Big-Laurel, Magnolia, or *Magnolia grandiflora*, of our Southern States has leaves evergreen, oval, thick, leathery : petals broad-obovate, abruptly narrowed into a claw. Cultivated.

F

HYACINTH.

JACINTH, HAREBELL, HYACINTHUS, JACINTHE-DES-FLEURISTES.

CLASS, Hexandria, from *hex,* six, *aner,* stamen.

ORDER, Monogynia, from *monos,* one, *gune,* pistil.

Because these flowers have *Six Stamens,* and *One Pistil,* and are consequently of the *Sixth Class* and *First Order* of Linnæus.

Hyacinthus orientalis,	Garden Hyacinth.
,,	*botryoides,*	Grape Hyacinth.
,,	*racemosus,*	Harebell Hyacinth.
,,	*muscari,*	Musk Hyacinth.

Besides these, there are a few other species of this flower growing in the Eastern and Middle States of North-America.

THE EMBLEM OF CONSTANCY.

A HYACINTH lifted its purple bell,
From the slender leaves around it,
It curved its cup in a flowing swell,
And a starry circle crowned it ;
The deep-blue tincture, that robed it, seemed
The gloomiest garb of sorrow,
As if on its eye no brightness beamed,
And it never in dearer moments dreamed
Of a fair and calm to-morrow.   *Percival.*

While I, with grateful heart, gather him yellow
Daffodils, pinks, anemones, musk-roses,
Or that red flower, whose lips ejaculate
Wo ! and form them into wreaths and posies.   *Ovid.*

This charming flower is found in many varieties of red, blue, and purple.   The blue varieties of the flower are campanulate, or bell-form. This plant is very frequently alluded to by the poets. Clarke, in his travels in the East, tells us it is found there in the richest abundance, where it spreads its beautiful flowers lavishly in spring over all the fields. It loads the air, in these places, with its spicy odours wafted on every gale. Those who examine this flower will observe the graceful curling or folding of its petals or flower-leaves: the poets have hence spoken of 'hyacinthine locks of hair,' of youths ' whose locks divinely spread like vernal hyacinths,' and of ' hyacinths handsome, with clustering locks.'

This flower by culture frequently becomes very double ; and is often seen of the size of a dollar, of a dark porcelain-blue, some-times rosy or red, and occasionally pure white. It is sometimes found variegated. The single-flowered are generally considered the handsomest. Several fine varieties of this plant are brought from Holland with other bulbous roots. They naturally flower in May, but may be made to blossom at almost any season of the year, by proper attention. They are handsome parlour flowers when made to bloom in glasses. The Hyacinth of the ancients is supposed to be the *Martagon Lily* of modern times. This, Mar-tyn tells us, is marked with many spots of a darker colour than the flower itself, which often run together, so as to form the letters *ai.* This is a Greek interjection, meaning *wo* or *alas.* Hence the poet tells us of ' the red flower, whose lips ejaculate *wo !* '—of the ' languid hyacinth, who wears his bitter sorrows painted on his bosom,' and ' mournfully strives to show *ai, ai,* the more, amidst his sanguine wo.' The origin of this flower is thus described : Ajax Talemon, the bravest of the Greeks, except Achilles, disputed with Ulysses the claim to the arms of Achilles after his death. He found them adjudged to Ulysses, and stabbed himself with his own sword—from his blood sprang this flower. There is an-other story, that Hyacinthus was a youth, the affections of whom were sought both by Apollo and Zephyrus. That Apollo's love was not reciprocated, for which he slew Hyacinthus, and changed his blood into this flower, placing his body among the constella-tions. The term *hyacinth* is from the Greek *ai,* alas, and *anthos,* flower. The *purple hyacinth* has therefore become the emblem of SORROW, and the *red* and *blue* of CONSTANCY. The *Hyacinthus, Hemerocallis, Asphodelus, Allium, Ornithogalum,* and two or three other genera, belong to the same *natural* order ASPHODELI.

The Garden Hyacinth, or *Hyacinthus orientalis,* has its corol funnel-form, half-six cleft, ventricose at the base.

YELLOW PRIMROSE.

EARLY PRIMROSE, POETIC PRIMROSE, COPPER-COLOURED
PRIMROSE, PRIME VERE, PRIMA VERA, PRIMULA VULGARIS.

CLASS, Pentandria, from
pente, five ; *aner*, stamen.

ORDER, Monogynia, from
monos, one ; *gune*, pistil.

Because these flowers have *Five Stamens*, and *One Pistil*, and are consequently of the *Fifth Class* and *First Order* of Linnæus.

Primula acaulis,	Primrose.
.. *veris,*	Gowslip Primrose.
.. *elatior,*	Oxlip Primrose.
.. *auricula,*	Auricula Primrose.

There are *twenty species*, with many varieties, of the Primrose ; several of which are
found growing in the Eastern and Middle States of North-America.

THE EMBLEM OF VIRTUE IN THE SHADE.

Mild offspring of a dark and sullen sire !
Whose modest form, so delicately fine,
Was nursed in whirling storms, and cradled in the winds,
Thee, when young Spring first question'd Winter's sway,
And dared the sturdy blusterer to the fight,
Thee on this bank he threw, to mark his victory.
In this low vale, the promise of the year,
Serene thou openest to the nipping gale,
Unnoticed and alone thy tender elegance :
So virtue blooms, brought forth amid the storms
Of chill adversity ; in some lone walk
Of life she rears her head, obscure and unobserved ;
While every bleaching breeze, that on her blows,
Chastens her spotless purity of breast,
And hardens her to bear, serene, the ills of life.   *Kirk White.*

This charming flower, so often alluded to by the poet, and so much esteemed for the richness of its fragrance, is among the earliest of spring flowers. It is almost unequalled in fragrance. The genus is called *primula*, from the Latin *primus*, first ; because this is one of the first, or earliest flowers in spring. The term Primrose is from *primus*, first, and *rosa*, a rose, unitedly signifying the first or earliest rose. It is truly an ' offspring of a dark and sullen sire' ; for its parent seems to be winter, or at least, as the poet tells us, it seems ' nursed in whirling storms, and cra-- dled by the winds.'

The purple, deep blue, violet, and early yellow or poetic primroses, are among the varieties most admired. The Primrose has but one flower upon a stalk ;—the Oxlip and Cowslip have several. The Oxlip, Cowslip, Auricula, and Polyanthus, are all primrose flowers. The American Cowslip is very different from the flower in England known by this name. The American Cowslip is the *Caltha palustris.* Many of the blossoms of the primrose tribe of plants are of a pale yellow. The American Cowslip is found growing in our wet meadows, and is sometimes seen in flower before the snow and ice have all dissolved. The early yellow, or poetic primrose, is a native of Europe. It generally opens in early spring, in some sunny vale, or on the sunny side of a hillock : it ' opens its tender elegance ' to the nipping gale, while every bleaching breeze' blows without. Its ' modest form and delicate blossom flourish and diffuse their sweetness in defiance of the wintry blasts, and ' on its bank' it ' braves the rigours of departing winter.' The effect of cold seems only to ' chasten its spotless purity of breast.' It often is found growing in ' woodland glades.' From its retiring habit, rich fragrance, and hardihood, it has been made the emblem of *Virtue in the shade* or of *unpattronized merit.* The *Dodecantheon media* is often known by the name of *Cowslip.* The *natural* order LYSIMACHIÆ includes the *Primula, Dodecantheon, Lysimachia, Samolus, Huttonia, Buchnera,* and one or two other genera.

The Primrose, or *Primula acaulis,* has leaves rugose, toothed, hirsute beneath : scape one-flowered.

WALL-FLOWER.

STOCK-JULY-FLOWER, WALL-FLOWER, YELLOW STOCK, GIROFLII
JAUNE, BROMPTON QUEENS, LE-BATON-D'OR, PAVIENTARIA, CHEIRANTHUS.

CLASS, Tetradynamia, from *tes-*
sares, four ; and *dunamis*, power.

ORDER, Siliquosa, from
siliqua, a pod.

Because these flowers have *Six Stamens*, four of which are larger than the
other two, and have long slender *pods*, containing the seed, and consequently are of the *Fifteenth Class* and *Second Order* of Linnæus.

Cheiranthus cheiri,	Wall-flower.
.. *annuus*,	Stock-july-flower.
.. *fenestralis*,	Waved Wall-flower.

Besides these, there are one or two other *species* found growing in the Eastern and Middle
States of North-America.

THE EMBLEM OF CONSTANCY.

An emblem true thou art,
Of love's enduring lustre given,
To cheer the lonely heart !
Of love, whose deepest, tenderest worth,
Till tried, was all unknown,
Which owes to sympathy its birth,
And " seeketh not its own."
To me it speaks of loveliness
That passes not with youth ;
Of beauty, which decay can bless ;
Of *constancy* and *truth.*
Not in prosperity's bright morn,
In streaks of golden light,
Are lent her splendors, to adorn
And make them still more bright ;
But, in adversity's dark hour,
When glory is gone by,
It then exerts its gentle power,
The scene to beautify.   *Barton.*

This lovely flower " lends its splendours in adversity's dark hour," and strives to beautify " with its yellow blossoms, and streaks of golden light," dark and lonely ruins. It springs up spontaneously about the walls of dilapidated castles, churches, towers, and other ruins, " where the voice of revelry and the hum of business " hath long since ceased, and where " desolation and ruin greenly dwells." In Italy, France, Spain, and Switzerland, it is found native, growing about old buildings and ruins. It springs from the crevices of disjointed stones, ' et qua vides murorum moles prœruptaque saxa,' as the poet tells us. Cultivation has produced many very beautiful varieties of it, both double and single. The colour, most frequently met with perhaps, is that of a rich golden hue. These beautiful blossoms differ however in colour, from the pale yellow to the deep orange. None of the varieties excel the wild in fragrance. When this lovely plant is found clinging even to ruin and desolation itself, seeming desirous to hide deformity and decay, it seems a fit emblem of CONSTANCY ; and, as the poet in the above quotation says, " it speaks of loveliness that passes not with youth ; of beauty which decay can bless ; of constancy and truth." It has sometimes been etseemed the emblem of *Fidelity in Misfortune.*

Its blossoms are often found of a yellow-red, or iron-brown. Several varieties of this plant have been introduced into our gardens, where it is cultivated for its fragrance and beauty. When, in the sunny days of spring, its splendid tufts are seen rising along our garden walls, " in streaks of golden light," striving to brighten the scene, and to spread beauty and fragrance around, it may justly be said to claim our admiration.

The base of each of the short stamens of this flower are surrounded by a honey-cup gland. This causes the honied appearance of the cup you observe. The term *cheiranthus,* is probably a Greek compound, from *cheir,* the hand, and *anthos,* a flower, because these flowers spring out from the wall, clinging to its crevices, like the grasp of a hand. The genus is found mostly in Europe and Asia, but there are a few native *species* in America.

The *Cheiranthus, Lunaria, Sinapis, Thlaspi, Hesperis, Brassica, Cardamine,* and twelve or fourteen other genera, belong to the same *natural* order. The order CRUCIFERÆ embraces them all.

The Wall-flower, or *Cheiranthus cheiri,* has leaves lanceolate, acute, glabrous : branches angled : stem somewhat of a woody texture.

DOUBLE ANEMONE.

ANEMONE, WIND-FLOWER, L'HERBE-AU-VENTE.

CLASS, Polyandria, from *polus*, many ; *aner*, stamen.   ORDER, Polygynia, from *polus*, many ; *gune*, pistil.

Because these flowers have *Twenty or more disunited Stamens*, and *many Pistils*, and consequently are of the 13*th Class* and 7*th Order* of Linnæus.

Anemone hortensis,	Garden Anemone.
,, *virginiana,*	Wind Flower.
,, *nemorosa,*	Low Anemone.
,, *thalictroides,*	Rue Anemone.

Besides these, there are three or four other *species*, with several varieties, found **growing** in the Eastern and Middle States of North-America.

THE EMBLEM OF ANTICIPATION, OR EXPECTED PLEASURE.

Beside a fading bank of snow,
A lovely ANEMONE blew,
Unfolding to the sun's bright glow
Its leaves, of heaven's serenest hue ;
The snowy stamens gemmed them o'er.
The pleasing contrast caught my eye,
As, on the ocean's sandy shore,
The purple shells and corals lie.
'Tis spring, I cried, pale winter 's fled,
The earliest wreath of flowers is blown,
The blossoms, withered long and dead,
Will soon proclaim their tyrant flown.   *Percival.*

————I gathered rushes, and began
To weave a garland for you, intertwined
With violets, hepaticas, primroses,
And " *Bog-Anemone*," that ne'er uncloses
Her lips, until they're blown upon by the wind.   *Smith.*

Of this elegant and curious flower, there are several fine varieties abounding wild in New-England. They are among the earliest spring flowers. They are of various shades and colours, being of a white, red, blue, or purple tinge. They are sometimes found curiously intermixed and variegated. The various kinds growing native in this country, that adorn our fields and woods, generally blossom in the month of April. The *anemone nemorosa*, or Wood Anemone, is very abundant in spring, all about our woods and pastures. To a careless observer it bears some resemblance to the blossom of the strawberry. The term, *anemone*, is from the Greek word *anemos*, meaning *wind*, because these flowers were formerly thought to open their blossoms only when the wind blew. Pliny tells us, this flower is never known to open its lips except when the wind blows. This lovely and delicate flower of the winds is found not only in our country, but widely diffused over every quarter of the globe. In the Anemone, as in the Ranunculus, and many other flowers, the stamina often become obliterated, or transformed into petals, constituting what are called " double flowers," as in the one above.

Some of the finest double and single varieties have been introduced into our gardens, where they are cultivated for their beauty. They have been much improved by cultivation. This flower is said, by the poets, to wait *impatiently* for the breathing of the winds, and not unclose its lips,' or 'unfold its silken petals till blown upon.' One poet tells us, that ' in early spring, all wan and shivering in the gale, sadly, with head reclined, it waits for the gentle breathing of the zephyrs.' When they arrive however, he adds, ' their soft voice and balmy influence call forth its tender blooms. Their pencil paints it and their breath perfumes.' From its waiting for the breath of spring, and living in anticipation of a more congenial season, it has been made emblematical of *anticipation*, or *expected pleasure*. The Anemones are distinguished from the Ranunculus by the want of an empalement, which, in the latter, consists of five leaves. The essential characteristics of this genus are marked by the honey-cup. In some species it is a naked pore, in others it is surrounded by a cylindrical border, and in others it is inclosed by a scale indented at the end.

The Garden Anemone, or *Anemone hortensis*, has radical leaves digitate, divisions three-cleft ; cauline ones ternate, lanceolate, connate, subdivided : seed woolly.

G

DAMASK ROSE.

DAMSON ROSE, DAMASCUS ROSE, ROSA DAMASCENA.

CLASS, Icosandria, from *eikosi*, twenty, *aner*, stamen. ORDER, Polygynia, from *polus*, many, *gune*, pistil.

Because these flowers have *Twenty or more Stamens* inserted on the calyx, and *Twenty or more Pistils*, and consequently are of the *Twelfth Class* and *Sixth Order* of Linnæus.

Rosa damascena,	Damson or Damask Rose.
" *burgundiaca,*	Burgundy Rose.
" *semperflorens,*	Monthly Rose.
" *canina,*	Dog-Rose, or Canine Rose.
" *rubiginosa,*	Sweet Briar.
" *corymbosa,*	Swamp Rose.

Twenty or more *Species,* with several hundred indigenous and exotic *varieties* of the genus ROSA are found growing in the Eastern and Middle States of North-America.

THE EMBLEM OF BASHFUL LOVE.

If Jove would give the leafy bowers
A queen from all their world of flowers,
The ROSE would be the choice of Jove,
And blush the queen of every grove.
Sweetest child of weeping morning,
Gem, the vest of earth adorning,
Eye of flowerets, glow of lawns,
Bud of beauty, nursed by dawns.   *Sappho.*

A stream of tears upon her fair cheek flows,
As morning dew upon the *Damask Rose,*
Or crystal glass veiling vermilion ;
Or drops of milk on the carnation.   *Browne.*

It has been named in another place that the varieties of the different species of the Rose are so great, that their number in some of the English botanic gardens amounts to more than *fifteen hundred*. Such a variety in a single genus is truly surprising. Considering that this is deemed the queen of flowers, and one of the most fragrant as well as beautiful, we cannot but admire the beneficence of the invisible hand that has strown around us such a profusion of sweets. At the same time we are delighted with the richest of odours, the eye is regaled with the most exquisite blending of colours. In the deliciously sweet Damask Rose we meet with both white and red, and often with intermediate shadings of beautiful pink verging towards purple. The Damask Rose was so named because first brought from Damascus in Western Asia.

Among rosaceous plants are reckoned not only the Rose itself, but the apple, pear, quince, plum, cherry, laurel, almond, pomegranate, service, medlar, and several others. These are probably ranked among roses from the similarity of their inflorescence ; and though their flowers are less beautiful, the plants themselves are not less useful.

The Burgundy Rose, from its diminutive, shrubby stem and small blossom has been esteemed the emblem of *simple beauty* ; the Damask Rose, from the beauty, fragrance, and purity of its flower, the emblem of *youth* ; the Daily Rose, from its short-lived flower, the emblem of *frivolity* and *lightness* ; the deep-red Rose, from its blushing colour, the emblem of *bashfulness* or *shame* ; the China Multiflora, from its exuberance of flowers, the emblem of *grace* and *high mental cultivation* ; the common Dog-rose, or York-and-Lancaster Rose, of *war*, in consequence of its historical allusion : the red of this species having been adopted by the house of Lancaster, the white, by the house of York as a badge. The Thornless Rose, *rosa inermis*, is by some made the emblem of *ingratitude*, because Lemaistre tells us the thorns of other species have been produced by culture. A strange mode of reasoning this ! The White Rose, with little less reason has been made the symbol of *sadness* and *despair*, because its leaves are pale or white. The Rose was sacred to Venus, and of course to love Fable informs us, the flower was originally white, but Venus being wounded by its thorns, the blood

On the *white* rosebud being shed,
Made it forever after *red*.

The Damask Rose, or *Rosa Damascena*, has a calyx half-pinnate : germ ovate, turgid, (thickened near its top,) bristly : stem and petioles prickly : leaflets ovate, pointed, downy beneath.

LOVE-LIES-BLEEDING.

PENDULOUS AMARANTH, DROOPING AMARANTHUS, LOVE-LIES-BLEEDING, DISCIPLINE-DES-RELIGIEUSES, AMARANTHUS MELANCHOLICUS.

CLASS, Monœcia, from *monos*, one, and *oikos*, house.

ORDER, Pentandria, from *pente*, five, and *aner*, stamen.

Because these flowers are *not hermaphrodite*, but *androgynous ;* that is, those that *have the stamens, have no pistils*, and those that *have pistils, have no stamens*, the staminate flowers having *five stamens*, and consequently are of the *Twenty-first Class* and *Fifth Order* of Linnæus.

Amaranthus melancholicus,		Love-lies-bleeding.
..	*oleraceus,*	Pot Amaranth.
..	*tricolor,*	Three-coloured Coxcomb.
..	*albus,*	White Coxcomb.
..	*hypochondriacus,*	Spleen Amaranth, or False Princess Feather.

Besides these, there are eight or ten other *species*, with many varieties, of the *Amaranthus,* found growing in the Eastern and Middle States of North-America.

THE EMBLEM OF CONSTANCY.

A hero's bride ! this desert bower,
It il*l* befits thy gentle breeding :
And wherefore dost thou love this flower
To call—" MY-LOVE-LIES-BLEEDING ?"
This purple flower my tears have nursed ;
A hero's blood supplied its bloom :
I love it, for it was the first
That grew on Connocht-Moran's tomb.
Nor would I change my buried love
For any heart of living mould.
No, for I'm a hero's child—
I'll hunt my quarry in the wild ;
And still my home this mansion make,
Of all unheeded and unheeding,
And cherish, for my warrior's sake,
The flower of " *Love-lies-bleeding.*"   *Campbell.*

The beautiful lines from Campbell give a very fanciful origin to this flower. They are the "lamentation of O'Conner's child over the tomb of Connocht Moran." This flower is long and pendulous, with pink seeds and purple-red flowers. There is a close family resemblance between the White Coxcomb, Dwarf Amaranth, Pot Amaranth, Spleen Amaranth, Rough Amaranth, and Love-lies-Bleeding. Two or three varieties grow native among the weeds in our gardens. The term *amaranth* is from the Greek *a*, not, and *maraino*, to fade, these unitedly meaning 'not to fade,' or unfading, because these flowers are said never to fade or lose their colour when dead and dry.

The Bloody-Amaranth, or Prince's-feather, has a charming effect in our gardens about sunset, after a shower, or in the morning when bathed in dew. It then appears to stand sparkling in dewdrops, or rain-drops, like a cluster of rubies, or crimson coral, 'bedropt with thousand sparkling gems,' or 'diamonds bright.' The Crested Amaranth, or Coxcomb, is a noble plant. Its flowers are found sometimes yellow, red, pink, purple, and white. They are rich and beautiful in all their varieties. The name *coxcomb* is probably a corruption of *cock's-comb*, because the form of these flowers resembles the crest or comb of the cock. The heads are sometimes divided like a plume of feathers. These crests occasionally grow of immense magnitude. In Japan and India, they are said sometimes to be seen of a foot in length and breadth, of scarlet and other hues, exceedingly rich. The tree, or tri-coloured Amaranth, when in perfection, Miller informs us, is one of the handsomest of all plants. The *Gnaphalium*, or Life-everlasting, Indian Posy, Cud-weed, and Life-of-man, so common in our dry pastures, are handsome varieties of the Amaranth. Their flowers are often of a pearly or silvery white, but in Spain of a delicate yellow. There is a variety in England and southern Africa of a rose colour. Many of the varieties of the *Gnaphalium* exhale an agreeable odour, while some of them are quite scentless, or afford an unpleasant smell. The poetry quoted above, sufficiently explains why this flower is esteemed the emblem of CONSTANCY. The Love-lies-bleeding is often considered the symbol of *hopelessness without heartlessness.* Campbell, Milton, Shelly, Moore, and many other beautiful writers, frequently allude to the Amaranth ; and often form for us, amaranthine wreaths, chaplets, and bowers. ———

The Love-lies-bleeding, or *Amaranthus melancholicus*, has glomerules axillary, peduncled, roundish : leaves ovate-lanceolate, coloured.

TULIP.

TULIPE, TULIP, TULIPA, TULIPANA.

CLASS, Hexandria, from *hex*, six, *aner*, stamen.

ORDER, Monogynia, from *monos*, one, *gune*, pistil.

Because these flowers have *Six Stamens*, and *One Pistil*, and are consequently of the *Sixth Class* and *First Order* of Linnæus.

Tulipa suaveolens, Sweet Tulip.
.. *gesneriana,* Common Tulip.
There are *Five Species*, and many varieties of the Tulip, a number of which are cultivated, in our gardens in New-England.

THE EMBLEM OF PRIDE AND WORTHLESS BEAUTY.

Bright TULIPS, we do know,
Ye had your coming thither,
And fading time doth show,
That ye must quickly wither.
Your sisterhoods may stay,
And smile here for an hour,
But ye must die away,
E'en as the meanest flower.
Come, virgins, then and see
Your frailties,—and bemoan ye,
For lost like these,—'t will be
As time had never known ye. *Herrick.*

For brilliant tints to charm the eye,
What plant can with the *Tulip* vie ?
Yet no delicious scent it yields
To cheer the garden, or the fields,
Vainly in gaudy colours drest,
'Tis rather gazed on, than caressed. *Anonymous.*

This showy flower is found growing native in several parts of the Eastern continent, particularly in Persia. There are many varieties of it cultivated in our gardens. They blossom, most of them, in May or June. Tulips are truly rich in colour, but often destitute of fragrance. Many valuable varieties have been introduced into our country from Holland, and other parts of Germany. The Tulip, first from Asia, was originally introduced into Constantinople, thence it was brought to Western Europe, and at length to America, where it is now generally known and cultivated. This plant has a bulbous root, which in every respect resembles a bud, except in its being produced under ground. It includes the leaves and flower in miniature, which are to be expanded the coming spring. By carefully cutting through the concentric coats of the root, longitudinally from the top to the base, and taking them off successively, the whole flower of the next summer's tulip is beautifully seen. It is discoverable by the naked eye, with its petals, pistils, and stamens. Gardeners, in order to make a tulip striped or variegated, transplant it from a rich soil to one lighter. The powers of the plant become weakened and its colour changes, from its change of soil.

A Persian poet compares the cup of this flower to a drinking goblet. Churchill the poet calls the Tulip, 'full-drest and idly glaring to the view, the fop of flowers.' Another poet, cautioning a lady against pride in dress, tells her, 'she who chooses the tulip's splendid dyes shall own too late, when that decays, that vainly proud nor greatly wise, she only caught a short-lived blaze.' This certainly will be found true by those who depend wholly on dress for charms and attractions.

This flower among the Persians is considered emblematical of *perfect love.* When a lover presents one of these flowers to his mistress, he gives her to understand he is all on fire with her beauty ; by the black base of it, that his heart is burnt to a coal. The Tulip opens with the rising, and shuts with the setting sun. The essential characteristic of this genus is a corolla of six petals, bell-shaped, with no style. As these flowers ' flush the parterre with their glow,' and ' break upon the sight in the rich diversity of variegated dyes, of crimson and of gold,' yet being scentless, and nearly useless, they are strikingly emblematical of *pride* and *worthless beauty.* As the red variety of this flower is esteemed the symbol of a *declaration of love,* so the variegated is considered that of *beautiful eyes.*

The common Tulip, or *Tulipa gesneriana,* has a stem 1-flowered, glabrous : flower various-coloured, erect : petals obtuse, glabrous : leaves lance-ovate.

PERIWINKLE.

MOUNTAIN MYRTLE, EVERGREEN MYRTLE, VINE MYRTLE, PERIWINKLE, VIOLETTE-DES-SORCIERS, PERVINCLE, PERVENCHE, PERVINCA, VINCA.

CLASS, Pentandria, from
pente, five ; *aner,* stamen.

ORDER, Monogynia, from
monos, one ; *gune,* pistil.

Because these flowers have *Five Stamens,* and *One Pistil,* and are consequently of the *Fifth Class* and *First Order* of Linnæus.

Vinca minor, Periwinkle.
.. *major,* Greater Periwinkle.
There are several varieties of the Periwinkle. The *natural* order, " APOCYNEÆE," embraces the *Vinca, Asclepias, Apocynum, Nerium,* and several other Genera.

THE EMBLEM OF SINCERE AND EARLY FRIENDSHIP.

Through primrose tufts, in that same bower,
The PERIWINKLE trailed its wreaths,
And 'tis my faith, that every flower
Enjoys the air, that breathes.   *Wordsworth.*

Where bloom now
The king-cup. or the daisy ? where inclines
The harebell or the cowslip ? where looks gay
The vernal furze, with golden buskets hung ?
Where captivates the sky-blue *Periwinkle*
Under the cottage-eaves ? the Vinca's matted leaves ?
The Orchis race, whose varied beauties charm,
And mark the exploring *bee,* or fly's aërial form ?   *Hurdis.*

The Periwinkle, or *Vinca,* is a plant that may, usually, be found in almost any of our gardens.   Though not so much, or so often celebrated in poetry as some other flowers, it is not undeserving our attention, and fostering care.   Its flowers are blue, white,

and sometimes red. The centres of the red and white varieties
are generally yellow. It grows native in France and very abundantly. There, in the mystic language of nosegays and lovers, it
is sent in wreaths with other flowers, as presents, between friends,
as emblematical of SINCERE FRIENDSHIP. It belongs to the natural order, named *contorta*, from the Latin words, *con*, with, and
torqueo, to turn, or twist, because the divisions of the corolla are
turned to the same direction with the apparent motion of the sun.
The several varieties of the plant are distinguished chiefly by the
colour of the blossom. This plant was a great favourite among
the older English poets. Chaucer and Spenser make frequent
mention of its 'sky-blue flowers,' and 'trailing vine.' When it 'captivates, under the cottage-eaves,' with ' its cerulean bloom,' and is
seen ' with its matted leaves,' where the ' vernal furze looks gay,
with golden buskets hung,' it certainly must win our favour, and
seem poetic and delightful indeed.

Thetis, the daughter of Neptune, the god of the Ocean, was represented, by the ancients, as a female of dark complexion, with
dishevelled hair about her shoulders, wearing upon her head a
coronet or crown of *periwinkle*. This has been generally thought
however to be that beautiful sea-shell, rather than this plant. The
Periwinkle is, by the poets, often associated with kingcups, cowslips, daisies, and harebells. Its little vine, when twined with
other rich flowers into a wreath, is very pretty, and has a fine effect.

The flower of the periwinkle, though most frequently blue, is not
always so. It is salver-shaped. The segments are connected with
the top of the tube, which forms a figure of five sides. The general character of the order is a cup of one leaf. This is divided
into five segments. The flower is sometimes of one petal, and
funnel-shaped. It is furnished with a very curious nectary. The
Periwinkle is an ever-green vine. It usually blossoms early in
April. The Blue Periwinkle is considered the emblem of ' Early
Friendship'—the Red or White, of ' Pleasing Remembrance.'

The Blue Periwinkle, or *Vinca minor*, now naturalized among
us, is said to be a native of Egypt. Its flowers are scentless, with a
white centre. The *Vinca rosea*, or white and sometimes red Periwinkle, flowers a greater part of the year, bearing blossoms either
of a rose colour or pure white, with a rich crimson centre, and a yellow eye.   ——————

The Periwinkle, or *Vinca Minor*, has a stem procumbent : leaves lance-
oval, smooth at the edges : flowers peduncled : teeth of the calyx lanceolate.

H

CARNATION PINK.

PINK, BARBED DIANTHUS, CARNATION PINK, PRICKERY CAR-
NATION, DIANTHUS BARBATUS, DIANTHUS CARYOPHYLLUS.

CLASS, Decandria, from *deka*,   ORDER, Digynia, from
ten, and *aner*, stamen.   *dis*, twice ; *gune*, pistil.

Because these flowers have *Ten Stamens* and *Two Pistils*, and are consequently of the *Tenth Class* and *Second Order* of Linnæus.

Dianthus barbatus,	Sweet William.
.. *chinensis,*	China Pink.
.. *caryophyllus,*	Carnation Pink.

Besides these, there are two or three other *species* found growing in the **Eastern and Middle**
States of North-America.

THE EMBLEM OF PRIDE AND BEAUTY.

. . . . . Fair-handed Spring
Throws out the snow-drop and the crocus first,
The daisy, primrose, violet darkly blue,
And polyanthus of unnumbered dyes,
And yellow wall-flower, stained with iron brown,
And lavish stock, that scents the garden round.
Propitious Spring comes forth, in bright array,
With Venus, goddess of the vernal day :
Her mild precursor, Zephyr, wafts the breeze
With blooming wings, o'er all the budding trees,
Maternal Flora, with benignant hand,
Her flowers profusely scatters o'er the land.
These deck the vallies with unnumbered hues,
And far around their fragrant sweets diffuse ;
The broad CARNATIONS, gay and spotted pinks,
Are showered profuse along the river's brinks. *Gray.*

Of the Pink there are a great many species, with numerous varieties. We have them red, white, and beautifully variegated. *Four* only of the species, however, possess any great beauty as garden and pot flowers, or are generally cultivated ; but each of these have many beautiful varieties. They may be noticed under the following heads, 1st, the Carnation Pink, *Caryophyllus*, or Clove Gilliflower : 2d, the *Deltoides*, *Dianthus communis*, or common Pink : 3d, the *Chinensis*, Indian or China Pink : and, 4th, the *Barbatus*, or barbed Dianthus, Prickery Carnation, or Sweet-William Pink. The Clove Gilliflower includes all the varieties of the Carnation. The calyx or flower-cup of this kind is cylindrical and monophyllous, or one-leaved, with four little scales at the base. The fine purple Double Stocks of our gardens are totally disregarded by botanists, or considered as monsters. By rich culture, the stamens of these flowers have become mostly changed into petals, forming the beautiful Carnations of our flower-pots and parterres. The single Stock, in its natural state, has a cup of four pieces, commonly unequal by pairs : that is, there are two opposite and equal of a similar size, and two others also opposite and equal, but larger. Within this are four flower-leaves, which spread out at the top over the cup, at its edge, into a large flat border. The petals generally grow wide of each other, and exactly opposite, forming a figure resembling that of a *cross*. This has given them the name of *cruciform* or cross-shaped flowers. The petals of the corolla, and the leaflets of the calyx, are situated alternately : and this position prevails in all flowers, in which there is a correspondent number of petals and leaflets. The seed-vessel of one species is *unilocular*, or contains its seeds in one apartment. The root has trailing shoots. The term Dianthus is from the Greek *Dis*, Jupiter, and *anthos*, flower, unitedly signifying, Jupiter's Flower : It was so named from its extraordinary beauty and fragrance. This flower, when in perfection, is among the most beautiful and fragrant of flowers, and may well merit the emblematic assignation given it by the poet, that of *pride and beauty*. Originally simply red and white, the pink has become greatly enlarged in dimensions, and varied in its colours. The Mountain Pink has been considered the emblem of *aspiration*, and the Indian Pink that of *lasting loveliness*.

The Carnation Pink, or *Dianthus caryophyllus*, has flowers solitary : scales of the calyx sub-rhomboid, very short : petals crenate, beardless : leaves linear-subulate, channelled.

PERSIAN RANUNCULUS.

BUTTER-CUP, CROW-FOOT, KING-CUP, SPEAR-WORT.

CLASS, Polyandria, from *polus*, many, *aner*, stamen.

ORDER, Polygynia, from *polus*, many, *gune*, pistil.

Because these flowers have *many Stamens*, and *many Pistils*, and consequently are of the 13*th Class* and 7*th Order* of Linnæus.

Ranunculus acris,	Crowfoot,—Butter Cup.
.. *asiaticus,*	Persian Ranunculus.
.. *flammula,*	Spear-wort.
.. *sceleratus,*	Celery Crowfoot.
.. *fluviatalis,*	River Crowfoot.

Besides these, there are about twenty other species of the Genus *Ranunculus*, growing in the Eastern and Middle States of North-America.

THE EMBLEM OF WEALTH.

Bright-flowing *King-cups* promise future wealth—
The *golden King-cup* shines in merry May.　　*Southey.*

Fair is the King-cup that in meadow blows,
Fair is the Daisy that beside her grows——
Let weeds instead of *butter-flowers* appear,
And meads, instead of daisies, hemlock bear.　　*Gay.*

And fairies now, no doubt unseen,
　In silent revels sup ;
With dew-drop bumpers toast their queen,
　From *crow-flower's* golden cup.　　*Clare.*

The *natural* Order RANUNCULACEÆ embraces several different genera. The *Anemone Nemorosa, A. Virginiana,* and other Anemones belong to this natural order, as well as the Ranunculi,

or Butter-Cups. The *Hepatica* or Liver-wort, formerly called
Herb Trinity, sometimes Bog Anemone, and other *Hepaticæ*,
were formerly embraced in the natural order *Ranunculaceæ*, but
have of late been removed from it. The term Ranunculus, as observed in another place, is a diminutive of the Latin *rana*, signifying a *frog*, because these plants are often found in fenny or wet
places where frogs abound.

Prof. Eaton makes the Ranunculus of the 13th Class, 13th Order. The Persian Ranunculus (*R. Asiaticus*) or Asiatic Ranunculus includes many very beautiful varieties. These, with their
various-coloured double flowers of purple, yellow, pink, and crimson, are among the greatest ornaments of our gardens. They are
often nearly as large as roses, and come out very early in the season. They have been sometimes called English Ranunculi, probably from the circumstance of having been often brought to this
country from England. Asia, and particularly Persia, seems to be
their native situation, as it is of many other beautiful flowers, and
hence they have been called *Asiaticus*,—Asiatic and Persian Ranunculus. The roots of these, in a dry state, consisting of little
tufts of cylindric tubers, are commonly imported from Holland, the
great mart of the florist. Many of the largest of these flowers very
much resemble roses in their appearance to a casual and inexpe-
rienced observer. Most of the indigenous flowers of this extensive genus are of a bright yellow, the petals appearing internally
as if varnished. Some writers include in this extensive genus
ninety species. They are in flower all the summer months.

The *R. hispidus*, *R. cymbalaria*, and *R. filiformis*, have white
flowers oftentimes, as well as yellow, and the *R. nitidus*, I believe,
has white only. Most of the *species* of this genus of plants have
very *acrid* roots, producing a pungent or biting sensation when chewed. The common *Butter-Cup* of our New-England fields has been
esteemed the symbol of *Riches*, probably in consequence of its *golden flowers*. Perhaps in consequence of the golden season, in
which it makes its first appearance. If ' bright-flowing *King-cups*
promise future wealth,' we see no reason why this rich *species* of
Persian Ranunculus should not much more abundantly be also esteemed the emblem of *Wealth*.

The Crow-foot, or Buttercup *Ranunculus* has a five-leaved calyx : five
petals with a nectiferous pore, a small scale at the base on the inside : capsules numerous, ovate mucronated with the stigma, one-seeded.

ARUM,

CALLA-ETHIOPICA, WAKE-ROBIN, DRAGON-PLANT, MEADOW-PINK,
RAGGED-ROBIN, CUCKOO-PINK, LORDS-AND-LADIES, FRIARS-COWL, WILD-WILLIAM,
BLOODY-MEN'S-FINGERS, RAMP, INDIAN-TURNIP, BONNET DE GRAND PRETE.

CLASS, Gynandria, from *gune*, pistil, and *aner*, stamen.   ORDER, Polyandria, from *polus*, many, and *aner*, stamen.

Because these flowers have their *stamens arising from the pistil*, and *many stamens*, and consequently are of the *20th Class*, and *9th Order* of Linnæus.

Arum draconitum,	Green-Dragon.
,, *triphyllum,*	Wake-robin, or Indian Turnip.
,, *virginicum,*	Poison Arum.
,, *atrorubens,*	Brown Dragon.

There are upwards of *thirty species* of this plant,—one species without stems, with compound leaves, one species without stems, with simple leaves, and one species caulescent.

THE EMBLEM OF FEROCITY AND DECEIT.

Now peers the ARUM, from its spotted veil,
The hooded Arum, early sprouting up,
Ere the white thorn-bud half unfolds to view,
Arum, that in a mantling hood conceals
Her sanguine club, and spreads her spotted leaf,
Armed with keen tortures for the unwary tongue.
With net-wove sash and glittering gorget drest,
And scarlet robe, lappelled upon her breast,
Stern *Ara* frowns, the measured march assumes,
Trails her long lance, and nods her shadowy plumes,
While love's soft beams illume her treacherous eyes,
And beauty lightens through the thin disguise.   *Smith, Darwin, Clare.*

The *Aconitum Dracontium* is called Dragon Root. The *Maculatum* is the species known by the name of Cuckoo-pink, Wake-robin, and Lords-and-Ladies. This species, in Worcestershire, in England, is called Bloody-men's fingers.' Its root is pulverized, when dry, and sold by the French, as a wash for the skin, under the name of *Cyprus-powder*. The *Sanguineous*, sometimes called *Dumb-cane*, grows in the sugar islands of the West Indies, where it is used to bring sugar to a " good grain."

The root of the Arum, when filled with its juice, is exceedingly acrimonious or biting to the taste. It is not unfrequently used by roguish boys, by way of joke, upon their companions. They persuade them to taste it, and ascertain its fineness, when they pay for their curiosity, by the pain it gives them. It is found common in many of our meadows, or at least that species, called the *Arum dracumculis*. The Ragged-Robin, or Wild-William, is known by the appellation of Cuckoo-Pink, probably because it blossoms about the time of the return of this bird. The term *calla* is from the Greek *kallos*, beautiful ; *Calla ethiopica* signifying " the beautiful Ethiopian," because our cultivated garden Arum, or *Calla*, was originally from Africa. In the Calla we see a fine exemplification of what are termed the *spatha* or *spathe* and *spadix* of flowers. The cream-coloured monopetalous corolla is the *spathe*, and the central spike, elongated receptacle, or pistil, the *spadix*. The emblem of DECEIT is strikingly exemplified in this plant. For while it ' invites us, with its beautiful robes, and glittering gorget,' as the poet tells us, it conceals, within its mantling hood, a sanguine club, and, what is worse, ' is armed with keen tortures for the unwary tongue.' It has its pistil rising from the spathe, like a *club*. ‣This is singularly clothed with the *anthers*. Hence the poet's allusion, ' of the mantling hood, that conceals the sanguine club,' and of the ' measured march of Ara, while she trails her long lance, and waves her shadowy plumes.' The spadix, or receptacle of this plant, is itself of a white, cream-colour, or purple. It is often blotched with scarlet or black, and sometimes curiously streaked. The *Calla* has its spathe usually of a cream-colour, or white. The *Calla Ethiopica* is a native of Southern Africa, the West Indies, and, according to Sir William Jones, of Asia. The *Arum*, the *Calla*, the *Ictodes*, or Skunk's-Cabbage, the *Zostera*, and *Orontium*, are of the same *natural* order of plants. ———

The Indian Turnip, Wild Turnip, Wake-robin, or *Arum triphyllum*, is sub-coulescent : leaves ternate : leaflets ovate, acuminate : spadix club-form : spathe ovate, acuminate, peduncled, with the lamina as long as the spadix.

ICE-PLANT,

FICOIDES, MESEMBRYANTHEMUM CRYSTALLINUM, DIAMOND-
FIG-MARYGOLD, FIR-MARYGOLD, ICE-PLANT, DEW-PLANT.

CLASS, Icosandria, from *eikosi,*   ORDER, Pentagynia, from
twenty, and *aner,* stamen.   *pente,* five, and *gune,* pistil.

Because these flowers have *Twenty or more Stamens,* inserted on the cup,
and *Five Pistils,* and consequently are of the 12*th Class* and 5*th Order* of Linnæus.

Mesembryanthemum crystallinum,   Ice-Plant.
    mediflorum,   Fig Marygold.

There are *seventy-five species* of this curious plant, originally brought from **Greece.**

THE EMBLEM OF AN OLD BEAU.

Did you but know, when bathed in dew,
How sweet the little violet grew
   Amidst the thorny brake ;
How fragrant blew the ambient air
   O'er buds of many flowers fair,
Your pillow you'd forsake.   *Herrick.*

The snow-drop and the violet
Arose from the ground, with warm dew wet,
And their breath was mixed with fresh odours sweet
From the turf, like the voice and instrument.
Geranium boasts her crimson honours, and
The spangled beau FICOIDES glitters bright
The winter long—With pellucid foliage, the ICE-FLOWER gems
His rimy foliage and his candied stems.   *Darwin and Cowper.*

This curious plant, in several of its varieties, is found growing in our flower-pots and gardens. It has received the name *Ficoides* from the Latin *Ficus*, meaning a *fig*, because of the resemblance of its leaf to the fig. The Egyptian Fig-Marygold, or *Mesembryanthemum nudiflorum*, is a native of Egypt. It is there cut up, and burned for potash.

The Diamond-Fig-Marygold, or Ice-Plant, called also the Diamond Ficoides or *Mesembryanthemum crystallinum*, bears leaves covered with pellucid pimples, full of moisture. These, when the sun shines on them, reflect the light very beautifully, and appear like small bubbles of *ice*. Hence the origin of its names, *Diamond* Ficoides, Ice-Plant, Diamond-fig-marygold, and the like. Several species of it are exceedingly hardy, and the leaves of them remain green a considerable part of the winter.

The Dew-plant differs from the Ice-plant in having less of the frosted appearance. Its pellucid pimples, being less conspicuous, appear more like dew than bubbles of ice. The different species exhibit this frosted appearance more or less distinctly, and accordingly pass under the different appellations of *Dew-plant*, Frost-plant, Ice-plant, &c. These gem-like and brilliant elevations upon the foliage are nothing more than pellucid, gummy exudations from the surface of the leaves. The above plate exhibits the species that has generally been termed the Dew-plant.

The Ice-plant was anciently employed for medicinal purposes. Its medicinal virtues however, at present, are considered rather doubtful. The *natural* order, *Ficoideœ*, embraces the solitary genus, *Mesembryanthemum*. From the glittering and cold appearance of this plant the poet has considered it emblematical of an old BEAU. The Dew-Plant is emblematic of an Evening Serenade. There is hardly any thing can equal the Ice-Plant in richness of appearance when bespangled with its thousand glittering *gems*. The *red flowers* appear like *rubies*, set *among diamonds* in *emeralds*. This plant is very abundant in the Morea of Greece.

The Ice-Plant, or *Mesembryanthemum crystallinum*, is branching : leaves alternate, ovate, pappillose : flowers sessile : calyx broad-ovate, acute, retuse.

SWEET-WILLIAM.

PRICKERY CARNATION, BROAD-LEAVED PINK, BARBED DIAN-
THUS, ŒILET-DE-POETE, DIANTHUS BARBATUS.

CLASS, Decandria, from *deka*,
ten, and *aner*, stamen.

ORDER, Digynia, from
dis, twice ; *gune*, pistil.

Because these flowers have *Ten Stamens* and *Two Pistils*, and are consequently of the *Tenth Class* and *Second Order* of Linnæus.

Dianthus barbatus,		Sweet William.
„	*caryophyllus,*	Carnation.
„	*chinensis,*	China Pink.
„	*plumarius,*	Single Pink.

Besides these, there are two or three other cultivated *species* of the *Dianthus*, with numerous varieties, several found growing in the Eastern and Middle States of North-America.

THE EMBLEM OF PRIDE AND BEAUTY.

SWEET WILLIAMS, Campions, Sops-in-wine,
By one another neatly,
I'd twine to form this wreath of mine,
And finish it completely ;
For in every copse and sheltered dell,
Unveiled to the observant eye,
Are faithful monitors, which tell
How pass the hours and seasons by.
The green-robed children of the spring
As they, as the primroses they pass,
Mingle with leaves Time's feathered wing,
And bind with flowers his silent glass.   *Wilson.*

The barbed or prickery Dianthus, Sweet William, or Prickery Carnation Pink, is a very fine variety of this elegant flower. It rises with many thick, leafy shoots, crowning the root in a cluster close to the ground. The leaves are of a spear shape, and, in England, are evergreen. They are from a half an inch to two inches broad. The stems are upright and firm, branching, erect, two or three feet high.

All the branches and main stem are crowned with numerous flowers in aggregate clusters. These are of different colours and variegations, all springing from the same point. When this, as likewise the other Pinks, are sown in a light soil, their single flowers are always more numerous than their double ones. In order to raise these sweet and beautiful flowers in perfection, the seeds should be sown from about the 20th of March to the 15th of April. They should be deposited in a light sandy soil, mixed with manure and a little loam. Some of the branches should be pruned from the main stalk, should it be desired to obtain flowers of a large size.

There are cultivated, in some of the botanic gardens, not less than two hundred different varieties of the Pink.* These are arranged in the catalogues of plants, under different names. The Sweet William, Carnation, China, and Common Pink, are the four species, however, most generally cultivated. This, like the Carnation, to which it seems somewhat allied, has, like that flower, been sometimes esteemed as the emblem of " BEAUTY and PRIDE."

The Pink differs but very little in its generic characteristics from the *Soponaica,* or Soap-wort, sometimes known in our gardens by the appellation of Bouncing-bet. From this genus *Dianthus* the *Saponaica* differs in having a similar calyx naked at the base.

Dianthus belongs to the *natural* order CARYOPHYLLEÆ. The order embraces plants that are generally stimulent.

The Sweet William, or *Dianthus Barbatus*, has flowers fascicled : scales of the calyx ovate subulate, equalling the tube : leaves lanceolate.

* See Mr. Prince's catalogue of Carnations, in his Botanic Garden on Long-Island.

PURPLE PRIMROSE.

BLUE PRIMROSE, PURPLE POETIC PRIMROSE, PRIMULA PUR-
PUREA, PRIME VERE.

CLASS, Pentandria, from *pente*, five, and *aner*, stamen.　　ORDER, Monogynia, from *monos*, one, and *gune*, pistil.

Because these flowers have *Five Stamens*, and *One Pistil*, and are consequently of the *Fifth Class* and *First Order* of Linnæus.

Primula *farinosa*,	Bird's-eye Primrose.
" *auricula*,	Auricula Primrose.
" *elatior*,	Oxlip Primrose.
" *veris*,	Cowslip Primrose.
" *acaulis*,	Primrose.

There are *twenty species*, with numerous varieties, of the *Primula* or Primrose ; several of which are found growing in the Eastern and Middle States of North America.

THE EMBLEM OF VIRTUE.

In sunny April's joyous time,
I spoilt the daisy's earliest prime,
Robbèd every PRIMROSE root I met,
And oft-times got the root to set,
And joyful home each nosegay bore,
And felt as I shall feel no more.　　*Clare.*

As one who marked, with depth of thought,
How the bright day-flowers droop'd away,
An evening *primrose* home I brought,
Which opens at the close of day.
And when its blossom was ready to burst,
At the coolness of evening's hour,
I heard the hum of the murmuring bee,
As he wantoned from flower to flower.　　*Anthology.*

The yellow and copper-coloured varieties of Primrose are much admired for their fragrance and beauty. Though more fragrant, they are perhaps less beautiful, than the *purple*. They are found both single and double-flowered, yielding a very delicious perfume.

There is a *crimson* variety, with double flowers, and one or two varieties of double and single *lilach*, that are considered very beautiful. The purple variety is by some more admired, than any of the other kinds. Its colour is of a deep-blue violet, and, when in full bloom and perfection, it is exquisitely lovely. It is almost unequalled in beauty. Like the yellow, and all the other species of *Primula*, or Primrose, it is a very early flower. The stem is wanting in the Primrose, Daisy, and several other plants. They are said to be *acaulescent*. The flowers are supported by *scapes*, which spring immediately from the root. The *peduncle* springs from a stem. Wordsworth, alluding to the very early appearance of the various species of Primrose, says, " Spring may love them, Summer knows but little of them." The Primrose is called, " Nature's meek and modest child." If it be the meek and modest child of nature, possessed of so many endearing qualities, it is certainly entitled to its emblematic meaning of Virtue. When it " early paints the blushing mount, filled with morning's pearly dew," it was certainly an apt and beautiful comparison when the poet said to his mistress : " Pity, dear, is the primrose, wet with morning's tear." The whole tribe of these charming flowers are very beautiful in themselves ; and, as they appear, many of them before other flowers have made their appearance, they seem still more interesting and lovely on that account.

The Auricula Primrose, or *Primula Auricula*, has leaves serrate, fleshy, obovate : scape many-flowered : calyx mealy.

PROVINS ROSE.

BURGUNDY ROSE, PROVINCE ROSE, ROSA BURGUNDIACA, ROSA
PROVINCIALIS.

CLASS, Icosandria, from   ORDER, Polygynia, from
eikosi, twenty, *aner*, stamen.   *polus*, many, *gune*, pistil.

Because these flowers have *Twenty or more Stamens* inserted on the receptacle, and *Twenty or more Pistils,* and consequently are of the *Twelfth
Class* and *Third Order* of Linnæus.

Rosa rubiginosa,	Sweet-briar Rose.
" *multiflora,*	Japan Rose.
" *spinosissima,*	Scotch Rose.
" *burgundiaca,*	Burgundy Rose.

There are about 50 Species, and more than 1400 different varieties, of the Rose, found
growing in some of the gardens in Europe.

THE EMBLEM OF YOUTH, LOVE, AND BEAUTY.

Oh ! trust the mind,
To grief so long, so silently resigned.
Let the light spirit, ne'er by sorrow taught,
The pure and lofty constancy of thought,
Its fleeting trials eager to forget,
Rise with elastic power o'er each regret !
Fostered in tears our young affections grew,
And I have learned to suffer and be true.
Deem not my love a frail, ephemeral flower,
Nursed by soft sunshine and the balmy shower ;
No, 'tis the child of tempests, and defies
And meets, unchanged, the anger of the skies.   *Wilson.*

In velvet lips the bashful ROSE began,
To show and catch the kisses of the sun ;
Some fuller blown, their crimson honours shed,
Sweet smell the chives that grace their head.   *Fawkes.*

We are told of rosy cheeks, rosy blushes, rosy lips, rosy dawns, rosy clouds, rosy mornings, and rosy evenings. We are told of things, as red as the rose, as fresh as the rose, as fair as the rose, as sweet as the rose, and as soft as the rose's leaf. Whatever is chaste, or fair, or lovely, in poetry, is often, as chaste, fair, or lovely as the rose. Purity is also associated with the idea of this beautiful flower. Young, opening rose-buds are made to be emblematic of purity, youth, and dawning beauty. There would seem almost to be a spell in the very name of this fair and fragrant flower. It may truly be termed the ' Queen of Flowers.'

The mention of its name, like magic, seems to send the spirit, on an excursion of fancy, back or forward to the charming months of Spring. For a moment, we are surrounded with beauty and breathing pleasure. Percival, in telling us that " in certain lands they talk in flowers, and tell in a garland their loves and vows," informs us, that " the rose is the *sign of joy and love,*—young, blushing love, in its earliest dawn." It is *here* also the emblem of LOVE. About 9 or 10 species of the Rose are indigenous in America.

It has been a custom in some parts of France, in former years, for the youths of both sexes annually to assemble in the month of May and elect their *May queen,* or queen of the day. They crowned her with a chaplet of roses and other flowers. This is truly a crown of innocence, suited for the brow of youthful beauty. The first of May was formerly celebrated in England, by erecting a pole,—*May-pole,*—and wreathing it with festoons of the freshest and fairest flowers, gathered from the neighbouring woods. This pole was permitted to remain, for the whole year, untouched, except by the *seasons.* The fading emblem was deemed an acceptable offering to the *Goddess of flowers.* It was, in this manner, consecrated to her as such. The Provins Rose receives its name from a district of this name in France. It has often been termed the Province-rose, having been supposed to be named from this part of France ; but others have spelled it Provins, from a small town bearing this name. The deep-red Rose is esteemed the emblem of BASHFUL SHAME—the Burgundy Rose that of SIMPLICITY and BEAUTY—and the Bridal Rose that of HAPPY LOVE.

The Provins Rose, or *Rosa Provincialis,* has germs sub-glabrose : germs and peduncles hispid : leaflets ovate, pubescent beneath : coral small, full, fleshy-white, disk obscure : scattered reflexed prickles on the branches, and glandular serratures.

BUTTER-CUPS.

CROW-FOOT, KING-CUP, FAIR-MAID-OF-FRANCE, RANUNCULUS.

CLASS, Polyandria, from *polus*, many, *aner*, stamen.

ORDER, Polygynia, from *polus*, many, *gune*, pistil.

Because these flowers have *Twenty or more Stamens*, and *Twenty or more Pistils*, and consequently are of the 13*th Class* and 7*th Order* of Linnæus.

Ranunculus acris,		Crow-foot.
..	*abortivus,*	Butter-cup.
..	*flammula,*	Spear-wort.
..	*recurvatus,*	White Crow-foot.

Besides these, there are *Twenty* or *Thirty* other species, with many varieties of the *Ranunculus,* found growing in the Eastern and Middle States of North-America.

THE EMBLEM OF RICHES.

Bring corn-flag, tulip, and adonis-flower,
Fair ox-eye, goldy-locks, and colombine,
Pinks, goulands, *king-cups,* and sweet sops-in-wine ;
Blue hair-bells, paigles, pansies, calaminth,
Flower-gentle, and the fair-haired hyacinth ;
Bring rich carnations, fleur-de-lues, lilies,
Bring crown-imperials.   *Ben Jonson.*

Fair the *king-cup,* that in meadow blows,
Fair is the daisy that beside her grows,
Let weeds, instead of *butter-cups,* appear,
And meads, instead of daisies, hemlock bear.   *Gay.*

This beautiful little flower is so well known and so generally found in every part of New-England, as scarcely to need a description. There are many varieties of it. Those bearing the white and yellow flower are most common. Of these, the yellow is most generally to be met with. *Blue* varieties are however sometimes found. In May and June the yellow varieties are seen scattered all over our meadows and low pastures, giving them the appearance of being studded with amber.

The leaves, when spread, bear a tolerable resemblance to the foot of the *crow.* Hence its name *crows-foot.* The plant is said to blossom most, when butter is made in the greatest abundance. This circumstance, together with its yellow flower, probably gave rise to the name of *Butter-cup,* and Gold-cup. The generic term *Ranunculus* is derived from the latin word, *rana,* meaning a *frog,* because these flowers are said to grow most abundantly in low, marshy situations, that abound in frogs. Many species of the Ranunculus become much altered by cultivation. These, as well as the Anemones and many other flowers, have their *stamens* obliterated by culture, or rather changed into flower-leaves or petals, making their flowers extremely *double.* Our rich double varieties of Garden Ranuncules are all originally from the single-flowered wild one. The Butter-cup is a species of the Ranunculus. There are three kinds of it. Of the *Ranunculus,* there are FIFTY-NINE SPECIES. The *Ranunculus Aconitifolius,* or Aconite-leaved Crowfoot, is a very handsome species. It grows about three or four feet high, bearing a beautiful white flower, terminating each branch. The double-flowering kind of our gardens is known by the appellation of *Fair-Maids-of-France.* The white variety is native of the Alps, in Europe. The Persian Crowfoot, or Garden Ranunculus, has been much improved by cultivation. Many varieties of this species bear semi-double flowers, of large size and great beauty. Twenty or thirty flowers, of beautiful colours, and many of them finely scented, often grow upon a single plant of the last-named species.

The Persian Ranunculus, or *Ranunculus Asiaticus,* with its numerous and various-coloured double-flowering varieties, is one of the most brilliant ornaments of our gardens. The species presents varieties of brilliant-coloured flowers, nearly as large as roses. They come out at an early season in the year. The roots of the plant, in a dry state, consist of little tufts of cylindric tubers, and are commonly imported from Holland, the great mart of the florist.

The Crow-foot, Butter-cup, or *Ranunculus acris,* has hairs close-pressed: leaves three-parted, many-cleft, upper ones linear : peduncles terete : calyx spreading.

CARDINAL-FLOWER.

CARDINAL, LOBELIA, LOBELIA-CARDINALIS, INDIAN-TOBACCO.

CLASS, Pentandria, from *pente*, five ; *aner*, stamen. ORDER, Monogynia, from *monos*, one ; *gune*, pistil.

Because these flowers have *Five Stamens*, and *One Pistil*, and are consequently of the *Fifth Class* and *First Order* of Linnæus.

Lobelia cardinalis,	Cardinal Flower.
.. *inflata*,	Wild Tobacco.
.. *siphilitica*,	Indian Tobacco.

There are *Eight* or *Ten Species*, with several varieties of the *Lobelia*, found growing in the Eastern and Middle States of North-America.

THE EMBLEM OF MALEVOLENT ASPERSION.

O'er the throng Urtica flings
Her barbed shafts, and darts her poisonous stings,
And fell LOBELIA's suffocating breath
Loads the dark pinion of the gale with death.   *Darwin.*

Flowers are on the borders ; flags in blue
Carpet the hollow, roses on the knoll
Open their clustered crimson, CARDINALS
Lift, on the margin, spikes of fire.
Ranunculus, whose feathered stem, and starry bloom
Of glossy yellow, wafted on the flow,
Floats, like a sleeping Naiad, on the wave.

This flower is found growing in most parts of New-England, on the margins of brooks and rivulets. The extraordinary *red* appearance of it gives, at the first look of the beholder, the impression of a *cone of flame*. When " lifting on the shady margin of our brooks its spikes of fire," it is exceedingly handsome, and contrasts finely, with the deep verdure with which it is usually surrounded. This contrast, together with its reflection from the crystal wave, over which it often stoops, renders its appearance *highly poetic*.

The several species of the *Lobelia* are most of them poisonous. The species, bearing a *blue flower*, is known by the appellation of *Wild Tobacco*, or *Indian* Tobacco. It is considered extremely poisonous, though sometimes employed in medicine. This is called the *Lobelia inflata*. When taken in considerable doses, it is a powerful emetic and expectorant.

The red-flowered, the *Lobelia Cardinalis*, is said to be *anthelmintic*.

The *Syphilitica* species is emetic, cathartic, and diuretic, in its properties, but less so than the *inflata*.

All the species, growing in New-England, except the *Cardinalis*, bear a blue flower.

The generic term Lobelia is from *Lobel*, a distinguished botanist. The blue-flowered species is often, though improperly, termed the Cardinal-flower.

The *Lobelia syphilitica* was used by the Indians of this country in the cure of syphilitic disorders. Hence its name. It was considered by them a *specific*, in these disorders, and an important secret. Sir William Johnson purchased this secret of them, which has since been made public.

The root is the part used in medicine, and this in the form of decoction. A handful of its roots are steeped in three measures of water, and this proportion is taken morning and evening, till its emetic powers operate.

If, as the poet tells us, " fell Lobelia's suffocating breath loads the dark pinion of the gale with death," it is certainly not an unfit emblem of MALEVOLENT ASPERSION.

The Cardinal Flower, or *Lobelia Cardinalis*, is erect, simple, pubescent : leaves lance-ovate, acuminate, erectly-denticulate : racemes somewhat one-sided, many-flowered : stamens longer than corals.

COLUMBINE.

AQUILEGIA, GARDEN HONEYSUCKLE, WILD HONEYSUCKLE.

CLASS, Polyandria, from   ORDER, Pentagynia, from
polus, many, *aner*, stamen.   *pente*, one, *gune*, pistil.

Because these flowers have *many Stamens* and *Five Pistils*, and consequently are of the 13*th Class* and *Fifth Order* of Linnæus.

Aquilegia vulgaris,   Garden Columbine.
    ..   *canadensis,*   Wild Columbine.

There are only *Two Species* of the Aquilegia, yet described as growing in **New-England.**

THE EMBLEM OF DESERTION.

The *Columbine* in tawny often taken,
Is then ascribed to such as are forsaken.   *Browne.*

Mrs. Piony came in quite late in a heat
With the Ice-plant new-spangled from forehead to feet ;
Lobelia, attired like a queen in her pride,
And Dahlias, with trimmings new-furbished and dyed,
And the Blue-bells and Hare-bells, in simple array,
With all their Scotch cousins from highland and brae.
Ragged Ladies and Marigolds clustered together,
And gossip'd of scandal, the news, and the weather ;
What dresses were worn at the wedding so fine
Of sharp Mr. Thistle and Sweet COLUMBINE.
     Mrs. Sigourney's Party of the Flowers.

The term *Aquilegia* is from the Latin *aqua*, water, and *lego*,
to gather, because the leaves of this plant are so shaped as to retain

the water. The English name *Columbine* is from *columba*, signifying a Dove, because the five cornuted nectaries of these flowers, taken in connexion with the other parts, are supposed very much to resemble a nest of young doves. The Columbine, or *Aquilegia*, belongs to the same natural family with the *Delphinium*, or Larkspur. The flowers of this last genus are so named from *delphinium*, a dolphin, because they appear like a dolphin elevated on a pillar or filament. This genus, as well as the Columbine, possess a five-leaved peltoid calyx, and five very singular, hollow, tubular petals, or rather lepanthia, terminating below in spurs or horns, containing honey. The flowers are red, purple, blue, or white, with several intermediate tints. Our common coral-coloured flowering species (*A. canadensis*), like most of the genus, has bi-ternated or twice three-parted leaves, incisely or deeply toothed at the extremity. The scarlet flowers hang pendulous, with the styles and stamens exserted, and form, in rocky situations, one of the most elegant vernal ornaments of the season.

The *Aquilegia canadensis*, or Wild Columbine, so common in New-England in rocky situations, has often been called, though improperly, Wild Honeysuckle. This name probably originated from the copious secretion of honey in its horn-like nectaries. Small insects are often seen plunging headlong into these reservoirs, in order to rifle them of their sweet contents. Hence we hear, in poesy, of the " diving of the busy bee in the Columbine horn," and of the " elfin crew's hunting in the horns of these flowers to rifle from them their nectarious sweets."

The poet informs us " the *Columbine* is ascribed to such as are forsaken." It has therefore been properly deemed the emblem of DESERTION. Some writers make six or eight species of this genus. The indigenous or American species is very generally found from Canada, whence it has its specific name, as far south as the Carolinas. The plant grows native also in Siberia and several other parts of Europe.

The Columbine *Aquilegia, Delphinium, Aconitum, Anemone, Hepatica, Ranunculus, Helleborus, Clematis, Pæonia, Adonis, Nelumbium, Caltha, Podophyllum, Coptis, Zanthorrhiza*, and several other *genera* belong to the same *natural* order of Jussieu. The Order RANUNCULACEÆ embraces them all.

The Garden Columbine, or *Aquilegia vulgaris*, has its nectaries like incurved horns : leafy stem, and leaves glabrous : leaves decompound. Nectaries multiplied by culture.

MIGNONETTE.

DYER'S-WEED, FRENCHMAN'S DARLING, YOUNG NUN, DARLING,
MY LITTLE NUN, MY LOVE, MON AMI, HERBE D'AMOUR, RESEDA D'EGYPTE,
MIGNONETA, RESEDA ODORATA.

CLASS, Dodecandria, from *dodeka*,   ORDER, Trigynia, from *tres*,
    twelve, and *aner*, stamen.   three, and *gune*, pistil.

Because these flowers have from Twelve to Nineteen *Stamens*, and Three
  Pistils, and consequently are of the 11*th Class*, and 3*d Order* of
  Linnæus.

Reseda odorata,	Mignonette.
.. *luteola*,	Dyer's Weed.

Though this plant was thought to be indigenous in Africa alone, Professor Ives found the last named species growing near New-Haven, in situations which induced him to suspect it to be indigenous in New-England.

THE EMBLEM OF MEEKNESS AND AFFECTION.

For thee ! in Autumn, blows
The Indian pink, the latest rose,
The MIGNONETTE perfumes the air,
And Stocks, unfading flowers, are there.   *Smith.*

What are the casements, lined with creeping herbs,
The prouder sashes, fronted with a range
Of orange, myrtle, or the fragrant weed,
The *Frenchman's darling ?* are they not all proofs,
That man, immured in cities, still retains
His inborn, inextinguishable thirst of rural scenes ?   *Cowper.*

The casual observer of this lovely plant, unacquainted with its excellences, might be led to inquire,—" Why has it been so distinguished, and acquired so many endearing and tender appellations, since it possesses little more beauty, than the common pigweed ?" Its *fragrance* alone entitles it to our highest admiration. In this respect, it is hardly inferior to the Primrose itself. It should find a place among our pot-flowers in all our windows. When wet with the dews of morning, or after a shower, it fills the surrounding atmosphere with the most delicious fragrance. It breathes the richest of perfumes, and pours them forth in the greatest abundance. Though almost destitute of beauty, it has gained the esteem of all, who have ever breathed its sweets. It is a particular favourite among the French. Hence its great variety of French names. It is called by them *Reseda d'Egypte*, or Reseda of Egypt, because it was first introduced into France from Egypt, or from the northern countries of Africa. It has since become widely disseminated over Europe, and is now found " growing wild" there, in fields and pastures. It is cultivated in our gardens and flower-pots almost solely for its fragrance, usually blossoming in June or July.

Its flowers are generally white or yellow. Those of the *Reseda luteola*, or Dyers'-weed, are always yellow, and the *Odorata* both yellow and white. The former generally blossoms in August, and the latter in June. They are both *annual* plants, and consequently, in our climate, must be sown every spring.

The term *Mignonette* is from the French *mi*, my, and *nonette*, young nun. The other terms *Herbe d'amour, mon ami*, meaning the ' herb of love' and ' my friend,' sufficiently indicate the attachment of the French to this plant. Hence Cowper has called it the ' *Frenchman's darling.*' It should not be the darling of the Frenchmen alone, but of all who are fond of the cultivation of flowers. From the plainness and rusticity of its appearance, its meek and humble garb, together with its endearing qualities, it has been made symbolical of MEEKNESS and AFFECTION. It is by some esteemed the emblem of Worth and Loveliness. A quaint old poet tells us, " the adrous pea, with its wings up lightsomely," and " balsam, with its shaft of amber," and " mignonette, are for a lady's chamber." The latter, for its almost unrivalled fragrance, we should think peculiarly fitted for this place.

––––––

The Mignonette, or *Reseda odorata*, has leaves entire, and three-lobed : calyx equalling the coral.

SWEET TULIP.

TULIPE, TULIP, TULIPA, TULIPANA.

CLASS, Hexandria, from *hex*, six, *aner*, stamen. ORDER, Monogynia, from *monos*, one, *gune*, pistil.

Because these flowers have *Six Stamens*, and *One Pistil*, and are consequently of the *Sixth Class* and *First Order* of Linnæus.

Tulipa suaveolens,   Sweet Tulip.
 ..   *gesneriana,*   Common Tulip.

There are *Five Species,* and many varieties of the Tulip, a number of which are cultivated, in our gardens in New-England.

THE EMBLEM OF PERFECT LOVE.

Fair-handed Spring
Throws out the snow-drop and the crocus first,
The daisy, primrose, violet darkly blue,
And polyanthos with unnumbered dyes,
And yellow wall-flower, stained with iron-brown,
And lavish stock that scents the garden round,
Anemone, auriculas, enriched with shining meal,
O'er all their velvet leaves,
And full ranuncules, of glowing red.
Then comes the TULIP race, whose beauty plays her idle freaks.

The Tulip is called, in the Turkish language, *Lale.* The Turks are particularly fond of it. Their nobility cultivate it with the greatest care. They make great sacrifices to procure uncommon kinds of it of the newest and most beautiful varieties. These are presented to the Sultan, on a certain day in the year· The ceremony is exceedingly splendid, and is called *Zeafit-lalesi ;* that is to say, ' the festival of tulips.' When the tulips were in full bloom in their gardens, they intermixed them with small lighted lamps, and cages in which they enclosed nightingales, taught to sing. Thus they endeavoured to gratify both the senses of seeing and hearing. This they called *cieragan,* i. e. the *illumination.*

Tulips have been in so great request at Constantinople, that several Sultans have ordered roots to be brought them from all countries, in order that they might have every possible variety of these flowers. They endeavoured to produce a *blue* variety of tulip, by putting into the bulb the flowers or buds of the *syringa cærulea.* This experiment, as may well be supposed, was unsuccessful.

The Sweet Tulip is called *Odorata,* from the fine odour which it yields.

There are perhaps no flowers that assume a greater variety of colours and shades than tulips. The Sweet-scented Tulip, *Tulipa gesneriana,* is a native of Persia, and in its wild state bears crimson flowers. The circumstance of its being the custom in Persia to consider the crimson variety of this flower as emblematic of PERFECT LOVE, and its gaudy hues making it emblematic of POMP or PRIDE, as explained in a previous page, renders it unnecessary to remark further on its emblematical meaning.

The Sweet Tulip, or *Tulipa suaveolens,* is small : stem one-flowered, pubescent : flower erect : petals obtuse, glabrous : leaves lance-ovate.

L

CHRYSANTHEMUM.

ANTHEMIS GRANDIFLORA, CHINESE CHRYSANTHEMUM, EARLY
CHRYSANTHEMUM.

CLASS, Syngenesia, from *sun*,   ORDER, Polygamia Superflua, from
with, and *genesis*, generation.   *polus*, many, and *gamia*, nuptials.

Because these flowers *have their anthers united at top into a cylinder,* and
florets in the centre bisexual, and those in the circumference female, and
consequently are of the *Nineteenth Class,* and *Second Order* of Linnæus.

Chrysanthemum leucanthemum,	Ox-eyed Daisy.	
..	*coronarium,*	Garden Chrysanthemum.
..	*parthenium,*	Fever-few, or Febrifuge.
..	*carinatum,*	Three-coloured Daisy.

There are Fifty or Sixty Species of this plant, with many varieties—several of them from China.

THE EMBLEM OF FLATTERY.

Return, Apheus, the dread voice is past,
That shrunk thy streams ; return, Sicilian Muse,
And call the vales, and bid them hither cast
Fair bells and florets, of a thousand hues.
Ye vallies low, where the mild whispers are
Of shades and wanton winds, and gushing brooks,
On whose fresh lap, the swart sun sparely looks,
Throw hither all your quaint enamelled eyes,
That on the green turf suck the honied showers,
And purple all the ground with vernal flowers.   *Milton.*

Spring, bright Chrysanth'mums, let your flowers be seen
To star the fields, and gild the shining green.   *Anonymous.*

These plants are found in many varieties. The name Chrysanthemum is from the Greek *chrusos*, meaning gold, and *anthemon*, a flower, because many flowers of this species resemble gold in their colour. By some, the term Chrysanthemum has been applied to *all* flowers of a golden colour, including all the marygolds, sunflowers, &c. Many of the Chrysanthemums of our gardens are natives of China and Japan. Excepting the purple varieties, they have, many of them, been recently introduced into Europe, and this country.

In 1787, the *first* Chrysanthemum was brought from China into France. We have now more than forty different kinds, represented by original drawings, recently made in this country from growing specimens.

Twelve of these, and perhaps of the varieties least estimable, are of a kind bearing *white* flowers. The remaining varieties are pink-and-white, yellow, red, purple, and lilach, in a great variety of appearances. The florets of several kinds are quilled, expanded, and long, or short so as to form a globose flower. The early crimson variety of this flower is among those most admired. Whether we regard the period of its flowering, the abundance of its flowers, or their rich colour, we cannot but consider it as exceedingly interesting, and among the most valuable of the species. This variety, unlike the others, is not a strong and hardy one, but throws up many stems, each with many branches, and every one of the branches producing many beautiful *crimson flowers.* Their rich hue accords exactly with Werner's Red Lake, but may fairly be called *light crimson.* The blossoms are often pendent, and two or three inches in diameter. They have an odour, strongly resembling that of the *Anthemis nobilis*, or Chamomile. These flowers, commingled with others, in our flower-pots and gardens, have a most splendid effect. The common White-weed of our fields, or Ox-eye Daisy, so troublesome to farmers, is of the genus Chrysanthemum. It however with its Daisy-like white-rayed flowers adds great beauty to our New-England landscape in spring. The *Chrysanthemum, Bellis, Gnaphallium, Solidago, Aster, Anthemis, Helianthus, Coreopsis, Calendula*, and several other *genera*, belong to the same *natural* order.

The Garden Chrysanthemum, or *Chrysanthemum coronarium*, has leaves bipinnatifid, acute, broader outwards : stem branching.

DOUBLE HYACINTH.

JACINTHE, HYACINTHUS.

CLASS, Hexandria, from *hex*, six, *aner*, stamen. ORDER, Monogynia, from *monos*, one, *gune*, pistil.

Because these flowers have *Six Stamens*, and *One Pistil*, and are consequently of the *Sixth Class* and *First Order* of Linnæus.

Hyacinthus orientalis,	Garden Hyacinth.
.. botryoides,	Grape Hyacinth.
.. muscari,	Musk Hyacinth.
.. comosus,	Purple Grape Hyacinth.
.. racemosus,	Harebell Hyacinth.

There are Six or Eight cultivated *species* with several varieties of the Hyacinth found growing in the Eastern and Middle States of North America.

THE EMBLEM OF CONSTANCY.

The *Hyacinth*'s for constancy
Wi' its unchanging blue. *Burns.*

Let his crook be with *Hyacinths* bound,
So Phillis the trophy despise ;
Let his forehead with laurel be crowned,
So they shine not in Phillis's eyes.
The language that flows from the heart
Is a stranger to Paridel's tongue. *Shenstone's Pastorals.*

The *Hyacinth* purple, white, and blue,
Which flung from its Bells a sweet peal anew,
Of music so delicate, soft, intense,
It was felt like an odour within the sense. *Shelley.*

This charming flower is very beautiful in all its varieties. The double-flowered variety is esteemed less so than the single by many. This, as likewise the Double Larkspur, is not so beautiful when double as when single. In doubling, the flower appears to have lost in some degree its beautiful and curious form, and to present to the eye a confused and unshapely mass of petals. The single varieties are endowed with the most exquisitely-formed and delicate corolla imaginable, and pour forth the richest fragrance.

Such flowers as have been *doubled* by cultivation are, however, generally esteemed much more beautiful than the single. This is the case with the Rose, the Pink, the Chrysanthemums, the Anemones, and almost every other kind of flowering plant. Some prefer the single-flowered *Dahlia* to the double, on account of its beautiful form. Flowers generally become doubled by cultivating them in a rich soil. Their *stamens* and *pistils* become converted into petals or flower-leaves. The *anthers* and *stigmas*, in these cases, are generally obliterated. These plants by botanists are termed *monsters*, because they lose their sexual characteristics.

The poet Homer informs us, that this flower was formed from the blood of Ajax, who killed himself in consequence of his defeat in a contest with Ulysses for the arms of Achilles. Not obtaining the armour of the dead hero, he stabbed himself, and from the blood sprang this flower. Hence Dr. Young tells us, that " from Ajax' streaming blood arose, with grief inscribed, a mournful flower."

Another story of the origin of the Hyacinth is, that Zephyrus, or the south-west wind, through jealousy caused the death of a youth of this name, beloved by Apollo, or the sun, the latter of whom changed his blood into this flower, and placed his body among the heavenly constellations.

Ovid, so famous for his metamorphoses of plants, tells us that

> " in the flower he weaved
> The sad impression of his sighs ; which bears
> Ai—Ai—displayed in funeral characters."

The word *Ai* is a Greek interjection, signifying *Alas !* The Martagon Lily is supposed by many to have been referred to in this passage from Ovid. Keats calls this flower " the sapphire queen of May," and Miss Landon tells us that " in the hyacinthine bells every summer odour dwells." Many *species* of this beautiful and fragrant flower have curling petals, that turn gracefully backward. Hence the expression " hyacinthine locks," often met with in poetry.

The Hare-bell Hyacinth, *Hyacinthus racemosus*, has flowers thick, ovate, those at the top sessile : leaves lax, pendent, linear, carinate.

CONVOLVULUS.

MORNING GLORY, BIND-WEED, MECHOACAN, IPOMEA.

CLASS, Pentandria, from *pente*, five, and *aner*, stamen.   ORDER, Monogynia, from *monos*, one, and *gune*, pistil. Because these flowers have *Five Stamens*, and *One Pistil*, and are consequently of the *Fifth Class* and *First Order* of Linnæus.

Convolvulus,	*stans,*	Dwarf Morning Glory.
..	*tricolor,*	Three-coloured Bindweed.
..	*jalapa,*	Jalap.
Ipomæa	*purpurea,*	Common Morning Glory.
..	*nil,*	Morning Glory.
..	*quamoclit,*	Jasmine Bindweed.

Of these two genera, there are fifteen or twenty *species*, both indigenous and exotic, found growing in the Eastern and Middle States of North-America.

THE EMBLEM OF AFFECTIONATE ATTACHMENT.

Yon clambering vine, that courts our walls
With gay fantastic flowers,
And winds in graceful wreaths along
The fragrant garden bowers,
Still glows with brilliant gems,—till fall
Blights nature's sweetest charms,
Then leaves its grasp,—and dies
With all that spring from Flora's arms.
Though long *Ipomea's* close embrace,
With flowers and beauties bright,
Hath lent yon bower its matchless grace,
Her charms are sunk in night.   *Anon.*

The different species of the *Ipomæa* have flowers yellow, red, purple, white, blue, and variegated. The genus *Ipomæa* was formerly united with the *Convolvulus,* or Climbing Morning Glory. To this it appears to have a near family alliance. The Common Morning Glory (*I. purpurea*) generally bears a blue or purple flower ; the Jasmine Bindweed, or Cypress Vine, (*I. quamoclit*) a red or white one ; the *I. bona-nox*, or *Bel-de-nuit* of the Southern States, a white one ; and the *I. coccinea*, a yellow or red flower. The *I. lacunosa* of the Southern States bears flowers both purple and white. The *bona-nox* and *coccinea*, as well as the *quamoclit* or Cypress-vine, are often cultivated for their beauty. The fine linear *pinnatifid* leaves of the Cypress-vine, like those of the *Cupressus* or Cypress properly so called, have probably given this name to the plant of our gardens. Its red and white flowers contrast finely with its beautiful green foliage.

The *natural* affinity between this genus and the *Convolvulus* has probably been the cause of their both receiving the common name of Morning Glory. This last term undoubtedly originated in the circumstance of these flowers opening only in the morning-sunshine. They are said to wither before noon. This is not, however, invariably the case, for they often expand several days in succession before they wither. They frequently open also in the evening as well as morning. This at least is the case with several of the species.

The *Convolvulus* is so called from *con*, with, and *volvo*, to roll, because many of them climb upon their supporters by a twisting or twirling motion of their slender stems. Their bell-shaped blossoms, before and after opening, resemble a twisted cone. The *Convolvuli* have two stigmas, and the *Ipomœa* only one.

The Tri-coloured Bindweed (*C. tricolor*) grows prostrate, does not twine, and has a corolla or blossom of beautiful bright blue, with a white eye, or centre, edged with yellow. The Purple Bindweed has rough heart-shaped leaves, with flowers commonly of a fine purple, sometimes red, bluish, or white, with fine purple lines.

The Jasmine-bind-weed, *Ipomea quamoclit*, called also sometimes Cypress-Vine, flowers in August. Its leaves are *pinnatifid* linear : flowers sub-solitary ; corolla sub-tubular. This, from its beauty and dependence for support on surrounding objects, has sometimes been esteemed the symbol of ' Female Affection.'

The Blue Convolvulus, a natural relative of the *Ipomea*, is considered the emblem of ' Repose :'—the pink, the emblem of ' Worth sustained by tender Affection :'—and the *Ipomœa* has sometimes been esteemed the symbol of ' Affectionate Attachment.'

The Three-coloured Bindweed, or *Convolvulus tricolor*, has leaves lance-ovate, glabrous : stem declined : flowers solitary.

ROSE-MALLOWS.

MALLOW, HOLLYHOCK, HIBISCUS, ALTHÆA, MALVA.

CLASS, Monadelphia, from *monos*, one, *adelphos*, brother.

ORDER, Polyandria, from *polus*, many, *aner*, stamen.

Because these flowers have the filaments of their stamens united at the base into *one substance* or brotherhood, *and many Stamens*, and consequently are of the 16*th Class* and 13*th Order* of the reformed system of Linnæus.

Hibiscus	*moscheutos*,	Marsh Mallow.
,,	*phœniceus*,	Phenician Mallow.
Althæa	*rosea*,	Hollyhock, or Rose Mallow.
,,	*ficifolia*,	Fig-Hollyhock.
Malva	*arborea*,	Tree-Mallow.
,,	*alcea*,	Vervain Mallow.

These three *Genera* embrace Eighteen or Twenty *Species* that are found growing in the Eastern and Middle States of North-America.

THE EMBLEM OF AMBITION.

Aspiring Alcæa emulates the rose. *Evans.*

The rich array of brilliant flowers,
That spread along yon garden bowers ;
The dazzling hues and colours bright
That meet the eye in lines of light,
Are but the pageants of an hour,
The splendors of a worthless flower.
Vain *Alcæa* there her robe displays,
And shines with meretricious blaze
In vain—no charms her lovers find—
Her gifts, when known, are soon resign'd. *Anon.*

The family MALVACÆA embraces the *Althæa, Hibiscus*, and *Malva* or Mallows, as well as the Cotton (*Gossypium*), the Silk Cotton (*Bombax*), the *Barringtonia*, the Hand-tree (*Chierostemon*), Soursop (*Adansonia*), and several other genera.   On inspecting a flower of the Hollyhock or Mallows, which will serve as a type of the whole family, it will be seen that the numerous stamens are united, by thin filaments into a column, to which the corolla adheres. This family was therefore formerly termed *Columniferæ*, or column-bearing. In the centre of this hollow column of stamens, when slit open, will be found the *styles*, disposed in *another bundle*.

To this family belongs the Soursop of Africa, (*Adansonia*,) one of the largest and longest-lived trees in the world. It was so named from Adanson, who travelled into this country and first described it. The base of its trunk has been often found of the enormous diameter of *twenty-five feet*, and sufficiently large, when hollow, to afford shelter to several negro families. Adanson states that they endure for *six* or *seven hundred years*. Professor Smith, who died in Congo, thinks, from the softness of its wood, this tree must be of quicker growth.

The Hollyhock (*Althæa rosea*) is native in China, Africa, Hindostan, and Siberia. Its flowers are both single and double, and of every variety of colour. They are red, purple, bluish, scarlet, white, yellow, pink, and sometimes almost black. The double varieties of this flower are generally esteemed the most beautiful. They bear some resemblance to roses, and this plant has hence often been called the *Rose Mallows*. The annexed plate represents one of the single-flowered varieties. These usually have but *five petals*, or flower-leaves.

The *Hibiscus* of the family *Malvacæ* is a genus embracing several beautiful species. They are remarkable for the magnitude and elegance of the colour of their flowers. The *H. palustris* is one of the finest of the genus, and is a tall *perennial*, growing in marshy grounds, flowering about August. The *H. syriacus*, Syrian Hibiscus, sometimes called the *Althæa frutex*, or simply the Althæa, is one of our common ornamental shrubs, with both single and double flowers. These are of various colours. They are often white or purple, with a deeper coloured ring in the centre.

The Hand-tree of Mexico (*Chierostemon*) has a flower with spreading linear stigmas, inclined to one side, not unaptly resembling the *hand* or *paw* of a monkey, whence its name. The *Barringtonia* is a native of the tropical islands of the Pacific. It is a tall, magnificent tree, full of large and most beautiful flowers of a brilliant white and purple.

The Hollyhock, or *Althæa rosea*, has a stem erect : leaves rough, heart-form, five to seven-angled, crenate.

M

NARCISSUS.

DAFFODIL, DAFFODILLY, DAFFODOWNDILLY, JONQUILLE, NARCISSUS, NARCISSE, NARCISO.

CLASS, Hexandria, from *hex*, six, *aner*, stamen.   ORDER, Monogynia, from *monos*, one, *gune*, pistil.

Because these flowers have *Six Stamens*, and *One Pistil*, and are consequently of the *Sixth Class* and *First Order* of Linnæus.

Narcissus poeticus,	Poet's Narcissus.
.. *jonquilla,*	Jonquille.
.. *tazetta,*	Polyanthos.
.. *pseudo-narcissus,*	Daffodil.

There are *Fifteen Species* of the Narcissus, with many *varieties*, several of which are found growing in our gardens in New-England.

THE EMBLEM OF SELF-LOVE AND EGOTISM.

Pride of gardens, charming flowers,
Fleeting are your little hours ;
Often does a summer day
Give ye life, and take away :
Ah ! I'll disturb not your reposes,
Gallant JONQUILLES, fair tuberoses,
For short is your sweet life.
The daughter of the flood has searched the mead
For violets pale, and cropped the poppy's head,
The short *Narcissus*, and fair *Daffodil*,
Pansies to please the sight, and cassia sweet to smell.
There, round about, grew every sort of flower,
To which sad lovers were transformed of yore,
Foolish *Narcisse*, that likes the watery shore.
Gay, motley'd pinks, and sweet *Jonquilles* she chose,
The violet blue, that on the moss-bank grows,
And, sweet to sense, the beauteous, flaunting rose. *Shakspeare and Spenser.*

Of this rich and fragrant flower there are many varieties, that pass under different names, but all under the general name of Narcissus. The Daffodil and Jonquil are species of the Narcissus. These flowers are often confounded by the poets, or their names are used indiscriminately. The common Daffodil has a white flower and a yellow cup, or a yellow flower and golden cup. The poetic Narcissus is pure white. It has a delicate yellow cup, edged with purple, or crimson border round the nectary. It affords a most delicious odour, especially in the morning when wet with dew. The cup, in the centre of this flower, was said to contain the tears of NARCISSUS, a youth, who, seeing his own image reflected in a fountain of clear water, became so enamoured of himself, that he pined, and at last, in despair, killed himself. His blood was changed into this flower.

The Primrose Daffodil has petals of a cream colour, with a yellow cup rising from the centre.

The Fragrant Narcissus, or Great Jonquil, is a valuable variety of this plant, and its flower yields a most exquisite odour. The Narcissus has a lily blossom, and belongs to that class of plants that diffuse sweeter perfume at evening, than during the daytime. Persia abounds in several rich varieties of the " odorous jonquil," as it does in roses, and other fragrant and beautiful flowers.

The Polyanthos Narcissus, or *Narcissus tazetta*, is a native of Spain, France, and Italy. Its *scape*, or flower-stalk, from twelve to eighteen inches in height, bears very fragrant flowers, of a white, or yellow colour. These flowers are clustering, from seven to ten of them, coming out of one *spathe*. The Daffodil has only one flower produced from the same spathe.

The general character of these flowers consists in *six petals*, or flower-leaves, forming a superior corolla, and a funnel-shaped honey-cup of one leaf, containing the stamens, which are fixed to its tube. The old poet Spenser has often confounded this flower with the *Asphodel*, and white Water Lily. Other poets have, very erroneously, made the Daffodil and Lily the same flower. Milton, in his Lycidas, very beautifully alludes to this flower. In their ' flowery rites' on May-day, on the banks of the Severn, these flowers, among others, were strown upon the stream, as an offering to Flora, the Goddess of Flowers.

The Poet's Narcissus, or *Narcissus poeticus*, has a spathe one-flowered; nectary wheel-formed, very short, scarious, (red,) crenulate : leaves inflexed at the margin.

BLUE-BELL.

VENUS' LOOKING-GLASS, CANTERBURY-BELL, CAMPANULA, HARE-
BELL, GREAT-BELL-FLOWER, FLAX-BELL-FLOWER.

CLASS, Pentandria, from   ORDER, Monogynia, from
pente, five, *aner*, stamen.   *monos*, one, *gune*, pistil.

Because these flowers have *Five* stamens and *One* pistil, and are consequently of the Fifth Class and First Order of Linnæus.

Campanula grandiflora,	Great Bell-flower.
.. *crinoides,*	Prickly Bell-flower.
.. *rotundifolia,*	Hare-bell, or Flax Bell-flower.
.. *speculum,*	Venus's Looking-glass.
.. *medium,*	Canterbury-bells.

There are Eight or Ten *Species* of the genus CAMPANULA, found growing in the Eastern and
Middle States of North-America.

THE EMBLEM OF GRATITUDE.

To me there's a tone in the BLUE-BELL-FLOWER,
With her blossoms so fresh when the storm is o'er,
As she thanked the sun for his beams the while.—
That flower has taught me to repay
The friends, who have cheered my stormy day,
With a grateful brow, and a sunny smile.   *Anon.*

    The *Hare-bell*—as with grief depressed,
    Bowing her fragrance.   *Gisborne.*

The generic term *Campanula* is a diminutive from the Latin
campana, a bell, because these flowers resemble little bells in their
form. They all partake more or less of this shape. They belong
to the fifth Linnæan class, which is a very extensive one and em-

braces more than one fourth of the whole vegetable kingdom, if we include the class *Syngenesia*, where the *five stamens* are combined together. That is, more than one fourth of all vegetables possess *five stamens* either free or combined together. The Harebell (*Campanula rotundifolia*), called also sometimes the Flax-Bell-flower, is a very beautiful species of this flower. It is very abundant in Scotland, and grows in rocky situations. It is often alluded to in poetry, and associated with other interesting flowers. Its flowers are generally blue, as are many other species of this genus, being pendulous and nodding, hanging like little bells. An indigenous *species* of the Hare-bell, having a blue flower, is found in most parts of New-England, in rocky situations. It blossoms in June. The *C. acuminata* and *C. crinoides*, or Prickly Bell-flower, both bear blossoms that are white and those that are blue.

The Blue-bell is found much more generally in Europe than in America, though there are a few species found among us. The term Blue-bell is often applied indiscriminately to the several *species* of the CAMPANULA, probably because these flowers are generally *blue*, and resemble a *bell* in their form. The Canterbury-bells (*C. medium*) bears its blossoms erect. The varieties of this species are extensive, and are said to be mostly *indigenous* to Europe. Only two species are described as having yet been found in South America. These flowers are *monopetalous*, or having *one petal*, and are sometimes blue, purple, or white. The flowers of the *Campanula parviflora*, or Clasping Bell-flower, are blue and very small. The *C. americana* is two or three feet in height, bearing two or three small blue flowers, generally in the axils of the leaves. The *Canterbury bell* (*C. medium*) has generally been esteemed the emblem of GRATITUDE. If, as the poet tells us,

> That flower has taught him to repay
> The friends who have cheered his stormy day,
> With a grateful brow and a sunny smile,

it certainly has been the *cause* of Gratitude, and is not an unapt *emblem* of it also. " The *Hare-bell*, as with grief depressed," bowing its fragrance, explains why this flower should have become the symbol of GRIEF itself. The *Campanulacæa* have a calyx adhering to the germ, limb divided. Corol inserted near the top of the calyx. Stamens inserted on the calyx below the corol. Leaves alternate. The *natural* order CAMPANULACÆA embraces the *two natural* genera *Campanula* and *Lobelia*.

The Great Bell-Flower, or *Campanula grandiflora*, has leaves ternate, oblong, serrate : stem, one-flowered : flowers spreading.

GERANIUM.

CRANES-BILL, HERB-ROBERT, STORK'S-BILL, DOVE'S-FOOT.

CLASS, Monadelphia, from *monos*, one, and *adelphia*, brotherhood.   ORDER, Decandria, from *deka*, ten, and *aner*, stamen.

Because these flowers *have their filaments united in one body, at bottom,* and *Ten Stamens,* and consequently are of the *Sixteenth Class,* and *Tenth Order* of Linnæus.

Geranium sanguineum,		Bloody Geranium.
··	*maculatum,*	Crow's-foot Geranium.
··	*washingtoneum,*	Washington's Geranium.
··	*robertianum,*	Herb Robert.
··	*zonale,*	Horse-shoe Geranium.
··	*graveolens,*	Sweet Rose Geranium.

There are at least *Forty* or *Fifty Species,* with numerous varieties of the Geranium, many of which are found growing in the Eastern and Middle States of North-America.

THE EMBLEM OF GENTILITY.

The fig-tree and the vine,
Which o'er the rocky entrance downward shoot,
Were placed by Glycon. He with cowslips pale,
Primrose, and purple lychnis, decked the green
Before my threshold, and my shelving walls
With honeysuckles covered. The sweet syringa,
Yielding but in scent to the rich orange,
And *Genteel* GERANIUM, with its leaf ;
For all that come, here boast in pride
And crimson honours, while the spangled beau
Ficoides, glitters bright the winter long.   *Akenside and others.*

The numerous species of *Pelargonium,* as well as of *Geranium,* are well known by the common name of Geraniums. Many *exotics* of this genus of plants are cultivated in our flower-pots and gardens for their beauty and fragrance. The leaves of several kinds are particularly fragrant.

The term Geranium is from the Greek *geranos,* a crane : so called because its pistil is long, like the bill of a crane. The species of this extensive genus of plants grow wild in very great abundance in Great-Britain. Their qualities, as well as their appearances, are very various. The beautiful family, of which our greenhouses display such an amazing variety, came originally from the Cape of Good Hope. Our *native species* have a single *cup* of five leaves. The petals of the corolla correspond with them in number. The ten stamens are alternately longer and shorter, but all of them shorter than the blossom. They have one pointal terminated by five *stigmas,* longer than the stamens, and permanent as well as the *cup.* The Spotted Cranes-bill has a deep-purple blossom. Its leaves are downy, with five lobes, or scollops, and these again divided into small indentures. The Musk Cranes-bill has a very strong smell of *musk,* when bruised, whence its name. The leaves are winged and jagged. Several flowers grow on the same foot-stalk. The flower has *five stamens,* and the seeds are furnished with a kind of protuberance like the bill of the crane or stork, whence its name Cranes-bill, or Storks-bill.

It is said, the Geraniums of Europe do not approach those of Africa in point of stature, or beauty of flower. Many very beautiful varieties of the Geranium have, within a few years, been introduced into our gardens and conservatories. One has only to examine the collections of almost any florist, to become acquainted with their names and properties. The emblematic signification of this flower, GENTILITY, is explained in the poetry quoted above.

The *natural* order *Gerania* includes the *Geranium, Oxalis, Impatiens, Tropelolum, Erodium, Pelargonum* ; the second, third, and fourth of which are termed *Geranioids.*

The Horse-shoe Geranium, or *Pelargonium zonale,* has umbels many-flowered : leaves heart-orbicular, obsoletely lobed, toothed, with a coloured zone or band around near the margin.

HUNDRED-LEAVED-ROSE.

ROSA-CENTAFOLIA, ROSA-DAMASCENA, ROSA-PALLIDA, LA-ROSE.

CLASS, Icosandria, from *eikosi*, twenty, *aner*, stamen.

ORDER, Polygynia, from *polus*, many, *gune*, pistil.

Because these flowers have *Twenty or more Stamens*, and *numerous Pistils*, and consequently are of the *12th Class* and *6th Order* of Linnæus.

Rosa centifolia,	Hundred-leaved Rose.
.. *multiflora,*	Japan Rose, or Multiflora Rose.
.. *spinosissima,*	Scotch Rose, or Thorny Rose.
.. *alba,*	White Rose.
.. *gallica,*	French Rose.
.. *cinnamomea,*	Cinnamon Rose.
.. *pimpinellifolia,*	Burnet Rose.

Some writers make the genus ROSA embrace *Fifty or more Species,* nine or ten of which are indigenous to North-America.

THE EMBLEM OF DIGNITY OF SOUL.

Thou queen of flowers of thousand leaves,
And throne surrounded by protecting thorn,
Thou heaven-born ROSE.   *Kliest.*

Rose ! thou art the sweetest flower
That ever drank the amber shower ;
Rose ! thou art the fondest child
Of dimpled Spring ! the wood-nymph wild !
Resplendent ROSE ! the flower of flowers,
Whose breath perfumes Olympus bowers,
Whose virgin blush, of chastened dye,
Enchants so much our mental eye,
Oft has the poet's magic tongue
The Rose's fair luxuriance sung.   *Anacreon.*

There are at least twenty species of the Rose, *indigenous* and *exotic,* found growing in the Eastern and Middle States. Of these species the *varieties* are almost innumerable. In this extensive family are included many of the most beautiful ornaments of our gardens. They are of all the various colours, red, white, pink, crimson, yellow, and variegated, often blending these colours also and forming intermediate tints. The Hundred-leaved Rose, or *Rosa centifolia*, called also the *Rosa damascena*, or Damask Rose, and by some writers the *Rosa pallida*, or Pale Rose, is said by some to be the same. It is known by the name of Damson, Damask, or Damascus Rose, because it is said to have been first introduced from Damascus in Western Asia. Most of the Roses, though much cultivated in our gardens, are far from being distinctly characterized. These denominated *varieties* are extremely numerous, and often permanently uniform ; but the *specific* differences, as hitherto pointed out, are in many respects so inadequate to the purpose of satisfactory discrimination, that it becomes a difficult matter *to distinguish which are species and which are varieties only.* Hence the great disagreement among botanical writers in regard to the *number of species* of this flower, and hence the confusion of names. Gerard and Parkinson make the *Rosa centifolia* or Hundred-leaved Rose the same as the *Rosa damascena.* The Damask Rose, according to Du Roi and Miller, is another *species*, widely different from the *Centifolia.* Professor Eaton describes the *Centifolia*, or Hundred-leaved Rose, as exclusively a red rose : whereas the Damask, Damson, or *Rosa damascena*, is described as both red and white. The differences however are not very great.

The specific term *Centifolia* is from the Latin *centum*, a hundred, and *folium*, a leaf, unitedly implying that the flower has a hundred *petals*, or flower-leaves. The number of petals, on counting, will be found not exclusively to be a hundred, but exceedingly various. This flower is generally of a pale red colour, sometimes of a deep-red, and is very fragrant. Its magnificent size and rich odour, so extremely agreeable to most people, has caused it to be much used among other roses in nosegays. The Hundred-leaved Rose with its slpendid and finely-coloured corolla of the richest fragrance, ' surrounded by protecting thorns,' has generally been esteemed the emblem of *Dignity and Elevation of Soul.*

The Velvet Rose, with its crimson, pink and purple flowers, belongs to the same *species.* ———

The Hundred-leaved Rose, or *Rosa centifolia*, has germs ovate : germs and peduncles hispid : stem hispid, prickly : leaves pubescent beneath : petioles unarmed.

N

AURICULA.

PURPLE-AURICULA, AURICULA PURPUREA, OREILLE-D'OURS,
BEARS-EARS, PRIMULA.

CLASS, Pentandria, from
pente, five, *aner*, stamen.

ORDER, Monogynia, from
monos, one, *gune*, pistil.

Because these flowers have *Five* stamens and *One* pistil, and are consequently of the Fifth Class and First Order of Linnæus.

Primula, auricula,	Auricula Primrose.
„ *farinosa,*	Bird's-eye Primrose.
„ *veris,*	Cowslip Primrose.

There are *Twenty Species*, with numerous *varieties*, of the Primula, or Primrose, several of which are found growing in New-England.

THE EMBLEM OF PRIDE AND ELEGANCE.

Come you who would bind up flowers,
Blending their od'rous sweets,
All lovely, yet from each other
New graces borrowing,
Come and make up a nosegay
For her whose love you prize,
Choose what you will: have enough—
Wild blooms, and garden flowers.   *Anon.*

In comes AURICULA, arrayed she comes
In splendour, and in liveliest colours blooms.

Where rayed in sparkling dust, and velvet pride,
Like brilliant stars arranged in splendid row,
The proud *Auriculas* their lustre show.   *Kliest.*

The Auricula is of the primrose family of plants, as will readily be observed. It has been termed by the French, *Oreille d'ours*, or Ear of the Bear, from the close resemblance of this flower to the bear's ear.

The term auricula is of Latin origin, from *auricula*, a little ear, because this flower resembles the ear of several animals in its form. There are at least *forty* cultivated varieties of this flower. Among these are the crimson, large purple, blue, pink, and yellow. These flowers are also found in several beautiful varieties of red, and lilach. The generic term *primula*, given to all this tribe of plants, from the Latin *primus*, first, implies their early coming. The *Caltha palustris* of our meadows, known also in New-England by the name of Cowslip, is of the same *natural* family. It is one of our earliest, and most interesting spring-flowers.

The *Dodecantheon meadia*, or False Cowslip, grows upon the banks of rivers, bearing a purple or bluish flower, blossoming in May. Its generic name *Dodecantheon* is from the Greek *doodeka*, twelve, and *anthemon*, flower, because this plant is supposed to bear about twelve flowers on each stalk. This is not however generally the case, for the number of its flowers is extremely various, sometimes more and sometimes less than twelve. There are *four* described species of the *Caltha*, or New-England Cowslip, found growing in the Eastern States, all bearing a yellow blossom. The *C. palustris*, or American Cowslip, blossoms in April,—the *C. ficaroides*, or Fig-Cowslip, in June,—the *C. flabellifolia*, or Tooth-leaf Cowslip, in May and June,—and the *C. integerrima*, in May. The *C. palustris* has stem erect, corymbed : leaves heart-reniform ; lobes spreading, acute crenate all around : floral leaves sub-sessile : petals ovate. The English Cowslip is a very different plant from any of the preceding. The *Auricula* is a *perennial*, flowering early. Most of the kinds are Alpine flowers, and are of almost every colour.

The poet tells us, " the proud Auriculas come arrayed in splendour, like brilliant stars, in rows, shining in sparkling dust, with velvet softness." The plant has hence become the emblem of PRIDE, ELEGANCE, and BEAUTY.

The Auricula Primrose, or *Primula auricula*, has leaves serrate, fleshy, obovate : scape many-flowered ; calyx mealy.

ALTHÆA.

SYRIAN MALLOW, HOLLYHOCK, MARSH-MALLOWS, FIG-HOLLY-HOCK, HIBISCUS, ALCÆA, MALVA.

CLASS, Monadelphia, from *monos*, one, *adelphia*, brotherhood.

ORDER, Polyandria, from *polus*, many, *aner*, stamen.

Because these flowers have their stamens united by their filaments into a tube, or one clump, and have *many pistils*, and consequently are of the *16th Class* and *13th Order* of Linnæus.

Althæa	*officinales,*	Marsh Mallows.
..	*rosea,*	Hollyhock.
..	*ficifolia,*	Fig-Hollybock.

There are Three or Four *species*, with several varieties of the Althæa, found growing in the Eastern and Middle States of North America.

THE EMBLEM OF AMBITION.

Some as they went, the blue-eyed violets strew,
Some spotless lilies in loose order throw ;
Some the white ALTHÆA, wet with morning dew,
Some did the way with full-blown roses spread,
Their smell divine, their colour strongly red,
Not such as our dull gardens proudly wear,
Which weathers taint, and winds' rude kisses tear,
Such, I believe, was the first roses here,
Which at God's word in beauteous Eden grew.
Queen of the flowers, that made that orchard gay,
The morning blushes, of the spring's new day.   *Cowley.*

The *Althæa* is so called from the Greek word *altheo*, to heal, because of the supposed healing qualities of its leaves, as well as those of the *Malva*, or Mallows. The *Althæa* or *Hibiscus*, as also the Hollyhock, or Rose Mallows, and other varieties of the Mallows, belong to the same *natural* order. They are of the same class and order in the Linnæan system of plants. Most plants of the mallow tribe, with us, are *herbaceous*, or die down to the ground in winter. Those of hot climates are frequently either shrubs, or trees. The *Althæa* is a shrubby plant.

The *Hibiscus*, or Marsh Mallows, is so named from the Geaik word *ibis*, a stork, because the stork was anciently supposed to chew this plant.

The Syrian Malva, or *Althæa frutex*, is a shrubby plant, six or eight feet high, a native of the old world, with white, pensile, and red flowers.

The generic term *Malva*, applied to the mallow-tribe, is said to be so used, because of the softness (*quasi molva*, from *mollis*, meaning soft) of the leaves of this class of plants. Several varieties of the *Althæa* are cultivated in our gardens, as ornamental plants or shrubs. Some of the oriental varieties are very beautiful.

The *Malva*, or Mallow tribe is also very common in our gardens. Some of these plants are very ornamental. The Hollyhock, or Rose Mallows, is particularly fine.

The *Hibiscus trionum* is known by the common appellation of " The-flower-of-an-hour." It is sometimes called the Bladder Ketmia. The poet tells us, " Aspiring *Althæa* emulates the rose." If this be the case, we may easily see why it has become the emble of AMBITION.

The *Althea* has also been sometimes deemed the symbol of CONSUMING LOVE. This emblematic meaning probably originated in the fable of Althæa and her unfortunate son, who lost his life in consequence of his love for the charming Atalanta. The youth, as the fatal brand was burning, pined in hopeless love till death freed him from his sorrows.

The *Althæa* common about our court-yards and gardens is the *Hibiscus syriacus*, so called because first brought from Syria.

The *Hibiscus*, *Malva*, *Althæa*, *Gordonia*, *Gossipium*, and several other genera, belong to the *natural* order *Malvacæa*.

The Marsh Mallows, or ALTHÆA OFFICINALIS, has leaves downy, oblong-ovate, obsoletely-three-lobed, toothed.

GARDEN MARYGOLD.

BUDDS, MARIGOLD, CALENDULA, SOUCI DE JARDINES, CHRY-
SANTHEMUM, FRENCH MARYGOLD, GOULDS.

CLASS, Syngenesia, from *sun*,   ORDER, Polygamia necessaria, from
with, and *genesis*, generation.   *polus*, many, and *gamia*, marriage.

Because these flowers *have their stamens united at top into a cylinder*, and
some of their florets male, and others female, and consequently are of the
Nineteenth Class, and *Fourth Order* of Linnæus.

Tagetes erecta,	African Marygold.
,, *patula,*	French Marygold.
Calendula officinalis,	Pot Marygold.

There are Two or Three *Species* of the *Tagetes* found growing in our gardens in the Eastern and
Middle States of North-America.

THE EMBLEM OF JEALOUSY.

Lapsana Nymphæa fair,
And bright CALUNDULA with golden hair,
Watch with nice eye the earth's diurnal way,
Marking her solar and sidereal day,
Her slow mutation, and her varying clime,
And trace, with mimic art, the march of time,
Round his bright foot a magic chain they fling,
And count the quick vibrations of his wing.   *Darwin.*

Then ope afresh your round of starry folds,
Dry up the moisture from your golden lids,
For in these days your praises shall be sung
On many harps, which have been lately strung,
And when old Sol again your beauty kisses,
Tell him I have you in my world of blisses :
So haply, when I rove in some far vale,
His mighty voice may come upon the gale.   *Keats.*

In France, and other Catholic countries, the Marygold is conse-crated to the Virgin Mary. We often find it mentioned, as a bridal flower, in poetry. There are several different flowers that pass under this name. Two or three species of the *Tagetes* are known by the name of Garden Marygold. The *Calendula* is known by the name of Pot Marygold. Besides these, there are flowers, belonging to different *genera*, that pass under the name of Marygold. The Yellow Marygold, or *Calendula officinalis*, grows native in Europe, South America, and India. It was con-secrated to Venus. It is fabled of it, that it was stained by the blood of the aboriginal Mexicans, slain by the Spaniards. Its flowers are dark-red, or of a deep yellow inclining to purple.

The old poet Spenser, in alluding to this flower, bids us " crown the bride's adorned head, with roses dight, and GOULDS, and daffo-dillies." We not only find it mentioned in the bridal wreath, but sometimes associated with funereal flowers, and scattered over the tomb as the sad memento of sorrow.

It belongs to the *natural tribe* of Chrysanthemums, or gold-flowers. The *Calendula* has been so called from the same Latin word, meaning ' a little calendar,' because these flowers are said, like little calendars or almanacks, to give us an account of the pass-ing of time. Hence the allusion in the quotation of poetry above. They indeed seem to notify us of the passing of time by their al-ternately opening and closing their flowers, and by their changing aspects, varying with the sun in his course. They open their flowers in the morning, and close them at night. These, like many other sun-flowers, appear to be much under the sun's influ-ence, and to be greatly affected by the changes of light and dark-ness. Several varieties of the marygold are natives of the south-ern countries of Europe. The French call it *Souci des jardines*, or Solicitude of the Garden, probably in allusion to the light in which it is viewed by Catholics. The *Tagetes* is often called the French Marygold.

The poets have made it the emblem of JEALOUSY. The French Marigold is the emblem of Jealousy, the Yellow of Sacred Affec-tion. The above quotation of poetry, from Dr. Darwin, is all very ingenious and pretty, but perhaps rather extravagant.

The African Marygold, or *Tagetes erecta*, has leaves pinnate : leaflets lanceolate, ciliate-serrate : peduncles one-flowered, incrassate, sub-inflated : calyx angled.

SINGLE ANEMONE.

BLUE WIND-FLOWER, PURPLE ANEMONE, SINGLE-FLOWERED
ANEMONE, WIND-ROSE.

CLASS, Polyandria, from
polus, many, *aner*, stamen.

ORDER, Polygynia, from
polus, many, *gune*, pistil.

Because these flowers have 20 *or more disunited Stamens* on the calyx, and
many Pistils, consequently are of the 13*th Class* and 7*th Order* of Linnæus.

Anemone lancifolia,	Lance-leaved White Anemone.
„ *nemorosa,*	Wood Anemone.
„ *dichotoma,*	Forked-stem Anemone.

There are *Eight* or *Ten Species*, with several varieties of the Anemone, found growing in the
Eastern and Middle States of North-America.

THE EMBLEM OF ANTICIPATION, AND EXPECTED PLEASURE.

Flower ! the laurel still may shed
Brightness round the victor's head ;
And the rose in Beauty's hair
Still its festal glories wear ;
And the willow-leaves droop o'er
Brows, which love sustains no more :
But, by living rays refined,
Thou, the trembler of the wind,
Thou, the spiritual flower,
Sentient of each breeze and shower,
Thou, rejoicing in the skies,
And transpierced with all their dyes,
Breathing vase, with light o'erflowing,
Gem-like, to thy centre glowing,
Thou the poet's type shalt be,
Flower of scent, ANEMONE !   *Mrs. Hemans.*

There seems to be some confusion among writers with regard to the Anemone, it being often confounded with the *Flos Adonis*. This confusion has probably originated, amongst the poets, from the similar origin of the two flowers. They are both fabled to have had their rise from the blood of the beautiful youth Adonis, who was killed while pursuing a wild boar. He was greatly beloved by Venus, who is said much to have lamented his untimely fate. From his *purple* blood, that flowed upon the mountain where he fell, sprung the *Flos Adonis*, and some say the *purple Anemone*.

The *Flos Adonis* and Anemone are both of the same class and order in the Linnæan arrangement. This circumstance, together with that of their feigned common origin, has probably been the cause of their being confounded. One poet bids us look in the garden, where blooms the "*flos Adonis*, that memory keeps of him who rashly died, thereafter changed by Venus, weeping, to this flower."

Another, speaking of the same youth, says, " his sunbeam-tinted tresses drooped unbound, sweeping the earth with negligence uncouth, the *white* anemones, that near him blew, felt his red blood, and *red* forever grew."

Another tells us, that " in his blood, that on the ground lay spilled, a *purple* flower sprang up, chequered with white."

Thus they differ, in their account of the origin of this flower. Each flower has its champions, perhaps of nearly equal authority. As observed in another place, anemones are white, blue, red, purple, and, often, fancifully and curiously variegated.

The *Adonis autumnalis* is known by the name of Pheasants-eye, and blossoms in August. It is an annual. A species of *Hepatica* is sometimes called Bog Anemone.

The *Anemone hepatica* is one of our earliest spring flowers, and one of the most abundant of our wild flowers, in New England. The circumstance of the anemone's waiting for the blowing of the wind before it will expand its flowers, has caused it to become the emblem of ANTICIPATION, and EXPECTED PLEASURE.

The Garden Anemone, or *Anemone hortensis*, has radical leaves digitate, divisions three-cleft, cauline ones ternate, lanceolate, connate, subdivided : seed woolly.

o

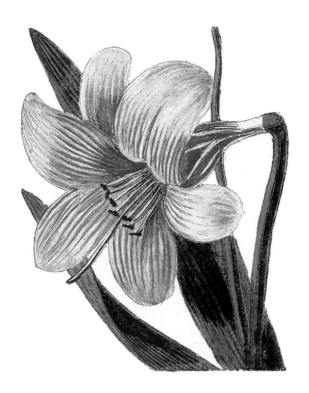

THE LILY.

DAY LILY, ORANGE LILY, YELLOW MEADOW LILY, CONVALLARIA,
FIELD LILY, LYS D'ORANGE, HEMEROCALLIS, LILIUM.

CLASS, Hexandria, from
hex, six, *aner*, stamen.

ORDER, Monogynia, from
monos, one, *gune*, pistil.

Because these flowers have *Six Stamens*, and *One Pistil*, and are consequently of the *Sixth Class* and *First Order* of Linnæus.

Lilium catesbæi,	Southern Lily.
„ *bulbiferum,*	Orange Lily.
Hemerocallis flava,	Yellow Day-Lily.
„ *fulva,*	Tawny Day-Lily.

There are several species of the *Lilium*, as well as of the *Hemerocallis*, found growing in
the Eastern and Middle States of North-America.

THE EMBLEM OF PLAYFUL GAIETY.

Take but the humblest ' LILY OF THE FIELD,'
And if our pride will to our reason yield,
It must, by sure comparison, be shown
That, on the regal seat, great David's son,
Arrayed in all his robes and types of power,
Shines with less glory, than that simple flower.   *Prior.*

And, night to night, yet added knowledge shows,
Far lowlier objects to the heart may reach ;
And wisdom's purest precepts may disclose,
Culled from the *Lily's* bloom, or gathered from the rose.   *Barton.*

Of this delightful flower, many varieties are very fragrant, and
their perfume almost incessant. Other varieties yield very little

fragrance. The splendid White Lily of our gardens is a native of Persia, the land of lilies and roses. It grows also in Japan, in great perfection and abundance. This is a very fragrant variety of the flower, and is called by the French, *Lys de Japan.* It often grows to a magnificent size in Palestine. Here the lily was formerly much admired, and composed many of the richest decorations of the Jewish temples. The red lily, as well as the orange and the white, is supposed to have originally been brought from Persia, that land of beautiful flowers. One of the chief cities of Persia, Shushan, is said to have received its name from the great abundance of these beautiful flowers, that grow native in its vicinity,—*Shushan,* in that language, signifying *the city of lilies.*

Frequent allusions are made in the sacred writings to the Lily. Russell tells us, that, " in these Eastern regions, a vivid verdure succeeds the autumnal rains, soon after which, the ploughed fields are covered with the Persian Lily, of a resplendent yellow colour."

The Martagon lilies are a fine variety of the lily, often cultivated in this country, as well as in England.

The *Lily of Catsby,* found native in South-Carolina, was first carried to England by him. It is prettily shaded, in red, orange, and lemon colours.

Anacreon calls the lily the " Venus of flowers." Pliny says, " the lily is next in excellence to the rose." In Eastern countries, it is often esteemed as an emblem of MORAL EXCELLENCE. The White Lily is esteemed the emblem of PURITY and BEAUTY ; the Scarlet Lily that of HIGH-TONED SENTIMENT. The Rose is said to be the handmaiden of *love,* and the Lily of PURITY.

The three different genera, *Convallaria, Hemerocallis,* and *Lilium,* all pass under the name of Lilies. The opposite cut represents one of the Genus *Lilium.* The *Convallaria* is the true Lily-of-the-Valley, so called. The generic term *Hemerocallis* is from the Greek *hemeron,* day, and *kallos,* beauty, unitedly meaning " the beauty of a day." *Convallaria* is from the Latin *con,* with or in, and *vallum,* a valley.

The Tulip, *Fritellaria,* or Crown Imperial, *Erythronium, Uvularia,* Hyacinth, Asphodel, and *Hemerocallis,* all belong to the same *natural* Order of plants.

The yellow Day-lily, or *Hemerocallis flava,* has leaves broad-linear, keeled : petals flat, acute ; nerves of the petals undivided.

BALM.

MELISSA, CALAMINT, GARDEN-BALM, CEDRANELLA, HIGH-BALM,

LOW-BALM, CITRAGO, CITRARIA, APIASTRUM, EROTIAN, COMMON CALLAMINT.

CLASS, Didynamia, from *dis*,   ORDER, Gymnospermia, from *gum-*
twice, and *dunamis,* superiority.   *nos,* naked, and *sperma,* seed.

Because these flowers have *Four Stamens, two longer than the other two,*
and *seeds naked* or *without an envelope,* and consequently are of the
Fourteenth Class and *First Order* of Linnæus.

| *Melissa* | *officinalis,* | Common Balm. |
| ,, | *nepeta,* | Callamint. |

There are but *Two* or *Three Species* of *Melissa*, with several varieties. described as found
growing in the Eastern and Middle States of North-America.

THE EMBLEM OF SOCIAL INTERCOURSE.

I paused at the sight of these blessed flowers,
No more could my tears restrain,
For it seemed that the purity and love
Of my childhood came again;
It seemed as sin and sorrow fled,
From view of the flower and tree,
And I thought what my blameless youth had been,
The same mine age might be.   *M. Hewett.*

Goes decking the green earth's dewy drapery
With BALM, that never ceases uttering sweets.   *Anon.*

The Balm, or *Melissa*, has received this appellation from the
Greek *mellissa*, signifying *a bee*, because the bees are very fond
of gathering honey from this species of flower.

The *Calamentha vulgare*, or common Garden Balm, is a well known plant, that is found growing in almost every garden. Its leaves are of an agreeable fragrance, and its flowers very handsome. Its generic name is from the Greek *kallos*, beautiful, and *mentha*, mint, meaning the Beautiful Mint.

The *Melissa officinalis* is another species of our Garden Balm, equally well known, and not less frequently cultivated. It is *native* of the southern countries of Europe. The flowers are sometimes white, or blue. The flowers of the *Nepeta* are red, and sometimes blue. Both species are perennial, or have roots that live during several successive seasons. The *nepeta* is known by the common appellation of Catnep, or Cat-mint.

The *officinalis* blossoms in July, and the *nepeta* in September. The leaf and stem of the Balm are of a roughish-aromatic taste, and have an agreeable smell, resembling that of the lemon. This plant is not unfrequently made into a tea, and used as a grateful drink, in fevers. The Calamint, or *Nepeta*, is also taken in decoction, against weakness of the stomach, flatulence, and hysterics. The poet tells us, " the balm is seen decking the green earth with dewy drapery, and never ceases uttering sweets." It has hence been made the emblem of SOCIAL INTERCOURSE, whose blessings are unceasing.

The term *Apiastrium* is from *apis*, a bee, because this is said to be a favourite flower with bees. They are often seen plunging their puny proboscis within the *ringent* florets of this fragrant plant. The flowers of the Balm and Calamint are situated in a semi-whorl, or are generally whirled half way round the stem. The Balm is said to be indigenous to Europe. Its flowers are both white and blue, and expand in June. Those of the *M. nepeta*, or Calamint, are blue and red, and blossom in September.

The *Melissa, Monarda, Mentha, Marubium, Rosmarinus, Hyssopus,* and *Lavandula*, with several other genera, belong to the same natural Order.

The Balm, or *Melissa officinalis*, has flowers whirled half way around, sub-sessile : bracts oblong, pedicelled : leaves ovate, acute, serrate.

JASMINE.

JASAMINE, JESSAMINE, JASMIN, JESIMA JASMINUM, NYNCTAN-
THES, EIGNONIA.

CLASS, Diandria, from *dis,*   ORDER, Monogynia, from
twice, and *aner,* stamen.   *monos,* one, and *gune,* pistil.

Because these flowers have *Two Stamens,* and *One Pistil,* and are consequently of the *Second Class* and *First Order* of Linnæus.

Jasminum fruticans,	Yellow Jasmine.
„ *officinalis,*	White Jasmine.

There are *Seventeen Species* of the Jasmine, with numerous varieties, a few of which are cultivated
in our gardens in New-England.

THE EMBLEM OF ELEGANCE AND GRACE.

There's a bright sunny spot, where the cinnamon trees
Shed their richest perfumes to the soft-wooing breeze ;
Where the rose is as sweet, and as bright as the sky,
As the balm of thy breath, and the glow of thine eye ;
And clouds pass as soon o'er that beautiful isle,
As the tear on thy cheek, dispersed at thy smile.
Far, far, midst its bowers, sequestered and lone,
Young love hath erected a JESSAMINE throne,
And sworn with an oath, which no mortal may say,
That none but the fairest its sceptre shall sway. *Geo. W. Patten.*

'Twas midnight—through the lattice, wreathed
With woodbine, many a perfume breathed.
From plants, that wake while others sleep,
From timid JASMINE buds, that keep
Their odours to themselves all day,
But, when the sunlight dies away,
Let the delicious secret out.   *Cromwell.*

This plant, as well as the Woodbine and Ivy, is much admired for arbours, and the decorations of walls. It is frequently alluded to in poetry. Several varieties of it grow luxuriantly in the Southern parts of the United States.

The *Bignonia sempervirens*, or Yellow Jasmine, is a very beautiful shrub or tree, bearing yellow, blue, and sometimes red flowers, often quite large. It is native in both the East and West Indies. That of the Southern States gives out a delicious fragrance in the night. In New-England it is reared with some difficulty. It is, however, generally found growing in our gardens, and is much admired. The white flowering variety is native of China and India, and several species of the genus are evergreen.

The *Bignonia radicans*, or Trumpet-Flower, is a most beautiful climbing shrub. It is often cultivated, and bears flowers both red and yellow. One species, the *flammea*, has yellow-scarlet flowers, and another bright scarlet.

The word Jasmine means ' fragrance,' and has with much propriety been applied to this flower. Retaining its delicious odours during the day, like the Honeysuckle and several other rich and valuable plants, it pours them forth at evening, when wet with dew, in the richest abundance. It fills the air with perfumes, breathing joy and delight to all who are near it. There is a species of Arabian Jasmine, the *Nyntanthes*, that expands a very beautiful flower. In its native situation, it blossoms and spreads its rich fragrance only in the night. Several of the Geraniums have this same property of yielding their fragrance only to the breath of evening. This is particularly the case with the *Geranium triste*.

The poet Churchill tells us, " the queen of flowers to charm her god, adorns his favourite bowers *with jasmine flowers.*" Another part says, " the Azores send their Jasmines, and remote Cafrara, foreigners from many lands, some like the silver spray, some like gold in the morning ray, to form a social shade." Herbert bids us, " mark how placidly the moonlight falls over that Jessamine palace, where the rose sits like a queen, with her pearly crown of dew. The White Jasmine is the emblem of Loveliness, —the Yellow of Grace.

The Yellow-flowered Jasmine, or *Jasminum fruticans*, has leaves alternate, ternate, simple : leaflets obovate, wedge-form, obtuse : branches angled.

MONK'S-HOOD.

CUPID'S CAR, VENUS'S SHELL, WOLF'S-BANE, ACONITE, THORA,
TOULOUPE, HERBE VENIMEUSE.

CLASS, Polyandria, from *polus*, many, *aner*, stamen.

ORDER, Trigynia, from *treis,* three, and *gune*, pistil.

Because these flowers have 20 *or more Stamens on the receptacle,* and *Three Pistils*, and consequently are of the 13*th Class* and 3*d Order* of Linnæus.

Aconitum uncinatum,   Monk's-Hood.
   ,,   *napellus*,   Wolf's-bane.

There are *Fourteen* Species of this plant, with many varieties, according to the last edition of Linnæus.

THE EMBLEM OF DECEIT.

And now arrives, unknown, Ægeus' seed,
Who, great in name, had two-sea'd Isthmos freed,
Whose undeserved ruin Medea sought,
By mortal ACONITE, from Scythia brought;
This from the Echidnean dog dire essence draws.
There is a blind steep cave, with foggy jaws,
Through which the bold Tyrinthian hero strained,
Dragged Cerberus, with adamant enchained,
Who backward hung, and scowling, looked askew
On glorious day, with anger rabid grew.
Thrice howls, thrice barks, at once with his three heads,
And on the grass his foaming poison sheds ;
This sprung, attracting from the fruitful soil
Dire nourishment, and power of deathful spoil;
The rural swains, because it takes delight
In barren rocks, surnamed it *Aconite.*   *Ovid.*

This is a very beautiful and curious plant, yet a most poisonous one. It is found in our gardens, amongst our flowers, in several fine varieties. The flowers are white, yellow, and blue. The common Monks-hood is a native of the woody and mountainous parts of France, Germany, and Switzerland. It is also found native in Siberia.

The term ' Monk's-hood' is derived from the circumstance of this flower's bearing a strong resemblance to the *hood* worn by the monks. The form of the flower is very various. It is composed of five irregular petals. These, united, resemble a helmet, or hood, worn upon the head. The upper petal represents the head. The two lower ones stand for that part which covers the jaws ; and the two wings conceal the temples. Thus it forms a complete helmet.

Most of the species of the Aconite are said to be poisonous. The ancients were afraid even to touch these plants. Hence the allusion in the poetry quoted above. The palace of Death is represented by the poetic Harte, as having this, together with *Stramonium,* Night-shade, Mandrake, and other poisonous plants, growing thickly about it. The huntsmen of the Alps, who pursue the wolves, and other wild animals of these bleak regions, are said to dip their arrows in the juice of this plant, to render the wounds occasioned by them mortal.

The effluvia of this plant has been known, if we may give credit to some writers, to produce fits of swooning and loss of sight. The beauty of its blossoms being inviting, yet the plant being exceedingly poisonous, has rendered it the fit emblem of DECEIT.

The *Aconite* of Theophrastus, Discorides, and Pliny, is probably not the same with ours, but should be referred to the genus *Ranunculus.* The term *Aconite* is said to be from the Greek *akone,* a whetstone, because this plant was anciently supposed to sharpen the sight, when taken, as that stone does cutting instruments.

There are but two described species growing in New-England, both bearing a blue flower, and both blossoming in June.

The *Adonis, Caltha, Aquilegia, Pæonia, Clematis, Hepotica, Anemone, Delphinium, Coptis, Podophyllum, Heleborus, Nelumbium,* and *Aconitum,* with several other genera, belong to the same *natural* order RANUNCULACÆE.

The Monk's-Hood, or *Aconitum unicantum,* has a stem flexuose : leaves palmate, three-to-five-parted, divisions rhomb-lanceolate, gash-toothed : upper lip of the corol lengthened.

P

FOX-GLOVE.

DIGITALIS, PURPLE FOX-GLOVE, PURPLE DIGITALIS, DIGITALIS
PURPUREA.

CLASS, Didynamia, from *dis*,   ORDER, Angiospermia, from
twice,and *dunamis*, superiority.   *angos*, a vessel, *sperma*, seed.

Because these flowers have *Four Stamens, two long,* and *two short,* and
have their *seeds contained in a covering or vessel,* and consequently are
of the *Fourteenth Class* and *Second Order* of Linnæus.

Digitalis *purpurea,*   Purple Fox-glove.
     „   *intermedia,*   Fox-glove.

These are nearly all the described *Species,* found growing in the Eastern and Middle States of
North-America.

THE EMBLEM OF INSINCERITY.

To later summer's fragrant breath,
Clematis' feathery garlands dance,
The hollow FOXGLOVE nods beneath,
Near the the tall Mullin's yellow lance.
Wound in the hedge-row's oaken boughs,
The Woodbine's tassels float in air,
And, blushing, the uncultured Rose
Hangs high her beauteous blossoms there;
Her fillets there, Celastrus graceful weaves,
And the Brionia winds her pale and scolloped leaves. *Smith.*

The Foxglove is an elegant plant, commonly found growing
native in England, and several other parts of Europe. This plant

grows in dry and elevated situations. The flowers are crimson, purple, yellow, and sometimes white. The Purple Digitalis, or *Digitalis purpurea*, is among the most splendid flowers that grow wild in England. The stem rises from three to six feet high, and is adorned with pendulous bell-shaped flowers. These hang one above another, in a very long spike. They are of a fine purple colour, elegantly mottled withinside with spots like eyes. The segments of the calyx are of an oval-pointed shape, and the leaves large and wrinkled. It is a *biennial*, or plant that vegetates for two years, and then perishes.

The term *Foxglove* was, perhaps, derived from the shape of its flowers. They are hollow, and somewhat in shape, like the fox's foot. The word *Digitalis* is of Latin origin, from *digitus*, the finger, and signifies something that regards the *fingers* of the hand.

The purple flowers, that hang from the stem, like little bells, by their peduncles, contrast very finely with the deep-green of the leaf. These, all together, give the plant a most lovely and inviting appearance. But, like INSINCERITY, of which it is the emblem, they only allure, to betray. It is in reality a most poisonous plant, notwithstanding its beauty. Its properties are of the *narcotic* kind. When taken in any considerable quantities, it will destroy life. In large doses, it brings on giddiness, loss of sight, and loss of intellect. Nausea soon follows, faintness, and at length death. Its leaves, however, are frequently used, in small doses, as a medicine. The purple variety has generally been introduced into our gardens for the beauty of its flowers. This variety is also extensively cultivated by the Shakers, near Albany.

The ancient physicians applied this plant, with others of its *natural* family, to wounds, externally ; and Parkinson, two centuries ago, used the *Digitalis* in the epilepsy, with great success.

The *Digitalis, Hemianthus, Dracocephalus, Mimulus, Gerardia, Antirrhinum, Collinsina, Urticularia, Gratiola*, and several other genera, belong to the same *natural* order. The Order SCROFULARÆA embraces them all.

The Purple Foxglove, or *Digitalis purpurea*, has leaflets of the calyx ovate, acute : corol obtuse ; upper lip entire : leaves lance-ovate, rugose.

AMARANTH.

GLOBE AMARANTH, GLOBE, BACHELOR'S-BUTTON, LOVE-LIES-BLEEDING, PRINCE'S-FEATHER, COXCOMB, RAGGED-SAILOR, HORSETAIL, FLOWER-GENTLE, LIFE-EVERLASTING, INDIAN-POSY, SPANISH WONDER, FLOWER-DE-JEALOUSIE, AMARANTHUS.

CLASS, Pentandria, from *pente*, five, and *aner*, stamen.

ORDER, Monogynia, from *monos*, one, and *gune*, pistil.

Because these flowers have *Five Stamens*, and *One Pistil*, and are consequently of the *Fifth Class* and *First Order* of Linnæus.

Gomphrena globosa,	Globe Amaranth.
Polygonum oriental,	Prince's Feather.
Gnaphalium margaritaceum,	Life Everlasting.

There are *twenty-two Species* of the Amaranth, with many varieties, according to the Encyclopedia.

THE EMBLEM OF CONSTANCY.

Hail to thee ! hail, thou lovely flower,
Still shed arou.'d thy sweet perfume,
Still smile amid the wintry hour,
And boast e'en then a spring-tide bloom.
Thus hope, 'mid life's severest days,
Still smiles, still triumphs o'er despair ;
Alike she lives in pleasure's rays,
And cold affliction's winter air.   *Anstor.*

Immortal AMARANTH ! a flower which once
In Paradise, fast by the tree of life,
Began to bloom ; but soon, for man's offence,
To heaven removed, where first it grew, there grows
And flowers aloft, shading the fount of life ;
And where the river of bliss, through midst of heaven,
Rolls o'er Elysian flowers her amber stream ;
With these, that never fade, the spirits elect
Bind their resplendent locks, inwreathed with beams.   *Milton.*

The various plants, enumerated under the above head, all pass under the general name of Amaranth. They are, however, of different Genera. The term *amaranth* is from the Greek *a*, *non*, or not, and *maraino*, to fade, meaning *unfading*, because the flowers never fade. They look as bright, and fair, when dead and dry, as when full of life, and growing in their greatest beauty. This all have remarked who have observed them when dry.

The red or white Field Campion, or *Lychnis diocece*, is by some called Bachelor's-Button. A species of *Gomphrena* also goes by this name. The term *Lychnis* is from the Greek *luknos*, a light, because this plant was anciently used for torches. The Prince's-Feather belongs to the genus *Polygonum*, from *polus*, many, and *gone*, joints or knees, because this tribe of plants have many joints. The biting Ars-smart, or *Hydropiper*, called also the Poor-man's-pepper, Lake-weed, and Water-pepper, belongs to this Class. Its name is from the Greek *hudor*, water, and *piper*, pepper.

The *Amaranthus melancholicus*, or Two-coloured Amaranth, when cultivated in the open air, bears a leaf of a dingy-purple colour on its upper surface, but, when cultivated by a stove, the *whole plant* is purple-coloured. The Ragged Sailor is of the genus *Polygonum*.

The Tree Amaranth, or *Amaranthus tricolor*, is a native of Guinea, Persia, China, and Japan. Its variegated leaves form a sort of pyramid, and, when in full lustre, cause the plant to appear very beautiful. This, together with the Livid Amaranth, and some other varieties, are usually disposed in pots, with Cocks-combs, and other showy plants, for adorning court-yards, and the environs of the house. The Tree Amaranth often grows to a large size, and makes a very fine appearance.

The Globe Amaranth, whose flowers resemble heads of clover of deepened hue, exists in several varieties of white, purple, speckled with gold, and variegated. From the flowers of this species remaining unchanged, even when dead and dry, they have been made the emblem of CONSTANCY. By some the Amaranth is considered as a symbol of Immortality. In poetry, we find ' ama-ranthine bowers,' ' amaranthine wreaths,' 'and amaranthine flow-ers'. The churches in Portugal, in winter, are adorned with the Globe Amaranth. In Spain, the shepherdesses often interweave it with laurel, for crowns and chaplets. The same is done in Sumatra. Milton often alludes to these charming flowers, as also Southey, Pope, Darwin, and Cowper.

The Globe Amaranth, Bachelor's-Button, or *Gomphrena globosa*, has a stem erect : leaves lance-ovate : heads solitary : peduncles two-leaved.

COREOPSIS.

CORYOPSIS, TICK-SEED SUNFLOWER, NUTALL-WEED, COREOPE
DE VIRGINIE.

CLASS, Syngenesia, from *sun*, ORDER, Polygamia frustranea,
with, and *genesis*, generation. from *polus*,many,*gamia*,marriages.

Because these flowers *have their Stamens united at top by the anthers
into a cylinder,* and *some of their florets hermaphroaite and others neuter,* and consequently are of the *Nineteenth Class,* and *Third Order* of
Linnæus.

Coreopsis *alternifolia,*	Meadow Coreopsis.	
„ *virginiana,*	Coreopsis.	
„ *tripteris,*	Tick-seed Sun-flower.	
„ *dichotoma,*	Swamp Coreopsis.	

This plant has, within a few years, been introduced into our gardens from the **Arkansaw**
Territory. Five or six Species of this genus grow in New-England.

THE EMBLEM OF CHEERFULNESS.

She sat in her twilight bower,
A temple formed of leaf and flower,
Rose and myrtle formed the roof,
To a shower of April proof,
And primroses, pale gems of spring,
Lay on the green turf glistening,
Close by the violet, whose breath
Is so sweet in a dewy wreath.
And oh ! that myrtle, how green it grew,
With flowers as white as pearls of dew
That shone beside—that GEM was there,
With fringe of gold and ebon centre fair. ANON.

The Coreopsis of Virginia, now cultivated among our garden flowers, is an indigenous plant of North-America, and a very beautiful one. It is said to grow wild abundantly in several of our Western States, and particularly in the prairies, or immense natural meadows of the Arkansaw Territory. The Tickseed Sunflower, or *Coreopsis tripteris,* so common in our fields in New-England, is a species of this genus. The genus embraces about thirty or thirty-five *species.*

Some of the species are cultivated in our gardens, and have yellow flowers. Many of them belong to the milder latitudes, but they are all peculiar to America. In the open swamps of New-Jersey, there is a low, narrow-leaved species with rose-coloured flowers. The most beautiful yet known is the *Coreopsis tinctoria,* an *annual* or *biennial* plant, originally from Arkansaw Territory, but now common in our gardens. Its flowers come out in May, and are of a fine orange-yellow, with a brown centre, as in the above plate. This variety has recently been introduced into our gardens as an ornamental plant. It continues in flower till frost comes. The ray florets are of the richest tinge of yellow, while the centre often appears almost of a jet black. The stalk rises to the height of three or four feet, giving off its branches in various directions, each of which is crowned with a fine little flower. The petals are usually eight in number, indented at the borders. Cultivation with this flower, like many others, has produced surprising changes. Growing in fine soil, it decorates the parterre with a rich beauty, having a wreath for spring, a garland for summer and autumn, and almost for winter itself. The plant gives a reddish-yellow, indelible stain to cotton, and this, as well as the *Coreopsis senifolia,* might be employed for dying. From the universality of its diffusing joy through each successive season, it has been considered the emblem of UNIFORM CHEERFULNESS.

Further, we are told by the poet that " the Coreopsis is cheerful as the smile that brightens on the cheek of youth, and sheds a gladness o'er the aged." It has therefore been sometimes deemed the emblem of BENEFICENCE.

The Tick-seed Sunflower, or *Coreopsis tripteris,* is glabrous, leaves opposite, petioled, lanceolate, entire, radical ones pinnate, cauline ones ternate : seeds obovate, naked at the apex.

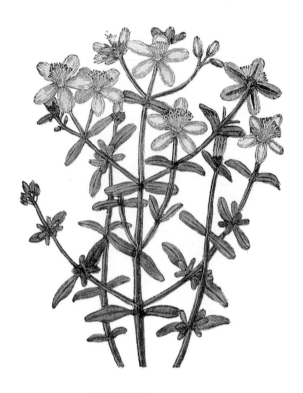

HYPERICUM.

SAINT-JOHN'S-WORT, FUGA DEMONUM, SCARECROW-OF-DEVILS,
ANDROSÆNUM.

CLASS, Polyadelphia, from *polus,*   ORDER, Polyandria, from *polus,*
many, and *adelphia,*brotherhood.   many, and *aner,* stanem.

Because these flowers *have their filaments united, forming three or more
bodies,* and *Twenty or more Stamens,* and consequently are of the *Eighteenth Class,* and **13***th Order* of Linnæus.

Hypericum ascyroides,	St. John's Wort.
,, *perforatum,*	Common Hypericum.
,, *virginicum,*	Purple St. John's Wort.

There are ten or twelve *species* of the *Hypericum,* with numerous varieties, found growing
in the Eastern and Middle States of North-America.

THE EMBLEM OF ANIMOSITY.

HYPERICUM, all bloom, so thick a swarm
Of flowers, like flies, clothing her slender rods,
That scarce a leaf appears : Mezereon too,
Though leafless, well attired, and thick beset
With blushing wreaths, investing every spray.
Althæa, with the purple eye ; the Broom
Yellow and bright, as bullion unalloyed,
Here blossoms in the myrtle shade.
Hypericum was there, the herb of war,
Pierced through with wounds, and seamed with many a scar. *Darwin.*

The *Hypericum*, or John's-Wort, is a common plant in most places in New-England. The *Hypericum perforatum* is that species so common in our fields, and so troublesome to farmers. It bears a yellow blossom, and rises from one to three or four feet in height. The stem gives off numerous branches, in various directions, each of which are again divided into smaller ones, that are crowned with many flowrets. They are often so numerous, that the flowers seem like a swarm of yellow flies, " clothing the slender rods so thick, that scarce a leaf appears."

It was formerly supposed that this plant possessed some hidden powers against evil spirits, and hence it was called *Fuga Demonum*, or Devil-Scarer.

The *Hypericum perforatum*, or Perforated Hypericum, appears as if pierced with numerous holes. Hence the fancy of the poet, when he tells us, " Hypericum was there, the herb of war, pierced through with wounds, and seamed with many a scar." And hence its emblematic signification of ANIMOSITY.

The genus *Hypericum* is a very extensive one. It is said to embrace more than one hundred *species*. These numerous species are scattered over the whole world. Though the species most generally bear a yellow flower, the *Hypericum virginicum* bears a purple one, and blossoms in August. Most of the other New-England species flower in June and July. They are all very hardy, and are perennial, excepting the *H. canadense*, which is an annual. The *H. prolificum* seems to be a woody plant.

The *Hypericum*, *Drosera*, *Dionæa*, and *Ascyrum*, belong to the same *natural* order of plants, viz. the Order HYPERICA.

The Common St. John's Wort, or *Hypericum perforatum*, is erect, branching : stem two-edged : leaves oblong, obtuse, transparently-punctate : panicle terminal, brachiate, leafy : petals twice as long as the acute, lanceolate calyx.

R

WATER-LILY.

LOTUS, NYMPHÆA, POND LILY, WHITE WATER-LILY, SWEET LILY, WATER-ROSE, LIS DES ETANGES, NUPHAR LOLE.

CLASS, Polyandria, from *polus*, many, and *aner*, stamen.

ORDER, Monogynia, from *monos*, one, and *gune*, pistil.

Because these flowers have *many disunited Stamens, originating from the receptacle*, and *one Pistil*, and consequently are of the *Thirteenth Class*, and *First Order* of Linnæus.

Nymphæa odorata,	White Water Lily.
.. *rosea*,	Redish Water Lily.
Nuphar Lutea,	YellowPond Lily, or Toad Lily.

There are but *one* or *two* Species of the White Water Lily, or *Nymphæa*, found growing in New-England. There are three or four of the *Nuphar*.

THE EMBLEM OF BEAUTY AND PURITY.

There's a spring in the woods of my summer home,
And far from the dark sea's tossing foam,
And the large WATER LILIES, that o'er it shed
Their pearly hues, to the soft light spread,
They haunt me ! I dream of that bright spring's flow,
I thirst for its rill, like a wounded roe. *Mrs. Hemans.*

Within thy beauteous corols, full-blown bell,
Long since the immortals fixed their fond abode,
There, day's bright source, Osiris, loved to dwell,
While by his side enamoured Isis glowed.
Brilliant thyself in store of dazzling *white*,
Thy sister plants more gaudy robes unfold,
This flames in *purple*,—that, intensely bright
Amid the illuminated waters, flames in *gold*.
But, far beyond the bounds of Afric's bourne,
Thine honours flourished 'mid Tibetian snows,
Booah and Bramah on thy stock repose. *Maurice.*

There are Six Species of the *Nymphæa*, only two of which are indigenous to the United States.

The *Nymphœa alba,* or White Water-Lily, is a most fragrant and beautiful flower. It has a tuberous root, creeping at the bottom of muddy and still ponds, and sending up frequent stems, crowned with large white flowers. The petals are from sixteen to twenty in number. The flower has sixty or seventy stamens. It opens at about seven o'clock in the morning, and closes soon after four in the afternoon. These flowers expand in July and August. They repose on the surface until they have perfected their fructification, and then the stems, assuming a spiral form, drag them to the bottom, beneath the surface of the water. These flowers are generally found in our slow rivers and still ponds, in New-England. The petals are of the most unsullied whiteness, excepting the outside ones, which are greenish. This purity and whiteness they retain, even when growing in muddy waters. Hence this flower has become the emblem of *Beauty* and *Purity.*

Some species of the *Lotus,* or Water Lily, expand the flower about sunrise in the morning, while floating on the surface of the water, and close it at an early hour in the afternoon. This flower has a slender stem, frequently six feet in length, according to the depth of the water. The Nymphea, or *Lotus,* is found growing in almost every part of the world. There is a species of Red Lotus found in Bengal, in India. Another, of the *blue* variety of Lotus, very beautiful, is said to be found in Cashmere, and Persia. This kind is said to be found nowhere else. The Red Lotus of Bengal are larger than our White Water-lilies. They are esteemed sacred by the Hindoos and Bramins, who feign that this flower was dyed crimson in the blood of Siva. Dr. Shaw tells us, the Lotus was a favourite vegetable symbol among the old Egyptians. Hence the allusion in the poetry. It attends the motions of the sun, said they ; lies under the water in his absence ; and has its flowers of the same round figure, as that luminary.

The Lotus was consecrated by the Egyptians to *Isis* and *Osiris,* or the Sun and Moon. The Persians know it by the name of *Nilufer,* because it grew about the Nile, in Egypt. The Lotus of Homer is supposed to have been the Sugar-Cane of modern times. That of Linnæus is a *papilinaceous* plant. The term *Lotus* is from the Greek *loö,* 'greatly to desire,' because those were said, by the ancients, to lose all relish for every thing else, who had once tasted of the Lotus. ————

The Pond Lily, or *Nymphœa odorata,* has leaves round-cordate, entire, sub-emarginate : lobes spreading asunder, acuminate, obtuse : petals equalling the four-leaved calyx : stigma with 16 to 20 radiating erectish lines.

SUN-FLOWER.

GOLD-FLOWER, SUN-MARYGOLD, TURN-SOL, HELIANTHUS, SUN'S-CROWN, HELIOTROPE, L'HELIANTHE, FLEUR DE SOLIEL, CORONA SOLIS, CORONA DEL SOLE, GIROSOLE INDIANO.

CLASS, Syngenesia, from *sun*, with, and *genesis*, generated.　　ORDER, Polygamia frustranea, from *polus*,many, and *gamia*,marriages.

Because these flowers *have their Stamens united, at top, by their anthers, into a cylinder,* and *some of their florets hermaphrodite, and others neuter,* and consequently are of the 19*th Class,* and 3*d Order,* of Linnæus.

Helianthus	*annuus,*	Common Sunflower.
..	*tuberosus,*	Jerusalem Artichoke.
..	*atrorubens,*	Purple Sunflower.
..	*augustifolia,*	Wild Sunflower.

There are twelve or fifteen described *species,* with several varieties, of the *Helianthus,* found growing in the Eastern and Middle States of North-America.

THE EMBLEM OF WATCHFULNESS, FLATTERY, AND DEVOTION.

And see, the sun himself ! On wings
Of glory up the east he springs.
Angel of light ! who, from the time
These heavens began their march sublime,
Has, first of all the starry choir,
Trod in his Maker's steps of fire !
Where are the days, thou wond'rous sphere,
When Iran, like the SUNFLOWER, turned,
To meet that eye, where'er it burned ?　　*T. Moore.*

Great *Helianthus* climbs the upland lawn,
And bows in homage to the rising dawn,
Imbibes with eagle eye the golden ray,
And watches, as it moves, the orb of day.　　*Darwin.*

This splendid flower has received the name of Sunflower, probably, from two or three different circumstances.　First, it has been supposed to turn towards, and face the sun, and follow him in his progressive course during the day. Hence its name *Turn-Sol*, from the Latin *sol*, the sun. The term *Heliotrope* is from the Greek *helios*, the sun, and *trepo*, to turn, because it turns in the direction of this luminary. Second,—its magnificent *corol*, when fully expanded, with its glowing centre and yellow ray-florets, bears a strong resemblance to the rising sun, when viewed at evening, or in the morning, in the direction of the light. Thirdly, its yellow colour, resembling that of the light of the rising sun, when mostly shorn of his rays, causes it to bear a still stronger resemblance to the heavenly orb, whose name it bears, and to which it has been consecrated. Hence its name also of Goldflower, and Sun-Marygold.

From the fancied resemblance of this flower to a crown, it has received the appellation of *Corona solis*, or Sun's Crown. The term *Helianthus* is from the Greek *helios*, sun, and *anthos*, flower.

These plants often grow to a magnificent size. At a meeting of the Horticultural Society, in August, 1832, a Sunflower was exhibited, whose disk measured four feet and six inches in circumference. It is said that in Peru and Mexico, its native country, the *Helianthus annuus* often grows 20 feet in height, and bears flowers 2 feet in diameter. One or two species are indigenous to India and Egypt.

The general term Sunflower has sometimes been given to *all* those flowers that turn towards the sun, or follow him, in his daily course. The *Heliotrope* is a smaller flower than the *Helianthus*, and of a different genus. The Artichoke of our gardens is the *Helianthus tuberosus*.

The poetic notion of the *Helianthus'* turning in the direction of the sun is almost wholly without foundation. For, at any time in the day, we may observe flowers of this plant facing in all the directions of the cardinal points and intermediate points. Its supposed devotion, however, to the source of light has rendered it the emblem of *Watchfulness*, *Flattery*, and *Devotion*. The *Heliotrope* has a very small, delicate, fragrant blossom, of a faint purple, or white colour. *Flatterers* have often been compared to it, because it is said to open its flowers only to the sun, and shut them in cloudy weather. The leaves of the Annual Sunflower perspire nineteen times as much as a man, in twenty-four hours.

The Common Sunflower, or *Helianthus annuus*, has leaves all cordate, three-nerved : peduncles thickening upwards : flowers very large, nodding : six or eight feet high.

AMERICAN ALOE.

AGAVE D'AMERIQUE, ALOE, AGAVE AMERICANA.

CLASS, Hexandria, from *hex*, six, *aner*, stamen.
ORDER, Monogynia, from *monos*, one, *gune*, pistil.

Because these flowers have *Six Stamens*, and *One Pistil*, and consequently are of the *Sixth Class* and *First Order* of Linnæus.

| *Agave americana*, | Mexican Aloe. |
| .. *virginica*, | Virginian Aloe. |

Beside these, there are several Species of the ALOE, indigenous to Egypt and the Cape of Good Hope.

THE EMBLEM OF RELIGIOUS SUPERSTITION.

In climes beneath the solar ray,
Where beams intolerable day,
And arid plains in silence spread,
The pale-green ALOE lifts its head.—
The mystic branch at Moslem's door,
Betokens travel long and sore
In Mecca's weary pilgrimage.   *Flora's Dictionary.*

The American Aloe has been said to blossom only once in 100 years, and then immediately to die. This tradition has often been very beautifully alluded to in poetry. The tardy-flowering species of Mexico, the *Agave americana*, has indeed, in cold climates, been cultivated near a century, before flowering. It arrives at this state, however, in six or seven years in its native climate, and in the warmth of Sicily. Before this period, the plant presents nothing but a perpetually unfolding cone of long, rather narrow, but thick and fleshy leaves, pointed and beset on their margins with strong thorns. Before flowering this cone and cluster of leaves attains an enormous bulk and developement. If suffered to flower, it sends up a central scape, from *eighteen* to *thirty feet* in height, resembling a huge chandelier with numerous branches clustered. These bear several thousands of elegant but not showy flowers, of a greenish yellow colour. From these slowly drops a shower of honey.

With the flowering of the plant, its energies become exhausted, and it immediately perishes, however long it may have previously existed. It sends up, however, at the same time, numerous shoots, for the purpose of a viviparous propagation. The Mexicans cultivate this plant, and call it *Magui*. They tap it for the juice with which it abounds. Many gallons of sap are often drawn from a single plant. It continues to exude for a considerable time from this vegetable fount. The liquor, when fermented, is distilled for drink, and is much used in that country. The tenacious and abundant fibres of the plant afford a durable flax or hemp, and are often employed as such. One species of this plant grows native in Virginia and the Southern States of North-America.

The common *Aloes* of commerce is often known by the name of Socotrine Aloes, and is brought from the island of Socotra, in the Indian Ocean. This bitter medicinal substance is said to be extracted from the leaves of the plant.

The Aloe is said to grow plentifully in *Arabia Felix*. The religion of Mahomet enjoins upon every Musulman to perform a pilgrimage to the temple of Mecca once in his lifetime. This flower blossoms but once, and this sometimes only after a period equal to the age of man. Hence the practice of placing a branch before the door, in commemoration of having performed this pilgrimage, and hence its emblematic signification of RELIGIOUS SUPERSTITION. Some refer the *Agave*, or American Aloe, to the *natural* order BROMELIÆ, the same of that of the Pine Apple. Others make it a genus of the *natural* order NARCISSI, embracing the Galanthus, Amaryllis, Polyanthos, Narcissus, and the like.

The *Agave virginica*, ar American Aloe, is stemless : leaves with cartilagenous seratures : scape very simple.

HOUSTONIA CÆRULEA.

VENUS'S PRIDE, FORGET-ME-NOT, EYE-BRIGHT, HOUSTONIA,
BLUETTS.

CLASS, Tetandria, from   ORDER, Monogynia, from
tesseres, four, *aner*, stamen.   *monos*, one, *gune*, pistil.

Because these flowers have *Four Stamens* and *One Pistil*, and are consequently of the *Fourth Class* and *First Order* of Linnæus.

Houstonia cærulea,	Venus' Pride.
..	*purpurea,*	White Houstonia.
..	*longifolia,*	Purple Houstonia.

These three Species are very abundant in New-England, and are the only ones described
as growing here.

THE EMBLEM OF MEEK AND QUIET HAPPINESS AND CONTENT.

How often, modest flower,
I mark thy tender blossoms when they spread,
Along the turfy slope, their starry bed,
   Hung heavy with the shower.
    'Tis but a few brief days,
I saw the green hill in its fold of snow ;
But now thy slender stems arise and blow
    In April's fitful rays.
   Sweet flower, thou tellest, how hearts
As pure, and tender as thy leaf,—as low
And humble as thy stem, will surely know
    The joy that peace imparts.   *Percival.*

In New-England, when the cold storms of winter have passed
away, and early spring, with its " sunshine and showers," has

returned, this lovely and meek little flower is seen spreading over our pastures, and through the vallies. It stretches gaily along the turfy slope, forming a " starry bed" of pale blue, faint lilach, and sometimes of the purest white flowers. They are amongst the first flowers of May and June. They give great beauty to our fields and pastures, before the grass and herbage are sufficiently tall to hide them from the view.

They are among the smallest flowers that are found. They grow in great profusion in almost all our uplands, of lighter soils. The flower has four little petals, forming a Maltese cross. Its little yellow anthers, also forming a cross in the centre, give it the appearance of a tiny, or delicate little cup of gold, set in four beautiful pearls. Its generic appellation *Houstonia* was given in commemoration of an eminent naturalist by the name of Houston. The other names Eye-bright, Venus's-Pride, and Forget-me-not, had their origin undoubtedly in its curious and beautiful structure. It has sometimes, improperly, been called the ' American Daisy,' and is known occasionally by the name of ' Bestings.' The specific term CÆRULEA means sky-colour, or blue.

It is well selected as the emblem of MEEK AND QUIET HAPPINESS. For it tells ' how hearts as pure and tender as its leaf, as low and humble as its stem, will surely know the joy that peace imparts.' Perhaps those persons, who have not had this charming floweret particularly pointed out to them, will recognize it more readily, if they are reminded that it often grows in such abundance in the fields, in April and May, as to give them, at a short distance, the appearance of having been visited by a slight flurry of snow. On closer inspection, however, it will be seen that this whiteness proceeds from an innumerable multitude of little cross-shaped, blue, lilach, and sometimes white flowerets, of exquisite delicacy and beauty.

The plant is not peculiar to New-England, but is found growing in several other parts of the United States.

The *Houstonia, Mitchella, Rubia,* and *Gallium,* belong to the same *natural order* of plants, viz. the Order RUBIACEÆ.

The Venus's-Pride, or *Houstonia Cærulea,* has a stem erect, setaceous dichotomous : radical leaves spatulate, cauline ones oblanceolate, opposite : peduncles one-flowered, elongated.

s

ASTER.

CLASS, Syngenesia, from *sun*, with, and *genesis*, generation.　　ORDER, Polygamia Superflua, from *polus*, many, and *gamia*, marriages.

Because these flowers *are all compound, having their Stamens united, by their anthers, into a hollow cylinder,* and *florets* of the disk *perfect,*—those of the margin furnished with *pistils only,* and consequently are of the 19*th Class,* and 2*d Order,* of Linnæus.

Aster hyssopifolius,	Star-flower.
„ *chinensis,*	China Aster.
„ *Nova-Angliæ,*	New-England Aster.
„ *tardiflorus,*	Late-flowering Aster.
„ *æstivus,*	Summer Aster.
„ *humilis,*	Low Aster.

There are said to be more than *Sixty Species* of the Genus ASTER indigenous to the United States of North-America.

THE EMBLEM OF RELIGIOUS FAITH.

And varied as the *Aster's* flower,
The charms of beauty bless my eye—
For who would prize the coming hour,
If only like the hours gone by.　　*Anon.*

The generic term *Aster* is from the Latin *aster,* signifying a *star,* because these beautiful flowers resemble stars in their appearance.　 Their ray florets finely represent the radiance of these brilliant nocturnal luminaries.　 When these flowers are in motion on their stalks by the winds, we can easily fancy we see them twinkle in bright colours, like stars in a clear evening.　 They are scattered lavishly all over our fields in New-England in summer and autumn. The greater number of the indigenous species expand their flowers in August, though several kinds blossom as late as October and November, and some as early as July. They are of all the varieties of yellow, purple, blue, red, and white. They are generally small, especially the species native in New-England. Some of their flowers are not much larger than the head of a common-sized pin, and are of great beauty. In their general appearance they resemble the Sunflower. They are indeed of the same *natural* order. Though the flowers are generally small, the plants themselves are often large. They grow in almost all situations where the soil is good—often in the shade of bushes and trees.

The China or Indian species of Aster is the one most frequent in our gardens. Its flowers are much larger and much more beautiful than the American kinds. They are of almost every colour and shade. The American genus *Inula* or *Chrysopsis* is nearly related to the Aster. The *Solidago*, or Golden-rod, is distinguished from the *Inula*, or Elecampane, by the smallness of the flowers of the former. The *Inula* has also a small imbricated calyx, with the scales generally connivent. The term *Chrysopsis*, sometimes applied to the genus *Inula*, is from the Greek *krusos*, gold, and *optholmos*, eye, unitedly signifying "Golden-eye," because these flowers are yellow. The Asters are also nearly allied to the Daisy-like flower *Erigeron*, one species of which, the *E. bellidi-folium*, is often called Poor Robin's Plantain, and its leaves are chewed as a substitute for Tobacco. Another species of it is termed Flea-bane, or Pride-weed, having a white flower. The flower of the Ox-eye Daisy, or White-Weed, the *Chrysanthemum leucanthemum*, often called also May-weed, so abundant in our fields, is sometimes miscalled an *Aster* or Daisy. This plant, however, as well as the *Buphthalmum grandiflorum*, both pass by the name of Ox-eye, and are of the same natural family as the Aster.

The Asters indigenous to New-England are all *perennial*. The China or India Asters are generally *annuals*. The *A. nova-angliæ*, or New-England Aster, in rich soils often grows ten or twelve feet high, bearing blue and purple flowers, while the *A. rigidus* scarcely reaches the height of a foot. The *A. cyaneus*, with its blue and purple stars, that appear in August, is generally esteemed the handsomest of the American species. Its *natural* order is *Corymbiferæ*.

The *Aster hyssopifolius*, or Star-flower, has leaves linnear-lanceolate, three-nerved, punctate, acute, margin scabrous : calyx imbricate.

MORNING-GLORY.

CONVOLVULUS, CLIMBING MORNING-GLORY, WITHWIND, BIND-
WEED, IPOMÆA, MAJOR CONVOLVULUS.

CLASS, Pentandria, from ORDER, Monogynia, from *mo-*
pente, five, and *aner*, stamen. *nos*, one, and *gune*, pistil.

Because these flowers have *Five Stamens*, and *One Pistil*, and are consequently of the *Fifth Class* and *First Order* of Linnæus.

Convolvulus stans,		Dwarf Morning-glory.
..	*jalapa,*	Jalap.
..	*batatus,*	Sweet, or Carolina Potato.
..	*arvensis,*	Bindweed.

There are ten or twelve *species* of the *Convolvulus*, with many varieties, found growing
in the Eastern and Middle States of North-America.

THE EMBLEM OF WORTH SUSTAINED BY AFFECTION.

Among the loose and arid sands,
The humble arenaria creeps,
Slowly the purple star expands,
But soon within its calyx sleeps,
And these small bells, so lightly rayed
With young Aurora's rosy hue,
Are to the noontide sun displayed,
But shut their plaits against the dew.
On upland slopes the shepherds mark
The hour, when, as the dial true,
Chiconium to the tuning lark
Lifts her soft eyes serenely blue.
And thou, " WEE CRIMSON-TIPPED FLOWER,"
Gatherest thy fringed mantle round
Thy bosom, at the closing hour.
When night-drops bathe the turfy ground.   *Smith.*

This beautiful vine or climber exists in several species, native in
New-England.   It grows wild in our fields and pastures, often running upon hedges and fences.   Several kinds are cul-

tivated in our gardens, and under our windows, for the beauty of their flowers, which are found blue, purple, pink, white, and variegated. Sometimes they are seen white, delicately pencilled with blue or red. They are of a most delicate structure, and in shape somewhat resemble a speaking-trumpet, or fisherman's horn.

The genus *Convolvulus* consists mostly of plants, containing a milky juice, strongly cathartic and caustic.

It is called *Convolvulus*, from the Latin word *convolvo*, to roll together, or twist up, because the plants twirl or twist around, as they climb up their supporters.

The Jalap, of medicine, is a species of the Convolvulus. It is a curious fact that the Carolina or Sweet Potato, so delicious as an esculent, belongs to the same Genus as the Jalap, so nauseous as a medicine. The *Mirabilis Jalapa*, Marvel-of-Peru, sometimes called also Marvel, Four-o'Clock, Noon-Sleep, and *Bel de Nuit*, is often known by the appellation of Low or Dwarf Morning Glory.

The *Convolvulus*, or Morning Glory, French Bean, and many other plants having a *voluble* or twining stem, twist, or twirl around any thing that comes in their way, in a spiral manner ;— nor can any thing prevent them, from thus turning from *right* to *left*. No art or force can compel them to take a direction contrary to their natural one. Honeysuckle, on the contrary, and several other plants, turn their stems, in a different direction, from *left* to *right*, according to the apparent motion of the sun. These are equally refractory, in regard to taking a different direction.

The genus *Convolvulus* belongs to the *natural* order *Campanacæ*, or Bell-flowers. The blossoms of the Bind-weed are generally white. Bell-flowers have a honey-cup in the bottom of the blossom. The border or circumference of the flower of the Morning-Glory folds upon itself when sleeping. This generally takes place in the middle of the day, it being open morning and evening. To the same *natural* order belong the *Convolvuli, Ipomæa, Diapensia, Pyxidanthera*, and *Cuscuta*.

The Convolvulus is an extensive genus, and is indigenous to America, Europe, and India.

As the *pink* variety are emblematic of WORTH, *sustained by affection*, so the *blue* is emblematic of REPOSE. " Touch not this flower, 'tis sacred to repose."

The Dwarf Morning-Glory, or *Convolvulus stans*, is erect, downy : leaves lance-oblong, accuminate, cordate, hind lobes obtuse : peduncle one-flowered, long : bracts ovate, acute : floriforous below.

CHINA PINK.

INDIAN-PINK, CHINESE-PINK, DIANTHUS-CHINENSIS, ŒILLET
DE CHINA.

CLASS, Decandria, from *deka*,   ORDER, Digynia, from
ten, and *aner*, stamen.   *dis*, twice ; *gune*, pistil.
Because these flowers have *Ten Stamens* and *Two Pistils*, and are consequently of the *Tenth Class* and *Second Order* of Linnæus.

Dianthus chinensis,	China Pink.	
. *caryophillus,*	Carnation.	
.. *communis,*	Common Pink.	
.. *barbatus,*	Sweet-William.	

Beside these, there are Two or Three other species of the Dianthus, with numerous varieties, found growing in the Eastern and Middle States of North-America.

THE EMBLEM OF KINDNESS AND DIGNITY.

I stopped beneath the walls
Of San-Mark's old cathedral halls,
I entered :—and beneath the roof
Ten thousand wax-lights burnt on high,
And incense from the censers fumed,
As for some great solemnity.
The white-robed choristers were singing
Their cheerful peals, the bells were ringing,
Their deep-voiced music floated round,
As the far arches sent forth sound,—
The stately organ :—and fair bands
Of young girls strewed, with lavish hands,
Violets, and PINKS, the ancient floor,
And sang, while scattering the sweet store.   *Landon.*

The generic term *Dianthus*, applied to this plant, as observed
in another place, is from the Greek *Dis*, Jove, and *Anthos*, flower,

unitedly signifying " Jove's Flower." It was so named from its extraordinary beauty. Its specific appellations *Chinensis*, China, and Indian Pink, was given it, because first introduced from China and India. The cultivated *varieties* of Pink are very numerous, exceeding, according to the catalogue of Mr. Prince, two hundred. The China Pink blossoms about the last of June or first of July.

Its flowers appear in succession, till the middle of November, or first of December, affording beauty and fragrance in abundance, even after almost all other flowers have disappeared. Its stalk rises twelve or fifteen inches in height, firm and upright, branching out on every side. It bears its flowers on the top, solitary, and of all colours and variegations imaginable. This Pink, in our climate, is *annual*, or dies every autumn.

The Genus *Dianthus* includes the rich Carnation, with its spicy odour, the Sweet William, and the whole tribe of Pinks, in all their varieties. The blossoms of the Childing Sweet-William expand about eight in the morning, and close again about one in the afternoon.

Nearly allied to the Pinks are the *Scleranthus, Silene* or Catchfly, *Saponaria* or Soapwort, often called Bouncing-Bet, the *Cerastium* or Mouse-ear Chickweed, and *Agrostemma* or Cockle so common among corn. The *Silene behen* is known by the name of Campion. The Sweet William has its flowers incorporated, many of them unitedly forming a head, and the scales as long as the corolla, whereas in the Carnation they are short. The Carnation and Sweet-William, being *perennial*, are easily cultivated.

The China and Single Pinks are *annual*, and must be sown every year. A flower-garden would hardly be deemed perfect without its pinks. The poet says,

  " For us in autumn blows
  The *Indian pink*—the latest rose ;"

implying that its beauty and loveliness are displayed in our behalf and for our pleasure. It has therefore been deemed a suitable symbol of BENIGNITY and KINDNESS.

The China Pink, or *Dianthus chinensis*, has flowers solitary : scales of the calyx subulate, spreading, leafy, equalling the tube : petals crenate : leaves lanceolate.

NIGHT-SHADE.

SOLANUM, BITTER-SWEET, EGG-PLANT, LOVE-APPLE, TOMATOES, ATROPA-BELLADONNA, DAWLE, HORSE-NETTLE, THORN-APPLE, MAD-APPLE, GARDEN-NIGHT-SHADE, WINTER-CHERRY, PALESTINE NIGHT-SHADE.

CLASS, Pentandria, from *pente*, five, and *aner*, stamen.   ORDER, Monogynia, from *monos*, one, and *gune*, pistil.

Because these flowers have *Five Stamens*, and *One Pistil*, and are consequently of the *Fifth Class* and *First Order* of Linnæus.

Solanum nigrum,	Deadly Nightshade.
,,	*tuberosum*,	Potato.
,,	*lycopersicum*,	Love-apple, Tomatoes.
,,	*melongena*,	Egg-plant.
,,	*pseudo-capsicum*,	Jerusalem Cherry.
,,	*dulcamara*,	Bitter-sweet.

There are said to be more than One Hundred *Species* of this genus, Six or Eight of which are found growing in the Eastern and Middle States of North-America.

THE EMBLEM OF SUSPICION AND DARK THOUGHTS.

Mimosa sat trembling, and said with a sigh,
" 'Twas so fine she was ready with rapture to die."
And Cactus, the grammar-school tutor, declared,
It might be with the gamut of Orpheus compared ;
Then moved himself round in a comical way
To show how the trees once frisked at the lay.
Yet NIGHT-SHADE, the metaphysician, complained,
That the nerves of his ears were excessively pained ;
'Twas but seldom he crept from the college, he said,
And he wished himself safe in his study or bed.   *Mrs. Sigourney.*

Thy baleful roots, *Solanum*, must arise
From dismal, dark Tartarian shade.   *Flora.*

It is somewhat remarkable that the Potato, one of our most wholesome esculents, should belong to this poisonous genus—the

Solanum. The resemblance of its blossom, however, will readily be recognized in the annexed plate. The Potato of our fields is *indigenous* to South-America. It was introduced into England by Sir Walter Raleigh, and now forms a considerable part of the food of the poorer classes in England and Ireland. It was originally brought from the mountains of Peru, as likewise the Thorn-apple, Jamestown Weed or Apple of Peru, as it is sometimes called. This, the *Datura*, is also another genus of the family SOLANÆ. The *Solanum tuberosum*, or Potato, since its introduction into Europe, has become infinitely more valuable as an article of food both here and in the colder regions of North-America than it could ever have been in its native climate.

The Deadly Night-shade, Bitter-sweet, Tomatoes or Love-apple, Egg-plant and Jerusalem Cherry, are *species* of the genus SOLANUM. The term *Solanum* is from the Latin *soleo*, to console or comfort, because these plants, many of them being narcotics, give comfort by their stupifying qualities. The leaves of the Thorn-apple possess this property in a high degree. They are simmered with cream or lard and used as a healing ointment—the *Unguentum Stramonæ* of the apothecaries. The Ground Cherry (*Physalis*) and common Tobacco (*Nicotiana*), are very nearly related to this genus, as likewise the Henbane, or *Hyoscyamus*. Nearly allied to these also is the *Atropa Belladonna* of Linnæus, so called from the Italian ' bella donna,' a handsome lady, because the ladies of Italy use it to take away the too florid colour of their faces. The *Amaryllis formosissima* or beautiful Jacobean Lily, as likewise the *Amaryllis Atamasco* or Atamasco Lily, have sometimes, to their great discredit, been confounded with the *Atropa belladonna*. The *Atropa, Solanum,* and *Circæa*, all pass under the common name of " Nightshade." The latter is called "Enchanter's Nightshade." The term *Deadly* has been well applied to the *Atropa*, if not to the *Solanum*, for every part of the former is a deadly poison. The lives of children have been destroyed by eating the berries, which, in any considerable quantities produce vertigo, coma, and death. These plants belong to the *Lurida* or Lurid family, and from their dark and sombre hues probably received the appellation of " Night Shades." The flowers of several species are extremely beautiful.

The Deadly Night-shade, the *Solanum nigrum*, flowering in June, has a stem unarmed, erectish or erect ; branches angled, dentate : leaves ovate, repand, glabrous : racemes two-ranked, nodding.

T

NASTURTION.

STERTION, STORTION, INDIAN-CRESS, LA GRANDE-CAPUCINE,
NASTURTIUM PERUVIANUM, NASTURTIUM INDICUM, TROPEOLUM MAJUS, FLOS
SANGUINEUS MONARDI, ACRIVIOLA, CARDAMINEUM MINUS.

CLASS, Octandria, from *okto*,   ORDER, Monogynia, from
eight, *aner*, stamen.   *monos*, one, *gune*, pistil.

Because these flowers have *Eight Stamens*, and *One Pistil*, and consequently are of the *Eighth Class* and *First Order* of Linnæus.

Tropæolum majus,   Nasturtion.
     „   *indicum,*   Indian Cress.
There are *Five Species* of the Tropæolum, or Indian Cress, with several varieties, one or two
of which are cultivated in our flower-pots and gardens in New-England.

THE EMBLEM OF WIT.

—Beside him teems the earth
With tulips, like the ruddy evening streak'd,
And here, the lily hangs the head of snow,
And here, amid her sable cup,
Shines the red eye-spot, like one brighter star,
The solitary twinkler of the night ;
And here the rose expands her
Paradise of leaves,——
The lady lily, paler than the moon,
And roses laden with the breath of May,
Queens of the field, in milk-white mantle drest,—
Bright the NASTURTION glows, and, late at eve,
Light, lambent, dances o'er its sleepless beds.   *Southey.*

This curious plant is said to possess the extraordinary property
of *emitting flashes of light in the dark.* It exhibits an appear-

ance not unlike the gleam of distant lightning. The phenomenon has most frequently been observed during the evening twilight of the warmer summer and autumnal months. This often takes place likewise before sunrise in the morning. It is much stronger at some times, than at others. It is often so bright as to render the plant itself entirely visible. It is said that the eldest daughter of Linnæus, Elizabeth Christiana, was the person who first discovered this wonderful property in the plant. It was at Upsal, where she made this discovery while examining some flowers. This she communicated to the Academy at Stockholm soon after. From the near resemblance of this light to that originating from the combustion of phosphorus, the plant has sometimes been called the Phosphorescent Plant. The light does arise, undoubtedly, from what the chemist would term its phosphorescent property. This property is possessed by some other plants besides the Nasturtion, as the *Œnothera* or Evening Primrose.

The Nasturtion, or greater Indian-Cress, was first brought to France from South-America, in 1684. It is a native of Peru, whence it was brought and named *La Grande Capucine*, in honour of an order of monks. It is called Nasturtion, or *Nasturtium*, as we are told *quod nasem torquet*, because it emits, when bruised, a pungent odour, that causes persons "to turn away their noses." In its recent state, the plant, and more especially its flowers, have a smell and taste, resembling that of Water-cresses. When bruised, it emits a pungent odour, like that of the horse-radish. Its blossoms are generally of a reddish or golden yellow, or snuff-colour, very brilliant, but sometimes inclining to a brown, and very curiously formed. Linnæus called it *Tropæolum*, " the Trophy Plant." In this name he elegantly and fancifully alluded to its use for decorating bowers, and the resemblance of its peltate leaves to *shields*, as well as of its flowers to golden *helmets*, " pierced through and through and stained with blood." From its emitting flashes of light, it has a semblance to those flashes of intellect, termed wit. It has, therefore, been made emblematic of this intellectual quality—WIT. By some it has been deemed an emblem of PATRIOTISM and BRAVERY.

The Nasturtion, or *Tropæolum majus*, has leaves peltate, sub-repand : petals obtuse, some of them fringed.

OXALIS.

WOOD-SORREL, UMBRELLA-SORREL, UMBELLED-SORREL, LUJULA,
TRIFOLIUM-ACETOSUM, L'OSEILLE, SOREL, OXALIS ACETOSA.

CLASS, Decandria, from *deka*,   ORDER, Pentagynia, from *pente*,
ten, and *aner*, stamen.   five, and *gune*, pistil.

Because these flowers have *Ten Stamens* and *Five Pistils*, and consequently are of the 10*th Class* and *Fifth Order* of Linnæus.

Oxalis acetosella,	Wood-Sorrel.
,,	*violacea,*	Violet Wood-Sorrel.
,,	*stricta,*	Yellow Wood-Sorrel.
,,	*corniculata,*	Procumbent Wood-Sorrel.

There are Ninety-Six described *Species* of this plant, but five or six of which are commonly found
growing in the Eastern and Middle States of North America.

THE EMBLEM OF AFFECTION AND TENDERNESS.

Sorrel, that hangs her cups,
Ere their frail forms and streaky views decay,
O'er her pale verdure, till parental care
Inclines the short'ning stems, and to the
Shade of closing leaves, her infant race withdraws.   *Gisborne.*

See trim Oxalis, with her pencilled flower,
Close to the sheltering copse the maiden cleaves,
And coyly plaits her purple-tinted leaves.   *Evans.*

The coy Oxalis seeks the sheltering glade,
Where beamy light and sunshine never played.   *Anon.*

This delicate and curious little flower is very generally found
growing native, in shady places in New-England. It often grows

in woods, and moist, shady lanes. It has hence received the name of Wood-sorrel, or Woods-sorrel. The term *Lujula*, sometimes applied to it, is said to be a contraction, or rather corruption, of the word *Allelujah*, ' Praise the Lord,' so named from its supposed many virtues.

The plant is totally inodorous, but possesses a grateful acid taste. Hence its name *Oxalis*, from the Greek *oxus*, signifying acid or sour, like vinegar.

Linnæus remarked of it, that its leaflets, in wet weather, are erected, but hang down in dry weather. The Common Oxalis, or *Oxalis acetosella*, is native all over Europe. It has been said of the Oxalis, that it has the *leaves* of the Trefoil, the *taste* of the Sorrel, and the *flower* of the Geranium. Contrary to what might be expected, this plant thrives, both in mountainous and low situations. It is both an inhabitant of the Alpine regions of Switzerland, and of the low countries of France. This is accounted for by Linnæus, in the observation, that the clouds, resting upon the tops of mountains, produce nearly the same state of atmosphere, as the fogs, in low and marshy situations.

The flowers of the *Oxalis* are yellow, purple, red, white, and variegated. There is a kind in New-England, having a primrose-yellow floweret, most delicately pencilled with crimson. In Pennsylvania and Virginia, a species is found with a pink and lilac flower, lined with red.

Some beautiful China varieties have recently been introduced into our gardens.

Linnæus says, that ' as soon as this flower throws off its petals, it thrusts its seed-vessels under the contiguous leaves, with a motion seemingly almost convulsive, and voluntary. The footstalk of the flower turns, bending back, at a sharp angle, till it brings its seed-vessel to the shelter of the leaves, that seem provided by Providence for its protection.' Hence the allusion of the poets, in the opposite quotation. Hence also, from its affectionate and protecting care, its emblematic signification of TENDERNESS and AFFECTION.

The Yellow Wood-sorrel, or *Oxalis stricta*, is all over hirsute : stem erect, branching : peduncles umbelliferous, leaves ternate, obcordate : petals obovate : styles of the length of the inner stamens.

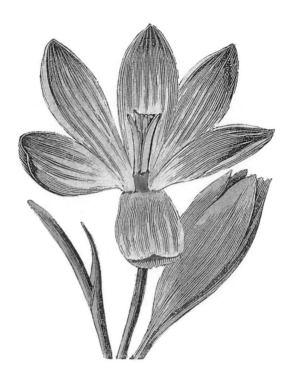

CROCUS.

SAFFRON, BLUE CROCUS, CARTHAMUS, CARTHAMUS TINCTORIUS,
CARDUUS SATIVUS, FLEUR DE SAFFRON, SAFFLOWER.

CLASS, Triandria, from   ORDER, Monogynia, from
treis, three, *aner*, stamen.   *monos*, one, *gune*, pistil.
Because these flowers have *Three Stamens*, and *One Pistil*, and consequently are of the *Third Class* and *First Order* of Linnæus.

Crocus *officinalis*,   Yellow Saffron.
..   *sativus*,   Blue Saffron.
The Carthamus and Crocus are different plants, though passing under the common name
of Saffron.

THE EMBLEM OF YOUTHFUL GLADNESS.

A flowery crown I will compose,
I'll weave the Crocus, weave the rose,
I'll weave narcissus, newly wet,
The hyacinth, and violet,
And myrtle shall supply me green,
And lilies laugh in light between.   *Meleager.*

Command my slaves to lead me forth
I will ; but they shall wear
The bridal saffron : all their locks shall bloom
With garlands ; and their blazing nuptial torch
And hymeneal songs prepare the way.   *Milman.*

The Crocus is found with flowers both yellow and blue, and
sometimes with violet and white ones. Several of them are very

handsome garden flowers. The generic term Crocus, applied to this flower, is from the Latin *crocus*, signifying *yellow*, because its blossoms are frequently of that colour. The stigmas are yellow also, and are pulled out and dried. In this state they are sold under the name of ' English Saffron.' The plant, known by the name of American Saffron, is of another Genus—the genus *Carthamus*. The florets of this kind are often used for the same purpose and sold under the name of " American Saffron."

It is a remarkable circumstance of this flower, that it keeps its petals expanded during a tolerable bright candle, or lamp light, in the same way as it does during the light of the sun. If the candle be removed, the flower closes its petals. This, it is said, it does, in the garden, when a cloud obscures the sun. When the artificial light is restored, the flower opens again, as it does on the return of the direct solar rays.

The Hyacinth, Narcissus, Amaryllis, Tulip, Iris, Crocus, and other bulbous-rooted plants, are often made to bloom in Water-Glasses in our parlours. The Roman Narcissus, Double Jonquille, Polyanthus Narcissus, Single Hyacinth, and Double Narcissus, may be brought forward so as to flower in the early part of winter, if properly managed. These are all exquisitely beauful flowers, well suited for glasses.

The *Calchicum autumnale*, so much used in the cure of rheumatism and gout, is called Meadow Saffron.

The origin of the Crocus is fancifully related, in the fourth book of Ovid's Metamorphoses, where a youth of this name was transformed into this pleasing little flower.

The remark of the poet, in the opposite quotation, authorizes us to esteem it, as the symbol of MARRIAGE ; but many have considered it more properly the emblem of YOUTHFUL JOY.

The *Carthamus, Carduus, Centaurea*, and several other genera, belong to the same *natural* order of plants, according to the arrangement of Jussieu—the Order CINAROCEPHALÆ. The Crocus belongs to the IRIDES—Flags or Irises.

The Saffron, or *Crocus sativus*, has leaves linear, with revolute margin : stigma exsert, with long linear segments : violet corals.

BLUE WATER-LILY.

BLUE LOTUS, ORIENTAL LOTUS, NUPHAR BLUEU, BLUE
WATER-ROSE.

CLASS, Polyandria, from *polus*,
many, and *aner*, stamen.

ORDER, Monogynia, from *monos*, one, and *gune*, pistil.

Because these flowers have *Twenty or more Stamens, on the receptacle,*
and *one Pistil,* and consequently are of the *Thirteenth Class,* and
First Order of Linnæus.

Nuphar cærulea,	Blue Water-Lily.
Nymphæa odorata,	Pond Lily.
.. *rosea,*	Reddish Pond Lily.

There are but *one* or *two* Species of the White Water Lily, or *Nymphæa*, found growing in New-
England. There are three or four of the *Nuphar.*

THE EMBLEM OF BEAUTY AND PURITY.

Bright bands of Egypt's fair young girls,
  To the lighted temple go,
With those LILIES wreathed in their glossy curls,
  By Nilus' dark stream that grow. *L. P. Smith.*

These virgin LILIES, all the night
Bathing their beauties in the lake,
That they may rise more fresh and bright,
  When their beloved suns awake. *T. Moore.*

From heaven's dim concave shot a golden ray,
Still brighter and more bright it streamed,
Then, like a thousand suns, resistless gleamed,
Whilst on the placid water blooming,
  And the sky perfuming,
An opening LOTUS rose, and smiling spread
  His *blue skirts* and vase of gold. *Sir Wm. Jones.*

There seems to be much confusion amongst writers, with regard
to the *Lotus.* Some modern writers, of high repute, make it the

Birds-foot- Trefoil, a papilionaceous plant, of the Decandria Class. Others, of equal note, tell us, it is an aquatic plant, a native of both Indies, and of Egypt. That it grows in abundance on the banks of the Nile, where its root is used for food.

The Lotus of Homer, as has been already observed, was probably the Sugar-cane of modern times. The Lotus of Linnæus is a papilionaceous flower. The plant, known among the Persians by the name of *Nilufer*, is doubtless the one formerly consecrated, in Egypt, to *Isis*. There is a species of it known by the name *Nelumbo*. The largest flowered plant in America is the *Nelumbium*, belonging to the natural tribe NYMPHÆACEÆ. It is an aquatic plant of the Southern and Western States, and grows also near Philadelphia. It is readily recognized by its large leaves, which are perfectly *orbicular* and *peltate*, or shield-shaped. These either float or rise out of the water. The peduncles always appear above the surface, each bearing a yellowish-white flower, having many concave petals. The pericarps, or nuts, of the American kind, are like acorns, each containing one seed, and are entirely immersed to the summit in a top-shaped or turbinate spongy receptacle. The pericarpium of one species is said to contain seeds, each of which envelopes the leaves of a perfect plant, in miniature.

The *blue* Lotus grows in Cashmire and Persia. The red and white in Bengal. Theophrastus, and after him Pliny, inform us, that the Lotus is found in the Euphrates, where it sinks under water at midnight, and rises again and expands its beautiful flowers in the morning. The natives of India, says Pennant, feign that "Camdeo, —the Indian Cupid, or God of love,—was first seen, floating down the river Ganges, on a leaf of *Lotus*." He has, say they, his abode in the flower of a *Lotus*. The *red* or *blue Lotus*, when floating on the calm stream, with its petals expanded to the blue sky, is exceedingly beautiful. The *white*, reflecting its light in the crystal waters, is scarcely less so. The Indian God *Brahma* wears earrings, bracelets, and a garland of *Blue lotus* flowers. The Brahmins, or priests, tell us, " this implies, that man should allay his fiery passions, as with cool waters, from the river's bed." When " Lilies, heaped like pearls from the sea, laugh on the blue or crystal waters, pure and spotless," they may truly be deemed the emblem of BEAUTY and PURITY. The plate represents the *Nuphar*.

The *Nuphar lutea*, or Water Lily, has leaves cordate, entire : lobes near each other, calyx five-leaved : stigma rapand, with 14 to 20 radiated lines, and a deep central hole.

U

CAMELLA-JAPONICA.

JAPAN-TREE-ROSE, INDIAN-TREE-ROSE, CHINA-ROSE, ROSE
OF INDIA, CAMELLA-INDICA.

CLASS, Monadelphia, from *monos*,   ORDER, Polyandria, from
one, and *adelphos*, brotherhood.   *polus*, many, *aner*, stamen.

Because these flowers have the filaments of their *Stamens* united laterally
into one groupe, and *many Stamens*, and consequently are of the
16*th Class* and 13*th Order* of Linnæus.

Camella Japonica,   Japan Rose, or Camella.
This shrub or tree, a native of China and Japan, has recently been introduced into our country.

THE EMBLEM OF UNPRETENDING EXCELLENCE.

The chaste CAMELLA's pure and spotless bloom,
That boasts no fragrance, and conceals no thorn.   *Roscoe.*

The rose was tossed by Zephyr's sighs ;
And Cupid stopped to gaze upon
The living gem, with raptured eyes:
It chanced a bee was busy there,
Searching for its fragrant fare ;
And, heedless, stooping there to sip,
An angry insect stung his lip,—
And, gushing from the ambrosial cell,
One bright drop on its bosom fell !
Weeping, to his mother, he
Told the tale of treachery ;
And she, her vengeful boy to please,
Strung his bow with captive bees,
And placed upon the ROSE's stem
The poisoned sting she plucked from them.
And none, since that eventful morn,
Have found this flower without a thorn.   *Anon.*

This beautiful shrub is a native of India, and particularly of Japan and several parts of China. It is there said to be a large, lofty tree, and an evergreen, bearing most magnificent flowers. These large and beautiful flowers in form resemble the rose, and exhibit a great variety of colours. The prevailing colour, however, is red or a dark purple, or crimson and scarlet. From its similarity to the rose, it has been termed the Indian or Japan Rose ; but is more generally known by the name of *Camella* or *Japonica*—the latter in allusion to its native country.

The *varieties* of the Japan Rose, or *Camella Japonica*, like those of most other flowers, are very numerous and pass under different names. More than fifty varieties are enumerated in the catalogues. They pass under different names, such as Lady Long's, Woods' Superb, Aiton's large, Chandler's striped, Pompone, Knight's Anemone-flowered, Lady Banks' tea-leaved, Grenville's-red, Lady Campbell's, Shell-flowered, Kew-blush, Nepaul, China Rose, Dwarf, Changeable, White, Pink, Coral-flowered, Hollyhock-flowered, White Pæony-flowered, Scarlet, Starry, Double-blush, Fringed, Single-white-oil-bearing, Double-crimson, Buff, Double-striped, Semi-double, Axillary, Fragrant-myrtle-leaved, Blotched, Spatulate, and so on, up to *Fifty Varieties*. Much attention has lately been given to the cultivation of the *Camella*, and many new *varieties* have recently been introduced. In most of them, there seems to be a succession of buds and flowers, following one another in regular gradation through the whole year.

This flower has been in such request, and so much admired, that Mr. Prince, the enterprizing proprietor of the Linnean garden at Long-Island, N. Y. recently purchased several plants at the high price of five guineas each. His collection is now large, comprising more than 3000 plants of all the beautiful varieties of red, white, purple, and striped. The flowers are both single and double. This shrub will endure a great degree of cold, and consequently needs very little care.

DENT DE LEON.

LION'S TOOTH, LEONTODON, DANDELION, TARAXACUM.

CLASS, Syngenesia, from *sun*, with, and *genesis*, generation.　　ORDER, Polygamia Equalis, from *polus*, many, and *gamia*, marriages.

Because these flowers *have their Stamens united at top, by their anthers, into a hollow cylinder,* and *all their florets hermaphrodite,* and consequently are of the 19*th* Class, and *First Order,* of Linnæus.

Leontodon taraxacum,　　Dandelion.

There are but One or Two Species of the GENUS Leontodon found growing in New-England.

" ONE OF FLORA'S TIME-KEEPERS."

Thine full many a pleasing bloom
Of blossoms, lost to all perfume,
Thine the DANDELION flowers,
Gilt with dew, like sun with showers.　　*Clare.*

At his departure, hangs her head and weeps,
And shrouds her sweetness up, and keeps
Sad vigils, like a cloistered nun,
Till his reviving ray appears
Waking her beauty as he dries her tears.　　*Moore.*

The Dandelion is very generally diffused over New-England. It is an early spring-flower, making its appearance sometimes in the early part of April, and continuing in flower till July or August. It bears a fine yellow or golden-coloured blossom, which, though destitute of the rich fragrance of many other flowers, appears very fine, when gemming the green turf of our pastures, sloping hill-sides, and meadows.

The term Dandelion is probably a corruption of the French *Dent-de-Leon*, signifying " the tooth of the lion," or lion's tooth. The appellation *Leontodon* is also two Greek words, *Leo*, a lion, and *odous*, tooth, which, united, signify the same thing, so called from its fancied resemblance.

It should be remarked, that, common and insignificant as this plant may seem, it is enumerated in the horologe of flowers. Linnæus reckoned it as one of Flora's *time*-pieces. It opens, regularly and punctually, during the summer months, at five or six in the morning, and closes its flower, with the same regularity, a little before sunset in the afternoon.

When its flowers have faded, the seeds present their curious feathery appendage, which unitedly give the appearance of a globular or round body, in place of the departed flower. The wind, however, soon disperses this aggregation, wafting each light seed through the air on its wings, scattering the meadows and fields with them, in all directions. In wet seasons, this plant blossoms early, and continues in flower during the whole summer and autumn. It is indigenous to Europe, but has become naturalized in America.

There is no flower, that more certainly opens and closes at a particular time, than this. Hence it has been placed among the first in the " HOROLOGE OF FLORA." From its bright-coloured and showy blossoms, that display charms to the eye, yet are destitute of all fragrance, affording only a sickly and nauseous smell, it has sometimes by the poets been deemed a suitable emblem of COQUETRY.

The *Leontodon, Hieracium, Sonchus, Lactuca, Prenathes, Cichorium, Krigia, Traximon, Apargia*, and several other genera, belong to the same *natural* order CICHORACEÆ.

The Dandelion, or *Leontodon taraxacum*, has the outer calyx reflexed : scape one-flowered : leaves runcinate with toothed divisions.

PÆONY.

PINY, PIONY, PEONY, PÆONIA, POIVIONE, DOUBLE-CRIMSON-
PIONY, PINA.

CLASS, Polyandria, from *polus*,   ORDER, Digynia, from *dis*,
many, and *aner*, stamen.   twice, and *gune*, pistil.

Because these flowers *have more than twenty disunited stamens, originating from the receptacle,* and *two pistils,* and consequently are of the
Thirteenth Class and *Second Order* of Linnæus.

Pæonia officinalis,	Red Peony.
„ *albiflora,*	White Piony.

There are *Five Species* of the Piony, with numerous varieties, several of which are cultivated in our gardens in New-England.

THE EMBLEM OF ANGER.

Fade, flowers, fade! nature will have it so,
'Tis but what we must in our autumn do!
And, as your leaves lie quiet on the ground,
So in the grave shall we as quiet lie,
Mirrored by those who loved our company ;
But some do so like thorns and nettles live,
That none for them can, when they perish, grieve.   *Waller.*

Pæonia round each fiery ring unfurls,
Bares to the noon's bright blaze her sanguine curls.   *Evans.*

These splendid flowers have of late attracted much attention.
They are among the most magnificent and brilliant ornaments of

our gardens. When fully expanded, some of the finest excel even the rose, the " queen of flowers," in beauty. The double crimson purple, and white kinds, are among those most admired. The rose-scented and Chinese kinds are esteemed for their fragrance and magnificent blossoms. The China kinds have received much attention of late in Europe, as likewise in America. Some of them are white, with a purple centre.

There are at least fifty varieties of this splendid genus, enumerated in the catalogues.

The generic term *Pæonia*, is from *Pæon*, the person who first applied it to medicinal purposes. In the time of Galen, and since, its dried roots, suspended about the neck as an amulet, were supposed to secure the wearer from attacks of the epilepsy.

The *Pæonia albiflora*, or White-flowered Piony, is a native of Siberia, and the northern countries of Asia. It bears a large milk-white flower, of an oval form, having about one hundred and fifty stamens, with yellow filaments and anthers.

The Mongols boil its root in their broth, and grind its seeds to put into their tea. The roots and seeds of the common red Garden Piony, when fresh, yield a faint, unpleasant smell, and are of a sub-acid and bitterish taste. Its roots and leaves are sometimes used in Medicine, being in a degree narcotic. The sanguine and fiery appearance of the Red Piony has induced the poets to esteem it the emblem of ANGER. The influence of the sun on this flower, when expanded, is remarkably small. Hence, Evans tells us, " *Pæonia* round each fiery ring unfurls, bares to the noon's bright blaze her sanguine curls." It never entirely closes after its petals are once open, but continues expanded, till its short-lived beauty decays, and its gaudy chaplet falls to the earth.

The varieties of this genus pass under different appellations, as Blush, Oxford, Vestal, Tartarian, Byzantine, Pallas, Grenville's, Anderson's, Doric, Cretan, Siberian, Spanish, Sabine's-crimson, Chinese-double-crimson, Chinese-purple, Tree, Chinese-poppy-flowered, &c. up to more than fifty varieties.

The Peony, Pina, or *Pæonia officinalis*, has leaves decompound : leaflets lobed, lobes broad-lanceolate : capsules downy. Petals red.

DAISY.

MOUNTAIN DAISY, DAY'S-EYE, DAISIE, SCARL, PEARL, DAUGH-
TER OF THE DAY, SPRING-TIDE FLOWER, LA BELLE MARGUERITE, GOWAN,
FIORE DI PRIMEVERA, BELLIS PERENNIS.

CLASS, Syngenesia, from *sun*,   ORDER, Polygamia Superflua,
with, and *genesis*, generated.   from *polus*, many, *gamia*, marriages.

Because these flowers *have their anthers united at top into a cylinder*,
and *florets in the centre bisexual, and those in the circumference female*,
and consequently are of the *19th Class*, and *Second Order* of Linnæus.

Bellis perennis,	Mountain Daisy.
„ *annuus*,	Sicilian Daisy.

There are only described *Two Species*, with several varieties of the Daisy, one or two of which
grow native near Pittsfield, in Massachusetts.

THE EMBLEM OF SIMPLE AND UNAFFECTED BEAUTY AND FONDNESS.

> There is a flower, a little flower,
> With silver crest and golden eye,
> That welcomes every changing hour,
> And weathers every sky.
> 'Tis Flora's page ;—in every place,
> In every season fresh and fair,
> It opens in perennial grace,
> And blossoms every where.
> O'er waste and ,woodland, rock and plain,
> Its humble buds unheeded rise,
> The rose has but a summer reign,
> The DAISY never dies.   *Montgomery.*

The term *Bellis*, applied to this genus, is from the Latin *bellis*, beautiful, *a bello colore*, named from its fair and beautiful colour.

There are several kinds of this fine little flower, so often alluded to by the poets. The Mountain Daisy, or *Bellis perennis*, is a native of most of the pasture lands of Europe. It often occupies a large share of these fields, to the exclusion of grass and more profitable plants. The taste of its leaves is somewhat acrid, and that of its root pungent. It is ungrateful to cattle and even to geese. It has nevertheless been a favourite flower among the poets. The older poets, Chaucer, Spencer, and Browne, seem never weary of chanting its praises, or of weaving it with their garlands and wreaths. In their poetry, we find it blooming on almost every page. It is a well-known fact, that it blossoms almost all the year, and closes its blossoms every night, and also in wet weather. Hence they tell us of the " *little daisy,* that sleeps as soon as the sun declines ;"—of " the sweet daughter of the day, whose opening flower invites the morning ray." They also tell us of " the daisy with its golden eye, whose bright flower, and home, is every where." Chaucer tells us, that Queen Alceste, who sacrificed her own life to preserve that of her husband, was, for this admirable virtue, " changed into a Daisy." That " Cybilla made the Daisy ;" and that Mars gave her a crown, " red, parde instede, of rubies set among the white." As it opens its leaves regularly, at sunrise in the morning, and closes them at sunset in the evening, it has received the name, *Day's-eye.*

The flowers are red, white, blue, and sometimes variegated. One of the finest varieties of the flower appears like a rich little ruby set among pearls. The common Daisy, or *Bellis perennis*, is a perennial root, and very hardy. The common Whiteweed of our Newengland fields, known by all the different appellations of *Bellis major, Buphthalmum majus, Oculus bovis, Chrysanthemum leucanthemum, Consolida media, Bellioides, Oxeye-daisy,* and *Maudlin-wort,* is often called simply the Daisy. It is in fact a large Daisy.

From the beauty, sweetness, lowly station, and simple loveliness of this flower, it has become emblematic of *Fondness, simple, unaffected Beauty, and faithful Love.* It has sometimes been esteemed the emblem of Beauty and Innocence.

The Daisy, or *Bellis perennis*, has leaves obovate, crenate : scape naked, one-flowered.

w

CHINA-ASTER.

STAR-WORT, FAIR LADIES' STARS, STAR-FLOWER, ASTERE,
ASTER, ASTERO.

CLASS, Syngenesia, from *sun*, ORDER, Polygamia Superflua,
with, and *genesis*, generation. from *polus*, many, *gama*, marriages.
Because these flowers have their *Anthers united*, and some of their *Florets
hermaphrodite, and others female only*, and consequently are of the
Nineteenth Class and *Second Order* of Linnæus.

Aster hyssopifolius,	Star-Flower.
.. *Chinensis*,	China Aster.
.. *solidaginoides*,	Golden-red-leaved Aster.
.. *nova-angliæ*,	New-England Aster.

There are at least *Seventy-Nine* North-American *Species* of the Aster, with numerous varieties,
Fifty or Sixty of which are found growing in the Eastern and Middle States.

THE EMBLEM OF RURAL HAPPINESS AND PIOUS ENJOYMENT.

Where are the flowers, the fair young flowers that lately sprung and stood
In brighter light and softer airs, a beauteous sisterhood?
The rain is falling where they lie—but the cold November rain
Calls not from out the earth those lovely ones again.
The wind-flower and the violet, they perished long ago,
And the wild-rose and the orchis died, amid the summer glow;
But on the hill the golden rod, and ASTER in the wood,
And yellow sunflower by the brook, in autumn beauty stood,
Till fell the frost from the clear cold heaven, as falls the plague on men,
And the brightness of their smile was gone, from upland, glade, and glen;
And now, when comes the calm, mild day, as still such days will come,
To call the squirrel and the bee from out their winter home,
When the sound of dropping nuts is heard, though all the trees are still,
And twinkle, in the smoky light, the waters of the rill,
The south wind searches for the flowers, whose fragrance last he bore,
And sighs to find them in the wood and by the stream no more.   *Bryant.*

The term Aster is from the Latin *aster*, a star. These flowers are so called, because, when fully expanded, they resemble stars. Their ray florets proceeding from a common centre, appear like the rays of light proceeding from the brilliant heavenly luminaries, that sparkle on the mantle of night.

Several species of the Aster are very gaudy flowers. One variety of the China Aster is known amongst the French by the appellation of *La Reine Marguerite*, or Queen Margaret. The Daisy is also sometimes known by this name, so that this term in French signifies " Queen Daisy."

The Aster does, indeed, somewhat resemble the Daisy in its form, though of a much larger size and more brilliant colour. The term *Marguerite*, as observed in another place, signifies a *pearl*, and the French appellation means, " A Queen of Pearls,' or " Queen Pearl." This kind is represented by the plate.

There are many varieties of the Aster in New-England. In the latter part of summer and in autumn, the different indigenous kinds are found growing all over our pastures and fields. Several species are very beautiful, putting forth delicate blue, lilach, yellow, and white flowers in corymb clusters. They finely mingle their bloom with the "gay Solidago," and other autumnal flowers.

The China varieties of this flower are those principally cultivated in gardens and flower-pots, as ornamental.

The Alpine and Italian Asters are easily propagated, by parting the roots in autumn. The Italian will propagate itself by seed.

The China Aster is an *annual*, and is propagated likewise by seeds. They must be sown in spring. Its varieties are in much request to adorn the late season with their profusion of specious flowers.

The China Aster, from " its garb of various hue," has sometimes been deemed the emblem of " *A Love of* VARIETY," and the American Star-wort, or Wild Aster of our New-England fields, the symbol of WELCOME RECEPTION. From its resemblance to the heavenly luminaries, the Aster by some has been considered an emblem of Immortality and a Future State.

The *Seventy-Nine* North-American Species of Aster, according to Muhlenberg, make *three-fifths* of the whole Genus.

The China Aster, or *Aster Chinensis*, has leaves ovate, thickly toothed, petioled, cauline ones sessile, at the base wedge-form, floral ones lanceolate, entire : stem hispid ; branches one-flowered : calyx foliaceous : flowers various-coloured.

LARKSPUR.

DELPHINIUM, ROCKET LARKSPUR, CALCARIS FLOS.

CLASS, Polyandria, from *polus*, many, and *aner*, stamen. **ORDER**, Digynia, from *dis*, twice, *gune*, pistil.

Because these flowers have *many Stamens* and *Two Pistils*, and consequently are of the *Thirteenth Class* and *Second Order* of Linnæus.

Delphinium consolidum,	Larkspur.
,, *ajacis,*	Rocket Larkspur.
,, *exaltatum,*	High Larkspur.
,, *azureum,*	Sky-coloured Larkspur.

Besides these, there are two or three other species of the Genus DELPHINIUM, described as growing in the Eastern and Middle States of North-America.

THE EMBLEM OF HAUGHTINESS AND FICKLENESS.

The LARKSPUR, plant of ancient name,
Advanced his haughty banners high. *Tales of the Flowers.*
Delphinium's purple flowers may grow,
A fickle type of those below
That cleave the azure flood—the brine,
Where dancing dolphins sport and shine
In sparkling gems, of liquid light,
Capricious as a wandering sprite— *Anon.*

The generic term *Delphinium* is from the Latin *delphinium*, signifying a dolphin, because these flowers, or rather their nectaries, are supposed to appear like dolphins elevated on little pillars. There is indeed in this flower and the Monk's-hood an appearance much of this sort. The English name, *Larkspur* originated from the circumstance of this flower's resemblance to the foot and toes of the lark. The projecting horn or spur, taken in connection with the other parts of the flower, possess indeed an appearance of this kind. The forms of the nectaries of flowers are very various. The hornlike projections of the Columbine have been supposed to resemble a nest of young doves ; the cornuted nectary of the *Delphinium*, that of a dolphin elevated on a pillar ; and those projec-jections of the *Aconite*, a *pair* of *little birds.*

The flowers of the Larkspur are of various colours. They are blue, white, pink, and sometimes of a greenish white. They are found both single and double, like those of many other plants. Culture produces changes in this respect.

The Larkspur is said to be indigenous to Siberia, the South of Europe, and America. The flowers are loosely spiked. The *Delphinium azureum*, or Azure Larkspur, is native in the Southern States. It is *perennial,* and blossoms in May, bearing a blue flow-er. The *D. consolidum* and *D. ajacis,* or Rocket Larkspur, are *annuals,* the former blossoming in July and the latter in August, bearing blue flowers. The *D. staphisagria* is a *biennial.* Though this genus has been placed in the Order *Digynia,* the flowers have from *two* to *five* pistils, and the order has often been termed *Di-Pentagynia* in allusion to this circumstance. The Monk's-hood, or *Aconite,* has no calyx or cup, but a corolla of five petals, and an inner set, or lepanthium, of two recurved and pedunculated petal-like processes. In the Larkspur there is but one bifid, sessile petal, continued backwards into a spur or horn, like the hind toe of the lark. In the Columbine there are five very sin-gular, hollow, tubular petals or lepanthia, terminating below in spurs or horns containing honey. These are shaped like the *cornu-copia,* or horn-of-plenty. Culture frequently increases their num-ber. It however generally diminishes that of the petals.

The poet informs us, " the Larkspur, plant of ancient name, advanced his haughty standard high." We are therefore author-ized to deem it the emblem of *Haughtiness,* and the poetry quoted explains its emblematic signification of FICKLENESS.

It belongs to the *natural* Order RANUNCULACÆA, which em-braces also the *Anemone, Aconitum, Adonis, Pæonia, Hellebo-rus,* and several other genera.

The *Delphinium consolidum* or Larkspur has nectaries one-leaved : stem sub-divided : three capsules : honey-cup cloven.

LABURNUM.

GOLDEN CHAIN, CYTISUS, BROOM, LE CYTISE, CITISO,
SPARTIUM, GENISTA.

CLASS, Diadelphia, from *dis*,   ORDER, Decandria, from *deca*,
twice, and *adelphia*, brotherhood.   ten, and *aner*, stamen.

Because these flowers have *their filaments united*, forming two bodies, and *ten stamens*, and consequently are of the *Seventeenth Class* and *Tenth Order* of Linnæus.

Spartium Scoparium,	Common Broom.
Genista juncea,	Spanish Broom.
Cytisus laburnum,	Laburnum.

The Broom and Laburnum, though nearly allied, are of different genera.

THE EMBLEM OF PENSIVE BEAUTY.

On the slope were five or six
White cottages ;—the roof reached not
To the LABURNUM's height, the boughs
Shook over them bright showers of golden bloom.   *Landon.*

The lily, with her snowy bells,
The gay jasmine, od'rous syringa,
Grateful woodbine, bloom-clad arbute,
 And other beauteous flowers, with grateful scents,
Regale the smell,—and to the enchanted eye
Mezereons purple, laurestinus white,
And the pale lilach's pendent flowers display
Their different beauties,—showers of golden bloom.
There LABURNUM's pensile tassels float in air,
Where thou within these topaz keels might'st creep
Secure, and rocked by lulling winds asleep.   *Smith, Dodsley.*

The term *Genista* is from the Latin *genu*, a knee or joint, so called from the inflection and angularity of its twigs.

Though there is a near alliance between these three genera, they differ in several respects. The Laburnum is the largest. Neither of them are natives of the United States, but both are here sometimes cultivated for the beauty of their flowers.

There are said to be *Thirty Species* of the genus *Cytisus* alone. Some make only twelve species. A kind of it is cultivated as a timber tree in England. The Broom, or *Genista*, is also cultivated there for its beautiful flowers. The *Spartium scoparium* is the Scotch Broom, and the *Spartium junceum*, the Spanish Broom.

The Brooms are generally evergreens ; the Laburnums, deciduous. Some of the Brooms are called indiscriminately, *Genista*, and *Cytisus*, though improperly. The Laburnum and some of the Brooms resemble, in appearance, a slender willow. One kind has drooping boughs, and bears a striking resemblance to the ' weeping-willow.' Pliny informs us that, in his time, " this shrub was used as food for cattle, causing cows to afford milk abundantly." The blossom is, generally, yellow. The *Genista Canariensis* of Linnæus, originally brought from the Canary Islands, is sometimes called *Rhodium*, from the Greek *rodon*, a rose, because its wood and roots afford a Rose-wood, that is said to smell like the most delicious Damask Rose. An essential oil is obtained from it and used as a perfume.

These shrubs are much admired by the cottagers in Scotland. Two kinds grow in Great-Britain,—one native, and the other cultivated. We often find these flowers mentioned in poetry, in connexion with the jasmine, lilach, lily, and rose. One poet tells us, " the dark-leaved laburnums, in drooping clusters, reflect, athwart the stream, their yellow lustres." When sweeping over the roof of the low cottage, and shaking over it its "bright showers of golden bloom," this shrub appears enchantingly sweet. Though its flowers, when gathered, soon droop and fade, they leave a pleasant memory. They have hence been made the emblem of GRACE AND REMEMBERED JOY. Others, from their drooping position, have deemed them ao emblem of PENSIVE BEAUTY.

The Spanish Broom, or *Spartium junceum*, has branches opposite, wand-like, bearing flowers at the end : leaves lanceolate, glabrous.

LILY-OF-THE-VALLEY.

MAY-LILY, LILY-CONVALLEY, LILLUM CONVALLIUM, LE LIS, LYS, LIS DES VALLIS, LE MUGUET (A FOP), GIGLIO CONVALLIS, MAIANTHEMUM.

CLASS, Hexandria, from *hex*,   ORDER, Monogynia, from
six, and *aner*, stamen.   *monos*, one, and *gune*, pistil.

Because these flowers have *Six Stamens*, and *One Pistil*, and are consequently of the *6th Class* and *First Order* of Linnæus.

Convallaria *majalis*,		Lily of the Valley.
"	*multiflora*,	Giant Solomon's Seal.
"	*angustifolia*,	Two-flowered Solomon Seal.
"	*racemosa*,	Spiked Solomon Seal.
"	*bifolia*,	Dwarf Solomon Seal.

There are *Twelve or Fifteen Species* of the *Convallaria*, with several varieties, found growing in the Eastern and Middle States of North-America.

THE EMBLEM OF SIMPLICITY AND MODESTY.

And there beside the babbling fount,
The date its welcome shadow threw,
And many a child was seen to mount,
And pluck the fruit that on it grew,
And with its broad and pendent boughs,
The thickly-tufted sycamore,
The image of profound repose,
Waved silently along the shore,
And many roses bent their limbs to taste
The wave that calmly floated by,
And showed beneath, as purely glossed,
A softer image of the sky.
And o'er the wilds that stretched away,
To meet the sands now steeped with rain,
The LILIES, in their proud array,
With pictured brightness gemmed the plain.   *Percival.*

The Lily of the Valley is a small delicate plant, bearing a bell-shaped flower. Keats tells us, " No flower amid the garden fairer grows, than the sweet *Lily of the lowly vale*, the queen of flowers."

The Genus *Convallaria* is divided into two parts, the first embracing the species having a cylindric corol, of a funnel-form, and stamens attached to the upper part of the corol. The second has corols bell or wheel-form, and stamens attached to the base of the corol. Most of the species of *Convallaria* are known by the appellation of Solomon's Seal. The single-flowered kind, that is known by *this* name, has a root which, when cut transversely, has the appearance of a *signet*, or *seal*. Hence its name of Solomon's seal. It is also called *Sigillum Solomonis* and *Lilium convallium*. The generic term *Convallaria* is from the Latin *con*, with, or in, and *vallum*, a valley, because these flowers often grow in valleys and marshes. The term *Maianthemum* is from *Maia*, May, and *anthos*, flower, meaning May-flower or May-Lily, because they are said to blossom in May. The common Lily of our fields of the genus *Lilium* is sometimes improperly called the Lily-of-the-Valley. The French term *Muguet*, Fop, is with much impropriety applied to this delicate flower.

The genus is often found growing in shady places. Hence the poet tells us, " Seek the bank where flowering elders crowd, where, scattered wide, the *Lily of the Vale* its balmy essence breathes, where cowslips hang the dewy head, where purple violets lurk, with all the lovely children of the shade." Wordsworth says, that the " *Lily of the vale* is a shy plant, that loves the ground, and from the sun withholds her pensive beauty, from the breeze her sweets."

Since " the Lily, in whose snow-white bells Simplicity delights and dwells," is delicate and sweet, and " screened from every ruder gale, in the lone copse or shadowy dale, it dwells the beauty of the vale," it has been made the symbol of MODESTY, SIMPLICITY, and BEAUTY.

The *Smilax, Asparagus, Trillium, Gyromia, Dracæna,* and *Convallaria,* are all of the same *natural* Order ASPARAGI.

The Lily of the Valley, or *Convallaria majalis*, has a scape naked, smooth : leaves oval-ovate.

X

MYRTLE.

MYRTUS, LE MYRTE, MYRTO.

CLASS, Icosandria, from *eikosi*, twenty, and *aner*, stamen.

ORDER, Monogynia, from *monos*, one, and *gune*, pistil.

.Because these flowers have *Twenty or more Stamens* inserted on the calyx, and *One Pistil*, and consequently are of the *Twelfth Class* and *First Order* of Linnæus.

Myrtus communis, Common Myrtle.

There are *Thirty-six Species*, with numerous varieties of the Myrtle.

THE EMBLEM OF HOPE AND LOVE.

Is this the way
To free man's spirit from the deadening sway
Of worldly sloth ?—to teach him, while he lives,
To know no bliss, but that which virtue gives,
And when he dies, to leave his lofty name,
A light, a landmark on the cliffs of fame ?
It was not so, land of the generous thought,
And airy deed ! thy godlike sages taught,
It was not thus, in bowers of wanton ease,
Thy freedom nursed her sacred energies :
Oh ! not beneath the enfeebling, withering glow
Of such dull luxury, did these MYRTLES grow,
With which she wreathed her sacred sword to dare
Immortal deeds ; but in the bracing air
Of toil, of temperance, of that high, rare,
Ethereal virtue which alone can breathe
Life, health, and lustre into Freedom's wreath.   *Prophet of Khorasen.*

The generic term *Myrtus*, Myrtle, is from the Greek *murta*, signifying myrrh, because several species of the genus are supposed to resemble myrrh in smell.

The genus is composed of small trees and shrubs. The common myrtle, or *Myrtus communis*, is well known, and is admired as an agreeable shrub. It is native of Asia, Africa, and Southern Europe.

It was a great favourite among the ancients for its elegant flowers, and its evergreen sweet leaves. It was sacred to Venus, the goddess of Love, perhaps on account of its growing near the sea, out of which she is said to have risen. The Bay-berry, or Tallow-tree, so common in Newengland, as likewise the Pepper-tree of Jamaica, (*Myrtus pymenta*) are both of the same genus Myrtle. The natural order *Myrtus* embraces the *Philadelphus* as well as the *Myrtus*.

The Myrtle and Willow are particularly poetic plants. The Jewish writers often mention them. The myrtle grows very plentifully in Syria. It flourishes most near the sea. Savary tells us it is very abundant near Catania, and that " Myrtle, intermixed with *Laurel roses*," abound in the vallies, and give peculiar beauty to the surrounding scenery. The leaf of the laurel, and flower of the myrtle, contrast with each other " very finely, and flowers of the latter emit perfumes more exquisite than the rose." They enchant every one, and the soul is filled with the softest emotions. Hence, and from its being sacred to the goddess of beauty and love, it has been made the emblem of LOVE.

The Myrtle was anciently used in medicine. Its leaves were used in cooking, and its branches were put into wine. Wreaths and garlands and crowns of Myrtle are to be met with every where in poetry. There we find the myrtle " diffusing its balmy essence" and " od'rous sweets," with " buds of roses, and a thousand fragrant posies."

The altar of Pan, the god of shepherds, was crowned with it, and the magistrates of Athens wore it as a symbol of authority. Spears were made of its wood, swords were wreathed with it, and bloodless victors were crowned with it. The first day of April, dedicated to Venus, was celebrated with flowers and myrtle wreaths.

The Myrtle, or *Myrtus communis* has flowers solitary : involucre two-leaved : leaves ovate.

MIMOSA.

SENSITIVE PLANT, HUMBLE PLANT, LIVING PLANT, HERBE VIVE, SENSITIVE HERB, MIMOSA SENSITIVA.

CLASS, Polygamia, from *polus*,   ORDER, Monœceia, from *monos*, many, and *gamos*, marriages.   one, and *oikos*, habitation.

Because these flowers are *hermaphrodite*, either upon the *same or different plants*, and also flowers of *one sex*, or *both sexes*, promiscuously are found on the plants, in a kind of *polygamy*, and this polygamy is on one and the same plant, and consequently the plants are of the 23*d Class* and 1*st Order* of Linnæus.

Mimosa sensativa,   Sensitive Plant.
   ,,   *pudica*,   Mimosa.

There are said to be *Eighty-Five* Species, with numerous varieties, of this curious plant already described.

THE EMBLEM OF PRUDERY, TIMIDITY, AND COURTESY.

A Sensitive Plant in a garden grew,
And the young winds fed it with silver dew,
And it opened its fan-like leaves to the light,
But closed them beneath the kisses of night.   *Shelly.*

Look, with nice sense the chaste Mimosa stands,
From each rude touch withdraws her timid hands.
Oft, as light clouds o'erpass the summer glade,
Alarmed, she trembles at the moving shade,
And feels alive, through all her tender form,
The whispered murmurs of the gathering storm;
Shuts her sweet eyelids to approaching night,
And hails with freshened charms the rising light.   *Darwin.*

Whence does it happen that the plant, which well
We name the *Sensitive*, should *move and feel?*
Whence know her leaves to answer her command.
And with quick horror fly the neighbouring hand?   *Prior.*

The generic term *Mimosa* is from the Greek *mimos*, a mimic or buffoon, because these plants were supposed to mimic creatures endowed with sensation.

Some of the *Mimosas* are of the size of large trees. There are one or two, of the numerous species of this wonderful genus found in our gardens, that present a very curious phenomenon. When the leaves or branches are touched, even the most slightly, they shrink and very briskly alter their position. The branches fall, and the leaves collapse, or fold together. This is done so instantaneously, that the plant seems almost as if endowed with life and sensibility. Hence the name " Sensitive Plant." The French call such plants *Herbes vives*, or living plants.

The *Mimosa sensitiva*, a native of Brazil, is a woody shrub, rising seven or eight feet in height, and bearing pale *purplish* flowers, on short *peduncles* or foot-stalks. The flowers generally make their appearance in three or four globular heads. The leaves of the plant, when touched, move slowly. The footstalks instantaneously fall.

There is a kind of this plant, growing on the plains in the East Indies, on the mountains of Yemen, and in several other parts of Asia, of a magnificent size, called the *Elcuya*. It is said to be so irritable, as to " bow to all who seek its canopy, or retire for shelter to its shade." When approached by any person, its branches collapse or drop, seeming to *bow* to the passing traveller, as in respect. Hence the name Humble Plant, and its emblematic signification *Courtesy*. The poetry quoted explains why it has been made the symbol of TIMIDITY and PRUDENCE.

The flowers of the *Elcuya* yield a rich fragrance. This, together with the pleasing shade it affords in these sultry regions, renders it a peculiar favourite. The poet tells us, " Mimosa's feathery leaves receive a shock, even if a breath of summer wind, when it has spent itself, blows on it." Naturalists, says Dr. Darwin, have not explained the immediate cause of the collapsing of the Sensitive Plant. " Perhaps it may be owing to a numbness, or paralysis, consequent to too violent irritation, like faintings of animals, from pain or fatigue." The most sensitive or irritable part seems to be the footstalks, between the stems and leaflets.

The Sensitive Plant, or *Mimosa sensitiva*, is prickly : leaves pinnate ; leaflets in pairs ; inmost ones minute.

STOCK-GILLIFLOWER.

GILLIFLOWER, DIANTHUS, OEILLET, GIROFLEE, JULY-FLOWER.

CLASS, Decandria, from *deca*,   ORDER, Digynia, from *dis*,
ten, *aner*, stamen.   twice, *gune*, pistil.

Because these flowers have Ten *Stamens*, and Two *Pistils*, and consequently are of the 10*th Class*, and 2*d Order* of Linnæus.

Dianthus plumarius,	Single Pink.
,, *deltoides,*	Maiden Pink.
,, *barbatus,*	Sweet William, or Poetic Pink.
Phlox subulatus,	Moss Pink.
Silene pennsylvanica,	Pennsylvania Pink.

There are Five or Six *Species* of the Genus DIANTHUS, described as growing in New-
England, embracing more than 200 *varieties.*

THE EMBLEM OF ASPIRATION.

The pretty pansy then I'll tie,
Like stones some chain enchasing,
And next to them, their near ally,
The purple violet placing,
The curious, choice CLOVE-JULY-FLOWER,
Whose kinds height the *Carnation,*
For sweetness of most sovereign power,
Shall help my wreath to fashion ;
Whose sundry colours of one kind,
First from one root derived,
Then in their several suits I'll bind,
My garland so contrived.   *Drayton.*

The *Phlox*, *Silene*, *Dianthus*, and several other genera, are known by the common appellation of Pink. The *Phlox* is often called the ' Moss Pink,' and the *Silene*, Catch-Fly. The former is also known by the name of *Lichnidia*, and the species *Phlox subulata* is called Mountain Pink. The generic term *Phlox*, sometimes improperly called Flock, is from the Greek *Phlox*, signifying a ' flame, or blaze of fire,' because these pretty little flowers were fancied, collectively, to represent a *blaze*. The common garden Pink, *Dianthus hortensis*, embraces several varieties, among which are the Double Pheasant-eyed, and several others. The Phlox is sometimes called Wild-Sweet-William.

The Musk Pink (*Dianthus moschatus*), and Caucasian Pink (*D. caucassicus*), as also the Sweet-Scented (*D. suaveolens*), and many others of this genus, are much admired as garden and pot flowers. The *varieties* of the different species of Pink are not always permanent. In this respect they are like many other flowers. The production of *new varieties* is mostly under the control of the gardener. In many flowers *these* are permanent, at least for a considerable time. A *species* is never *created* by the *art of man*. It consists in such traits as are supposed to have characterized the individuals from their first creation. There is probably not a *species* now in existence that did not exist at the creation of the world, though species may have become extinct. New *varieties*, on the contrary, are often produced from different species in various ways, and are called *Hybrids*. This is the case with Pinks, Chrysanthemums, Passion-flowers, &c. It is the case with the *Dianthus hybridus*, or Mule Pink, sometimes called Hybrid Pink. The different *varieties* of Pink, thus produced, are known among gardeners by different appellations, such as Glory, Fame, Phœnix, Parnassia, Pomonia, Sultana, Pampadour, Dulcinea, Suwarrow, Eucharis, Sappho, Cæsar, Hercules, Syren, Fairy, Enchanter, Incomparable, Supreme, Matchless, Perfection, Rifleman, Elysian, St. George, Arcadia, Cataline, Proserpine, Effulgent, Pluto, Leopold, Mars, and so on, up to 200 varieties.

The term Gilliflower or July-flower, originated from the circumstance of this flower's blossoming in July. It rises with many short trailing shoots from the root, garnished with long, very narrow, evergreen leaves ; and amidst them upright slender flower-stalks, from one to three feet high, emitting many side shoots, all of which, as well as the main stalk, are terminated by large solitary flowers, having short oval scales to the calyx, and crenated petals.   The Mountain-Pink is the emblem of *Aspiring Thoughts*, and the Double Red Pink of FEMALE AFFECTION.

The *Dianthus, Lychnis, Arenaria, Stellaria, Saponaria,* and several other genera, are embraced in the *natural* Order CARYOPHYLLEÆ.

The *Dianthus plumarius*, or Single Pink, has flowers solitary : scales of the calyx, sub-ovate, very short, and obtuse ; awnless, corol many-cleft with the throat hairy.

We conclude our description of flowers with the following beautiful lines, from a recent English publication, addressed to the "Melancholy Gilliflower, which is only fragrant during the night."

> Oh why, thou lone and lovely flower,
>   Deny thy sweetness to the day,
> And ever in night's hushest hour,
>   Still sigh thy fragrant life away ?
>
> The wild bee murmurs round each spray,
>   And kisses every flower but thine,
> No scent allures the vagrant's way,
>   Or tempts him to the golden mine.
>
> The glowing breath of gorgeous noon
>   Is swelled by every other sweet ;
> Why dost thou only the pale moon,
>   And chilly night-winds love to greet ?
>
> When young Endymion earliest dreamed
>   On that wild hill's enchanted ground,
> The flattering radiance fearful gleamed,
>   And cast a quivering light around.
>
> Still in his dreams did charmed sighs
>   Float trembling o'er his favoured head,
> And strange mysterious music rise
>   And hover round his mountain bed.
>
> Thine was the conscious flower that threw
>   Its lonely fragrance on the night,
> Thou only shed thy pallid hue
>   Beneath the silent flood of light.
>
> Thy sisters veil their foreheads fair,
>   And fold their bells on heath and dale,
> Nor on the misty evening air
>   Their breath of sweetness dare exhale.
>
> But thou dost long for holy eve,
>   To shroud thee from day's piercing eye,
> Night's chilly hours alone receive
>   The secret tear and perfumed sigh.

FLOWERS.

COLOURS OF FLOWERS AND LEAVES.

1.· PLINY, long ago, beautifully said that blossoms are the joy of trees, in the bearing of which they assume a new aspect, vieing with each other in the luxuriance and variety of their colours. Some of nature's richest tints, and most elegant combinations of colour, are reserved for the petals of flowers, which are among the most transient of created beings. But though we may be dazzled with the brilliancy of a flower-garden, we repose with pleasure on the verdure of a grove or meadow. Though we can account but imperfectly for the green, so universal in the herbage of plants, we gratefully admire the beneficence of the Creator in clothing the earth with a colour the most pleasing, and least fatiguing to the eyes. Of all greens, the most delicate and beautiful perhaps, is displayed in the rich foliage of the vegetable creation. This is much more permanent than the colours of the flowers ; for even during the short existence of the parts they decorate, the colours themselves are often undergoing remarkable variations.

2. Many yellow flowers, under the influence of light, become white. Numbers of red, purple, or blue ones, are liable, from some unknown cause in the plant to which they belong, to vary to white. Such *varieties* are sometimes propagated by seed, and are almost invariably permanent, if the plants be propagated by roots, cuttings, or grafting. The pretty little weed Scorpion-grass, *Myostis scorpioides*, and several of its natural order, have flower-buds of a most delicate rose colour, that turn to a bright blue, as they open.

3. The *leaves* of plants of an acid or astringent nature, often become very red by the action of light; as the Polygonum, Rumex, and Epilobium. It is remarkable that American plants in general, as well as such European ones as are particularly related to them, are distinguished for assuming various rich tints in their foliage, of red, yellow, white, or even blue, at the decline of the year. Fruits, for the most part, incline to a red colour, apparently from the acid they contain. The colour-

Y

ing principle of the Raspberry is a fine blue, turned red by the acid in the fruit.

4.   The Fungi, called *Boletus bovinus* and *Agaracus deliciosus*, almost instantly, on exposure to the air, change from yellow to a dark blue or green.   Light is undoubtedly a powerful agent in affecting the changes in colour of flowers and leaves.   Plants raised in darkness are generally of a sickly white.   The green colour of leaves is owing to the light.   Hence the practice of blanching Celery and other garden plants, called by the French *etoilation* (from *etoile* a star) by covering them up from the light.   When brought to the light, or even in the dark if exposed to the action of oxygen gas, they acquire their natural colour.   Tulips and Crocus-flowers have long been known to be coloured even when reared in the dark.   Their colour must depend on a different principle.

5.   It has been asserted by chymists, that all the colours of flowers arise from the mixture of sulphur with other substances.   That these differ, according to the different admixtures of salts with these sulphurs. The flowers of all plants abound in an essential oil and sulphur, and we know, that one and the same oil, the essential oil of Thyme, by such an admixture, may be turned to all the colours that we find in the different flowers of plants, from white to deep black, with all the intermediate shades of red, yellow, purple, blue, and green.   By the same law, the essential oils of plants while contained in their flowers may be so combined with the substances they meet, as to produce all their varieties of beautiful colours.

6.   The whole use and physiology of the *corolla* or flower has not yet been explained.   It is not true, as the poet says,

" Full many a flower is born to blush unseen,"

for we find that even the beauties of the most sequestered wilderness are not unobserved, nor made in vain.   Myriads of admirers, attracted by the charms of its "blossoms infinite," and rewarded by their treasures, that would perhaps be as useless to the plant itself as gold to the miser, throng these regions, and 'buzz and sip, and sip and buzz again,' among its flowers.   The services rendered by such visitants, are not unimportant to the plants themselves.

7.   Sprengel demonstrated some hundreds of instances, where the *corolla* served as an attraction to insects in pursuit of honey.   They are accommodated at once with a convenient resting-place and shelter, while they extract it.   This elegant, and curious accommodation may be observed

in almost every flower we examine. The protection of the *corolla* to the tender and important parts within it from wet, is by no means its only use. St. Pierre ingeniously supposed it to regulate the sun's influence on the fructification, by reverberating the solar rays upon the anthers and stigma: also by sheltering them from too intense heat.

8. Linnæus imagined it served as wings to waft the flower up and down in the air; and so promote the functions of the stamens and pistils. Dr. Darwin calls it the *lungs* of the *stamens* and *pistils*. It is generally much more durable or lasting in double flowers, than in single ones. The sunbeams have a powerful influence on it, often causing it entirely to close, frequently to expand. It is probable that the oblong summit of the *spadix* in the *Arum* answers the same purpose, with respect to air and light, as the petals in flowers.

9. To guard against the hurtful influence of nocturnal dews, or drenching rains, most flowers hang down their heads when the sun does not shine, and by this means their internal organs are sheltered.   Some always droop, as the Snowdrop or *Galanthus*, the Fritillaria, or Crown Imperial, and various species of *Campanula*, while their over-shadowing corolla keeps off the rain, and the air has free access underneath to blow the *pollen* to the *stigma*. This drooping is not caused by the weight of the flowers, for the fruit of many plants is much heavier, and yet erect, on the very same stalk.

10. Papilionaceous flowers, in general, spread their wings in fine weather, but close their petals at night, protected by the green leaves of the plant folding closely about them.   The Poor-Mans-Weather-glass *Anagalis*, and *Calendula*, shut their flowers against the approach of rain. Very sudden thunder-showers however often take such flowers by surprise, the previous state of the atmosphere not having been such as to give them due warning.

EFFECTS OF LIGHT UPON LEAVES AND FLOWERS.

11. The effect of light upon leaves and flowers is very great.   Many flowers of the compound radiated kind, as the Daisy, Sunflower, Marygold, &c. are peculiarly sensible to it.   In their forms, nature seems to have delighted to imitate the radiant luminary to which they are apparently dedicated, and in the absence of whose beams, many of them do not expand their blossoms at all.   The stately annual Sunflower, *Heli-*

anthus annuus, displays this phenomenon more conspicuously on account of its size, but many of the tribe have a greater sensibility to light.

12. The stem of these flowers is often in some degree compressed, to facilitate the movement of the flower, which, after following the small day, returns after sundown to the east, by its natural elasticity, to meet his beams in the morning. Dr. Hales supposed this caused by the heat of the sun contracting the stem on one side occasioning the flower to incline that way.

13. By observing similar flowers, others have imagined the impression to be made, on their radiated florets, which act as wings. They suppose they are contrived chiefly for this purpose, and frequently destitute of any other use. Leaves of trees nailed against a north wall turn from the wall though it be toward the north and in direct opposition to those on a southern wall over against them. A glaring example of the sun's influence on leaves is seen on looking upon a *clover-field,* whose myriads of leaflets are seen looking towards that luminary.

14. Some *pinnated* leaves display an extraordinary sensibility to the touch as well as to the light. The *Mimosa sensativa, Mimosa pudica,* and *Smithia sensativa,* as likewise the *Oxalis sensativa,* are extremely sensible to the touch of an extraneous body or sudden concussion. An impression made, even in the most gentle manner, upon one of their leaflets, is communicated in succession to all of them, evincing an exquisite irritability. It is in vain to attempt any mechanical solution of this phenomenon.

15. The *Hedysarum gyrans,* one of this tribe, has a spontaneous motion in its leaves, independent of any external stimulus, even of light. It requires only a very warm, still atmosphere, to be performed in perfection. Each leaf is ternate. The small lateral leaflets are frequently moved up and down, either equally or by jerks, without any uniformity or cooperation among themselves.

RELATIONS OF STAMEN AND PISTIL.

16. The stamens are most generally in the same flower with the pistil, lodged securely under the protection of the same silken veil. This is the case with at least a majority of our shrubs and herbs. The leaves being present might impede the passage of the pollen were it otherwise. The trees of cold climates, on the contrary, have generally sepa-

rated flowers, blossoming before the leaves come out, and in a windy season of the year.   When the roots are luxuriantly polific, flowers are in some measure defective, nature relaxing, as it were, in her usual solicitude for the propagation of the seeds.   She seems willing to indulge her children in a repose, and to allow them the abundance of good things about them.

17.   Thus plants have occasionally abortive stamens in one flower, and barren pistils in another, as the *Musa* or Plane-tree.   Linnæus says, five out of the six stamens of this tree are perfected in such blossoms as ripen no fruit, while those with a fertile germen contain only a single ripe stamen, five being ineffective.   The pollen and stigma of flowers are always in perfection at the same time.   The stigma commonly withers and falls off a little after the anthers, though the style often remains to become a useful appendage to the fruit.   The Jacobean Lily, or *Amaryllis formosissima* is provided with a drop of clear liquid, that protrudes from the stigma every morning, to receive the pollen, whose vapour renders it turbid, and at evening it is again re-absorbed.

18.   The usual proportion and situation of stamens with respect to pistils is well worthy of notice.   The former are generally shortest in drooping flowers, and longest in erect ones.   The barren blossoms stand above the fertile ones, in many flowers, that the pollen may fall on the stigmas.   Many curious contrivances of nature serve to bring the anthers and stigma together.   In the *Gloriosa* the style is bent at right angles from the very base, for this purpose.

19.   In Saxifrage and Parnassia, the stamens lean, one or two at a time, over the stigma, retiring after they have shed their pollen and giving place to others.   The filaments of the *Celosia* or *Cock's-comb* are connected at their lower part by a membraneous web, which in moist weather is relaxed, and the stamens spread for shelter under the concave lobes of the corolla.   When the air is dry the contraction of the membrane brings them together, to scatter their pollen in the centre of the flower.

20.   The elastic filaments of *Kalmia* and *Parietaria*, for a while restrained by the calyx, or the minute pouches in the corolla, relieve themselves by an elastic spring, which in both instances serve to dash the pollen, with great force, upon the stigma.   The curved germen of the *Medicago falcata*, releasing itself from the closed keel of the flower by a spring, accomplishes the same end.

21. The *Barberry-bush* bears a flower with six stamens, sheltered under the concave tips of the petals.   When touched on the inner part of their filaments, by the feet or trunk of an insect in search of honey, or by any other extraneous body, the irritability of that part is such, that the filament immediately contracts, and consequently strikes its anther full of pollen against the stigma.   Any other part of the filament may be touched without producing this effect.   After a while the filament returns gradually to its original position.   There exists no sympathy between the filaments themselves.

SAP OF FLOWERS.

22. It is supposed, though the portion of sap sent to the flower and fruit undergoes very remarkable and important changes for the purpose to which these curious organs are devoted, it is not returned from thence as from the leaves, to answer any further ends.   The existence of these organs is still more temporary and more absolutely limited to their own purposes, than even that of the leaves, from whose secretions theirs are very distinct.

23. There has not been made any distinct observation on the returning of the sap into the bark, after is is conveyed from the root into the flower and fruit.   It is pretty well determined however that no matter of increase is furnished from the flowers or their stalks, to the part of the branch below, or indeed to any other part.   There is no doubt however that certain parts of the flower perform functions, respecting air and light, analogous to those of the leaves; but entirely subservient to the benefit of the flower and fruit.   Their secretions, formed by the sap, are confined to their own purposes.

24. As soon as these are accomplished, a decided separation of vessels takes place, and the rich fruit, accompanied perhaps by its stalk, falls from the tree.   It has been tried in vain to give a flavour to fruit, by the most penetrating and volatile fluids conveyed through the sap vessels of the flower.   The laws of secretion are absolute in these organs, and their various results are, if possible, more strikingly distinct than even those of the leaves.

EFFLUVIA OF FLOWERS.

25. Mischief has undoubtedly arisen from flowers in a bedroom and other confined apartments.   This is attributed to their perfumed effluvia.

The bad effects of the *Lobelia longiflora* on the air of a hothouse, the danger incurred by those who sleep under the Machineel-tree or *Hippomane mancinella*, or, as is commonly believed, under a Walnut-tree, are probably to be attributed as much to poisonous secretions, as to the air these plants evolve.

26. Dr. Ingenhouz observed, that fruits and flowers almost invariably give out a bad or carbonic air, especially in the dark. This is particularly the case with leaves. Yet, as many believe, plants in the sunshine purify the air very quickly. This they do by a copious evolution of oxygen gas, which will often rise in streams, when leaves are immersed in an inverted tumbler of water placed in the sunlight. The *Nymphæa alba* or White Water Lily affords an extraordinary abundance of this gas.

27. Dr. Priestley found that plants would alter even unmixed inflammable air, or hydrogen. This was particularly the case with the *Hydropiper*, a species of Polygonum, and the *Epilobium hirsutum*. Mr. Ellis of Edinburgh however believes, from some experiments, that flowers, fruits, roots, and all parts of vegetating plants, at all times, both by day and night, whether in the sunshine or shade, consume oxygen from the atmosphere, and produce carbonic acid in its stead—that the production of oxygen from plants, is more than counterbalanced by its consumption, and the formation of carbonic acid. If this be true, vegetables deteriorate the atmosphere in a much greater degree than they improve it.

————

CUP OF FLOWERS.

28. Linnæus adopted the opinion that the calyx or cup, proceeded from the bark, because often similar in colour and texture. He supposed it proceeded from the outer bark, while the more delicate corolla or blossom originated in the liber or inner bark. Dr. Smith thinks this hypothesis totally inadmissible. When a flower has only one covering it is not always easy to say wether it be a calyx or corolla. When *green* and *coarse* like the cup, we call it a calyx ; when delicate and finely coloured, a corolla. The coloured leaves of the Tulip-flower were called a calyx by Jussieu, as likewise those of *Liliaceous* flowers, however beautiful. The segments of the cup are for the most part alternate with the stamens, and frequently equal to them in number. The spatha and calyx seem to run into each other, and both into a corolla as may be seen

in the Arum.   The *spatha* sometimes becomes a *Bractea*.   In general the distinction between these several parts can be pointed out only by the colour, for in most liliaceous plants the calyx and corolla are connected.   Of 1021 genera known in the time of Professor Alston, **673** had a perianth, **72** a spatha, **25** an involucre, **29** a glume, **18** an ament, **3** a clyptra, and 110 want a calyx altogether.

HONEY.

29.   The secretion of *Honey* is not absolutely confined to the flower. The glands on the footstalks of the Passion-flower yield it.   It exudes from the flower-stalks of some liliaceous plants.   There has been much diversity of opinion in regard to the use of this sweet viscid liquor.   Pontedra supposed it was absorbed by the seeds for nourishment.   Darwin supposed the honey to be the food of the stamens and pistils.   Dr. Smith supposes its sole use, with respect to the plant, to tempt insects who in procuring it, fertilize the flower, by distributing the dust of the stamens among the pistils.   It is often lodged in spurs, horns or cells, quite out of the reach of the stamens and pistils, and barren flowers produce it as well as fertile ones.   It is not therefore probably designed for the nourishment of those central organs.

DIFFERENT KINDS OF FLOWERS.

30.   Flowers, though various, may be distinguished in several respects into differently formed classes, having a common resemblance.   Several large and in some respects very natural divisions are sometimes made, into such as *Liliaceous* or Lily-like flowers, *Cruciform* or cross-shaped flowers, *Papilionaceous* or butterfly-shaped, *Labiate* or lip-shaped, *Personate* or mask-like, and *Ringent* or gaping.   There is also a large family that are termed Compound flowers, in opposition to those called Simple flowers, and another collection known by the name of *Rosacious* or Rose-like, because of their resemblance to the Rose.

31.   The Hexandrous class embraces by far the greater part of the *Liliaceous* tribe.   These flowers are generally destitute of a calyx or cup, that so frequently accompanies other flowers.   The stems are simple and unbranched, the leaves entire, never cut, or divided.   The Lily, Tulip, Hyacinth, Daffodil, Crocus, Snow-drop, Onion, Leek, &c. are of this class. The stamens are generally *six*, though sometimes only *three*, —six petals, a triangular germ, with three cells,—many of the roots partake more or less of the nature of bulbs, either *squamous* or *tunicated*. This being recollected, there will be little difficulty in recognizing a Liliaceous flower.

32. The *Cruciform* or cross-shaped flowers, from the Latin *crux* a cross, are mostly of the *Tetradynamia* or 15th class. They are readily known by the four petals they produce in the form of a cross, whence they have derived their name. Many of them have become very double, and are with difficulty distinguished, as the Pink, Rose, Stock, Wallflower, &c. in which the stamens have been transformed into petals, or given place, as in several pinks, to almost an innumerable quantity of petals or flower-leaves.

33. The *Papilionaceous* flowers derive their name from the Latin *Papilio*, signifying a butterfly, because these flowers are supposed to resemble butterflies. They are sometimes termed *Leguminosæ* because the *legumen* or *pod* is their uniform seed-vessel. The Pea, Bean, &c. are of this family. All flowers are said to be regular or irregular. These are termed irregular. Regular flowers present a symmetry and equality in all their parts, each portion forming the segment of a circle, as the Rose, Tulip, Pink, &c. There is no distinction into upper and lower part, or into right and left, as in the irregular, of which the Pea, Bean, Locust, and other *Papilionaceous* flowers, present us with examples. In the tribe of *Leguminosæ* or *Papilionaceous* flowers, are included, besides the Beans, Peas, &c. Lentils, Lupines, Vetches, Lucern, Saintfoin, Indigo, Liquorice, Honey-locust, Coffee-bean, Cassia, and many other flowers.

34. The *Labiate* flowers, are so named from the Latin *labium*, a lip, because their opening or expansion, or both, has been supposed to resemble the lips of the mouth. They were called *ringent* or gaping flowers by Linnæus, because they appeared to him like so many little projecting mouths, divided into an appropriate upper and lower lip. This tribe by some, has been separated into two orders. 1st, The *labiate*, or *ringent* properly so called, when the entrance into the corolla or blossom is always open. 2d. The *personate*, or *masked*, from the Latin *persona*, a mask, because the orifice of these is always closed by a prominent palate or mask. The Ground-Ivy, (*Glechoma hederacea*) Balm, Calamint, &c. are specimens of perfect Labiate flowers, and to this

z

family belong also the Rosemary, Sage, Thyme, Mint, Lavender, Horehound, Hyssop, Basil, Marjorum, Selfheal, Deadnettle, &c. To the *personate*, or masked division, belong the Foxglove, Toadflax, Snapdragon, Bignonia, Pentstemon, &c.

35. To the *Rosaceous flowers*, from the Latin *rosa* a rose, belong not only all the Roses, but the flowers of almost all our orchard fruit-trees. The stamens are numerous and are attached to the calyx, either immediately or with the corolla, which consists commonly of five petals, in the apple-tribe. The Apple, Pear, Quince, Prune or Plum, Laurel, Almond, Peach, Nectarine, Pomegranate, Service, Medlar, Raspberry, Dewberry, Thimbleberry, Strawberry, Potentilla or Cinquefoil, sometimes called Five-finger and Barren-Strawberry, wild Strawberry, &c. all belong to the *Rosaceous flowers*. They are so named from a general resemblance to the flower of the Rose.

36. Compound flowers have in part been explained in the Introduction. They are in fact an aggregation, often of some hundreds of minute flowers or florets, often provided with a corolla, stamens, styles, and seed of their own, all situated on a common basement or receptacle. The floscules in the centre are collectively termed the *disc* or *disk* of the flower, and those of the margin or border the *ray*. Each floscule or floret will be found, if we examine a Sunflower, or the head of an Oxeye Daisy or Whiteweed, to contain within its little tubular or tubelike corolla, another yellow tube, formed of five anthers in the form of a cylinder. At their base the filaments appear distinct, and are elastic. Through the centre of this tube of anthers, passes the style terminated by a bifid, reflected stigma. Below is attached the germ which becomes the seed. The seed in the Dandelion and many others is crowned with a downy plume for transporting the seed.

37. The white rays of the border that appear like bits of tape, are also so many distinct florets or little flowers. They are not so perfect as the central or tubular ones, for they are often wanting in one of the essential parts of fructification, viz the stamens or pistils. These marginal florets are commonly toothed or indented, and cleft open nearly to their base. Outside of these, is the common or general calyx or cup. These are the general features of a *Compound flower*.

38. The florets of compound flowers do not all expand at once, but begin at the margin, and open successively towards the disc, often during a period of several days. The florets of all compound flowers are

either tubular with a tooth border, or strap-shaped, appearing as if split open and spread out but retaining still the toothed extremity.

39. Some flowers are made up entirely of the semi-flosculous or *strap-shaped* florets, as the Dandelion, Succory or Blue-weed, Sow-this-tle, Lettuce, &c. and some are formed entirely of the tubular florets, as the Wormwood, Burdock, Artichoke, Thistles, &c. The former are termed *semi-flosculous* or halved flowers, and the latter *flosculous* flow-ers.

40. Some flowers are formed of them both, and are termed *radiate* or *rayed-flowers.* Of this kind is the Oxeye Daisy or Whiteweed, Sunflower, Marygold, and the like. The ray florets are often of a dif-ferent colour from those of the disk as in the White-weed and Sunflow-er. These ray florets are generally provided with a style and stigma, but are destitute of anthers. In some flowers, as the Sunflower, they are destitute even of a style, but in others as the Marygold, the flat rays afford the perfect seed, while the florets of the disk are abortive or bar-ren. The essential character of all compound flowers, is the union of the anthers into a tube. This circumstance sufficiently distinguishes this great natural tribe of flowers, that have been accordingly termed syngenesious.

41. There is a very natural assemblage of plants, termed *Umbellate* from the Latin *umbella* an umbrella, because they send off branches like the sticks or frame of an umbrella. The Carrot, Parsnip, Hemlock, Fennel, Dill, Carraway, Cheveril, Skerret, &c. are of this family. Some of them are very poisonous and some are used as articles of diet.

PROPAGATION OF PLANTS.

42. There are two methods of propagating plants. First, by *re-production*: Second, by *continuation.* A plant is reproduced when it grows immediately from the seed. The potato is reproduced, when the seed is taken from the berry, planted, and grows. Apple-trees are repro-duced in nurseries from seeds.

43. A plant is *continued,* when the parts taken from its roots, stem, branches, buds, or other parts, are transferred to different places, and so cultivated as to continue to grow in several places at the same time. Thus the living branches or twigs of the same apple-tree, may continue to grow from the original root, and from hundreds of other roots in dif-

ferent countries, at the same time : and it is a fact now well established, says Eaton, that these twigs or grafts, however recently inserted, feel the effects of age in the same degree, with the twigs remaining on the original stalk.   Dr. Smith thinks this hypothesis inadmissible.

44.   The operation called Grafting, consists in uniting the branches of two or more separate trees.   This is performed in various ways. A more common practice called budding or *inoculating* is performed by inserting a bud of one tree, accompanied by a portion of its bark, into the bark of another.   The tree thus engrafted upon, is called the *stock*. By this means different kinds of fruit, as, apples, pears, plums, and different flowers, each of which is only a variety accidentally raised from the seed, but no farther perpetuated in the same manner, are multiplied. The *buds* of the kind wanted to be propagated, may be engrafted on so many *stocks* of a wild nature.   It is of primary importance in these operations that the *liber* or young bark of the bud, and that of the stock should be accurately united by their edges.   The air and wet must of course be excluded.

45.   It is also requisite for the success of this operation that the plants should be nearly akin.   Varieties of the same species succeed best of all.   Apples and pears, however, two different species of the same genus, may be grafted on one stock.   The Fringe-tree succeeds well on the common Ash, and is thus often propagated in our gardens. There is a story of a Black Rose being produced by grafting a common rose on a black-currant stock.   The rose vulgarly reported to be so produced is the dark Double-Velvet-Rose, a variety of the *Rosa centifolia.*   Maltese Oranges, famed for their red juice, are said to be produced by budding the Pomegranate stock with the common Orange.   Dr. Smith thinks these reports of the Orange and Black rose, fabulous and without foundation.   The *Bergamot* tree is the *Orange* engrafted upon the *Pear.*

46.   The roots of potatoes continue in succession, in their native torrid regions, year after year, for a limited period, like the Malaxis, and some other of the Orchis family in our latitude.   Agriculturists and gardeners aid their progress by housing the roots in winter, and setting them in the earth again in the spring season.   In due time however, the effects of age become manifest to the cultivator, and he finds it necessary to *reproduce* this useful plant from the *seed.*   The Lombardy Poplar is becoming enfeebled by age, in our country so that very recent shoots will hardly withstand a severe winter. The reason, says Eaton, is manifest. " There has never been a pistilate tree introduced from Europe : consequently this tree has never been reproduced here, from the seed. We therefore see but the feeble limbs of an exile in dotage, though yet sustained in a thousand localities."

GROWTH OF PLANTS FROM SEED.

47. If a seed be immersed in warm water, for a considerable time and then subjected to a high magnifying power, the elementary form of the future plant may be seen. In some seeds, even the embryo of the future *flower* becomes manifest. Therefore it may not be absurd to say, that the germination and growth is affected by the developement of the embryo plant, contained in the seed. This developement goes on by means of successive supplies of nutriment, which are taken into the organized structure adapted to their reception.

48. Hence the importance of furnishing plants with suitable nutriment, and of placing them in situations where they may imbibe it for their growth. Hence the practice of manuring, mixing soils, watering, housing, and cultivating plants in all the various forms, and hence the origin of Green Houses, Hot Beds, and Hot Houses.

49. A certain degree of heat is essential to the germination and growth of plants. No plant can germinate, or grow, where the temperature is as low as 32 degrees of Fahrenheit. Accordingly Gardeners and Florists have created Green Houses, and Hot Houses, for maintaining a due degree of temperature in cold weather.

50. The temperature most favourable to vegetation ranges from 60 to 80 degrees of Fahrenheit. We therefore see most vegetation in the spring and summer months, when the weather is warm. The precise degree of heat required however varies with the nature of the plant. This circumstance accounts for the difference in the season of the year, at which different seeds begin to germinate, and different plants to grow. Too much heat, such as that of boiling water, which is 212 deg. Fahrenheit, prevents germination, and vegetation altogether, by depriving the germ and plant of the vital principle. Plants have a tendency to preserve a uniform temperature and to resist heat and cold. Hence fruits and leaves situated in the sun, preserve themselves cool, while surrounding objects are heated. In the island of Lu-

con, is a rivulet springing from the earth, the temperature of whose waters is 175 degrees Fahrenheit. Yet the *Vitex* and *Aspalathus* grow upon its banks, and sweep its waters with their roots. In the island of Tonna, near a volcano where the earth is heated to 200 deg. of Fahrenheit, the ground is covered with flowers. Again, in Sweden and Lapland near the North Cape, are Pines, Firs, and Birches, and in latitude 69 near the Frozen Ocean, the ground, in July is covered with grass and flowers, though it is not thawed above four inches from the surface, beneath which is a solid body of ice. There are at least thirty species of plants in the island of Spitzbergen. Moisture and the presence of oxygen gas are also necessary to vegetation.

51. The influence of light which is so favourable to all the subsequent stages of vegetation, is very injurious to the progress of germination. Therefore Seeds are buried in the earth when they are desired to germinate.

52. From what has been remarked then, it is apparent that when seeds are placed an inch or two under the surface of the earth, in spring, and are covered loosely, they are favourably disposed for germination. For the ground is warmed, by absorbing the solar-rays, to 60 or 80 deg. the seeds are moistened by occasional showers, the earth protects them from light, and by its porosity, at the same time, give free access to the air, which contains the oxygen required.

HOT BEDS.

53. Hot Beds are usually formed in March, by marking out a bed corresponding in size, with the size of the frame intended to cover it. This is often 6 feet in length, by 3 feet in breadth. It is covered with sashes of 12 panes each of 7 by 9 glass. The sashes are hung with hinges, upon the back side, for the convenience of opening. These sashes incline downwards, from the back side about 6 inches. The box or frame should be tight on all sides. It may be about 12 inches in height in front, and 18 in the rear.

54. The bed should be covered with litter from the horse-stable, well trodden down in several layers, until it is raised to the height wished. At last, cover this bed of layers with a layer of earth, or rich mould, from 9 to 12 inches in thickness, setting on the frame, and in the course of 8 or 10 days it will be ready for planting. It is sometimes necessary to admit fresh air, where the fermentation is very powerful.

55. The degree of heat may be ascertained by placing the hand upon the bed, or thrusting it into it. The temperature is easily lowered by raising the lights in the frame, until you have obtained the right degree.

56. Many tropical plants cannot endure the winter in our latitude. The Stock-Gillyflowers, Wall-flowers, Polyanthus, Scarlet Colutea, Auricula, Myrtle, and Carolina Jasmine, will require to be transplanted into flower-pots, and be housed. They should be kept where they can be exposed to the light, either in a warm cellar, or in a frame.

————

CULTIVATION OF FLOWERS WITH BULBOUS ROOTS.

57. Bulbous roots should, in general, be placed in a light, rich soil, mixed with a tolerable proportion of sea-sand. The compost commonly used is one third fine sand, one sixth rich loam, one third stable manure, and one sixth leaves of trees. The two last named articles are to be well rotted, and at least two years old. The beds should be formed two feet deep, being raised four or six inches above the garden, to turn off the rain. The best time for planting bulbs is in October or November, though it will do if delayed until the first of December.

58. The distance at which Hyacinths should be placed from each other is about six inches. The bulb should be placed in fine sea-sand, and covered with it. After they are thus planted, the bed should be carefully covered with earth four inches in depth. When winter sets in, or about the middle of December, cover these beds with straw, sea-weed or leaves four or five inches deep. A part of this ought to be removed, however, about the middle of February, and the remainder during the month of March. If there be too much protection, the bulbs will be injured.

59. When these plants blossom, their bells may be supported by small sticks. They should be protected from heavy rains and an intense vertical sun. When the blossoms are faded and the flowering season is over, the flower-stems should be cut off. The buds should be left, until the leaves are nearly dry, when the bulbs are to be taken up and the leaves cut off, half an inch from the top of the bulb. They are then replaced, (sideways) with the fibres on in the earth, and again covered with it. They should there be allowed to remain and gradually dry for a month, and then be taken up, cleared from the earth and fibres, and

each bulb wrapped in a separate paper, and kept dry, or packed in dry sand.

60. Should the flowers be desired to decorate the parlour in the winter, they ought to be planted in September. They should be placed in deep, narrow pots, six inches in diameter at the top, and about one third deeper than common flower-pots. The bulb should be just covered with the kind of soil before described. The watering should be from the top, but the pots may be allowed, twice a week, to stand in saucers filled with soft water. They ought to have as much sun and air as possible. They should never, however be allowed to feel the direct influence of fire. When the plants begin to blossom, the earth may be kept almost constantly saturated with moisture. The bulbs may be preserved, when they have done blossoming, as before directed.

61. The Single Hyacinth is generally preferable to the double, for early flowering. Many of them, are two or three weeks sooner in bloom. Their flowers are more numerous and brilliant than those of the double.

62. Tulips are hardier than Hyacinths. They are generally planted three or four inches apart, and covered with earth two or three inches deep.

63. The Polyanthus Narcissus, is among the most delicate and tender of bulbs. These bulbs should be very carefully protected from the frost. They may be planted six or eight inches deep, and about eight inches apart from each other. They ought to be taken up soon after blossoming, otherwise they are liable to suffer during the winter.

64. The Ranunculus, Anemone, Oxalis, and Dogs-tooth Violet, should be planted at the depth of one inch. The Bulbous Iris, Crocus, Arum, Small Fritillaria, Tiger-flower, Gladiolus, and Snowdrop, two inches. Tulip, Double Narcissus, Jonquille, Colchicum, and Snow-flake, three inches. Hyacinth, Amaryllis, Martagon, and other large Lilies, and Pæonies, four inches. The Crown Imperial, and Polyanthus Narcissus, five inches.

65. In making the estimate of these depths, admeasurement should always be taken from the top of the bulb. The rows should be eight or ten inches apart, and the roots about six or seven distant from each other, varying with the size of the flower. The bulbous roots most frequently selected for parlour flowers, in winter, are the Roman Narcissus, Double Jonquille, Polyanthus Narcissus, Double Narcissus, Crocus,

and Single Hyacinths. Some of the earliest Double Hyacinths are however sometimes selected, although they blossom some time later than the single.

66. Hyacinths intended for winter, should be placed in glasses, about the middle of November. The glasses should be previously filled with pure water. The bottom of the bulb when placed in the glass, may just touch the water. When thus situated, they are to be placed, for the first ten days, in a dark room, to promote the shooting of the roots. They then must be exposed to the light and sun as much as possible. Although they will blossom without the influence of the sun, the colours of the flowers will be greatly inferior, should they bloom in the shade.

67. The water, when it becomes impure, should be changed. The roots should be taken from the glasses, and their fibres rinsed in clean water, and the glasses well washed inside. Great care must be taken that the water in the glasses be not allowed to freeze, as it bursts the glasses and destroys the roots. Soft, clear rain water is preferable for such roots. Other pure water will, however, answer.

68. Nosegays when they have been kept for a considerable time, may often be, in a degree, restored in this way, by a change of the water in the glasses, in which their ends are inserted. They are benefitted by this change on the same principle as bulbous roots. Flowers almost dry, may sometimes be temporarily restored, by covering them with a glass bell or cup, or substituting warm water instead of cold.

69. The only advantage gained by taking up bulbs after blooming, (Tulips excepted) is, either to divide the roots, when too numerous, or to renew a worn-out soil. Neither of these can occur oftener than once in three or four years.

70. Bulbs are subterranean organs somewhat analogous to buds. They usually have numerous fibres or radicles attached to their inferior surfaces. Though they do not in all respects seem to belong to roots, they are usually regarded, and described as such.

71. *Three* varieties are commonly enumerated. 1st. The *scaly* bulb, as that of the Lily. 2d. The *tunicated* or *coated*, as that of the Onion. 3d. The *solid*, as that of the Crocus or English Saffron.

72. Bulbs, like buds, enclose the embryo of the future plant, and protect it until the period of its evolution arrives. In this respect they perform the office of buds. Many of them are composed of concentric

AA

scales, nearly allied to those of the buds which secure the tender leaves and flowers of northern regions from the rigours of winter, to which they would otherwise be exposed.

73. They also bear some analogy to the tuberous root, and, whether we consider them as buds or roots, the plants to which they are attached will always be regarded with peculiar interest, as among the most splendid ornaments of our gardens.

74. These plants are often among the earliest harbingers of spring, embracing the Snowdrop, Lily, Tulip, Hyacinth, and about 40 other beautifully flowering plants.

75. We cannot fail to observe, while examining the curious organization of different roots, with what apparent care the plants of another year are protected, and the species secured against the various chances of destruction.

ROOTS IN GENERAL.

76. Plants generally grow from the earth, and have a root that attaches them to it. The design of this is undoubtedly to fix the plant to its place, and to draw up nourishment for its support. It generally plunges into the earth, and its small fibres suck up the elements that eventually go for the growth and developement of the plant.

77. This appendage is very various in form, and has received different appellations according to its shape. When it plunges downward, tapering like the Carrot, Parsnip, and the like, it is said to be *fusiform*, or spindle-shaped, from the Latin *fusis*, a spindle.

78. Sometimes the root runs horizontally under the earth, as in the Mint, the root sending up frequent shoots or stems ; and is termed creeping (*repens*).   Sometimes like the stem it is divided, and is termed *branching*.

79. The small fibres that grow from the main root are termed radicles, from the Latin diminutive *radicula*, little root.   If the root consist of fleshy knobs, as that of the potato, artichoke, and the like, it is termed a tuberous root, from the Latin *tuber*, a knob.

80. Two or more of these *tubers* connected at their bases form what is termed the *palmate* root, from the Latin *palma*, the hand, because somewhat resembling the hand with the fingers extended.

81. Several roots bundled together are said to be *fasciculated* from

the Latin *fascicula*, a bundle of rods. The two last named varieties are exmplified in the different kinds of Orchis.

82. The root is occasionally found abruptly discontinued, appearing as if broken or bitten off, as in the Devils-bit. Such roots are termed abrupt or præmorse, from the Latin *præmordeo*, to bite off.

83. Several small knobs or grains are sometimes seen strung along the radical fibres like beads on a string, as in the roots of the Wood-Sorrel, or *Oxalis*. Such are said to be *granulated*, from the Latin *granula*, a grain.

84. If the root assume the form of a ball or bulb, as that of the Tulip, Hyacinth, and the like, and be composed of several concentric coats or layers, like the Onion, it is said to be tunicated, from the Latin *tunica*, a tunic or short coat.

85. When scaly, as in some grasses, it is termed *squamous* bulb, from the Latin *squamum*, the scales of a fish.

86. The *Epidendrum*, or Flower-of-the-Air, indigenous to the East Indies, is an extraordinary plant. It grows abundantly on the banks of the Ganges, where it is gathered by the Hindoo as an ornament to his cottage. It is said to vegetate for years, hung upon the ceiling of the Indian's dwelling, with no other nourishment than that which it derives from the air of the room. It communicates a delightful fragrance.

87. The Love-Vine or *Dodder*, is easily recognized by the golden colour of its thread-like and leafless stems. After springing from the earth, it seizes upon the first tree or plant in its reach. Rising, it penetrates the bark with its roots. The lower part of the plant then perishes, and it continues to derive its nourishment entirely from the supporter.

88. The Misletoe of our Southern States, and of Europe, never grows upon the earth, but upon other plants, such as the Apple-tree and Oak. It sends its roots deeply into the bark and wood of those trees to which it adheres, creeping extensively beneath their surface.

89. This plant abstracts the nourishment of its supporter and appropriates it to its own purposes. The Druids, deemed this plant sacred, especially when growing upon the Oak. They entertained the superstitious belief, that it was the " immediate gift of Heaven, sent down to avert the numerous evils to which men are in this life exposed."

90. Duhamel, Decandolle and others, have made some interesting ex-

periments on several of the tribe of *parasitic* plants. From observations, they entertain the opinion that the Misletoe, and several other
parasites, do not exhaust the plants on which they grow.

91. They believe them to increase the power of their supporters to
elevate the sap in the same degree as they take it from them by absorption, so that no loss is sustained by the plants to which they attach themselves. Some plants float in the water without any attachment of their
roots, and gather their food as they swim, from the surrounding element.
The Spanish Beard, *Tillandsia*, Beech Drops, and several kinds of
Moss, grow upon trees, and doubtless injure them by absorbing their
nourishment.

92. In determining the soil to which different plants are best suited,
some opinion may be formed from the shape of their roots. As a general rule we may say, that:

93. Those roots which descend deeply into the earth all require a deep
soil, and that the ground be deeply furrowed. 2d. Such as spread
widely and creep extensively near the surface, will flourish in a light
and thin soil, and do not require deep furrowing. 3d. Those that penetrate deeply for nourishment, being furnished with bulbs as a guard a-
gainst drought, and abundant radicles for the absorption of moisture and
food, will succeed on sandy plains, being suited to a dry soil. Such are
secured against the vicissitudes of moisture and dryness.

94. Too little attention has generally been paid to the time and
place of planting. Every seed has its proper time for germinating, as
well as its proper place for growth. It should ever be remembered,
that to every seed there is a requisite degree of heat, and moisture, beyond which it will not grow or thrive. The patches of vegetation
that stud the deserts of Africa, with here and there a verdant spot,
could no more flourish in Greenland, than the snows of the latter could
remain undissolved beneath the vertical sun of the former.

95. The degree of heat necessary to make the seed of a parsnip,
turnip, or cabbage germinate, will rot that of a cucumber, melon or
squash, and where the latter would grow and flourish, the seeds of
many tropical plants would perish, without manifesting signs of vegetation. Most vegetables thrive better to shift the ground, every year, alternately for different sorts. Each kind, is supposed to draw a somewhat different nourishment from the soil. Some crops, however, as the
Onion, do better to continue cultivating them continually on the same
spot.

SOWING OF SEEDS.

96. The seeds of annual plants must be sown in a rich earth, finely pulverized. The season of sowing should be regulated by the species of plants. The borders of gardens and walks, where they are to be sown, should be previously well dug with a trowel or small spade. The earth, after being broken, must be made light and the surface even. The seeds ought to be covered with fresh earth, an inch or two in depth, small seeds not so deep as this, and some few large ones a little deeper.

97. The most delicate plants are often sown in pots, as the Mignonette, Cypress-vine, &c. Plants should not be allowed to grow too thickly, and if they are so, should be regularly thinned, to give room for their more luxuriant growth. When the ground becomes dry it may be watered with soft water, poured from a watering pot, finely pierced, that it fall not heavily and harden the ground.

98. Pot plants should not be exposed to the sun all day, but only till 11 or 12 o'clock in the forenoon. They may then be removed to the shade. Some persons sift the mould intended for pots, through a coarse wire sive. Many plants as the Balsams, Asters, Globe Amaranths, Ice-plants, Marygolds, Chrysanthemums, Coxcombs, Stocks, Eternal-flowers, &c. may be transplanted from beds into Flowerpots, in June or early in July.

99. Many biennnial and perennial plants diffuse a most agreeable odour, especially in their season of flowering. This renders them desirable objects for flower-gardens, and shrubberies. Their flowers communicate to a nosegay a delicious fragrance. When placed in a vase, or jar, of water, they fill an apartment with the most exquisite perfume. They should be placed in water immediately after they are gathered, as many of them, from their extreme delicacy soon droop, and wither without this precaution.

100. Their seeds may generally be sown during the months of April and May, in borders of walks or in beds of rich earth, three or four feet wide. The earth should be finely pulverized, as for those of annuals, and made smooth, even, and light. They may be transplanted, if wished, for the sake of diversifying a garden. This should be done in August or September: Scoop Trowels will be found useful, in general, in shifting the locality of plants.

101. Transplanting should be done in moist or cloudy weather, and watering frequently practised until the plants have taken root. A considerable quantity of earth is generally taken up with the root. A piece of shell or broken earthen may be placed over the hole in the flowerpot, to make room for the water to drain off. It should be borne in mind that Biennials and Perennials do not blossom the same year that they are sown. The biennials put forth their blossoms on the following year. To ensure a constant supply of the flowers of annuals and biennials, therefore, they must be sown yearly.

PROPAGATION OF FLOWERS.

102. In regard to the culture of plants of every description, it may be said generally, that they should stand at such distances from each other as that the air may circulate freely about them, and that the sun may have its proper influence in bringing them to perfection.

103. In order to accomplish this, the distances to be observed in planting must vary with the size of the plant. When too thickly planted, they should be properly thinned while small. The earth must be kept loose about them with a prong-hoe, or other instrument.

104. Weeds of every kind ought to be removed on their first appearance. Ploughing, hoeing, and removing the earth should be done in dry weather. Stirring it when wet renders it clammy and hard.

105. Plants, particularly those of the shrubby kind, that have dead and decaying branches, should be deprived of them by pruning. The suckers, that shoot up about them from time to time, should also be taken away.

106. The best soil for a garden is a deep loam, which may easily be made rich by old rotten manure. The earth must be well pulverized, and not too wet or too dry, varying with the nature of the plant. A level plat of ground, gradually sloping toward the south, is deemed best for a garden.

107. Though most plants may be propagated in several modes, viz. by *seeds*, by *cuttings*, by *layers*, by *parting the roots* and *transplanting*, by *budding* and *grafting*, some are propagated with greater facility in one of these ways and some in others.

108. Among those often propagated by *suckers*, by *shoots* and *slips*, and *dividing the roots*, are enumerated by florists the Almond, Daisy, Chrysanthemum, Dahlia, Eupatorium, Geranium, Glycine, Honeysuckle, Hydrangea, Iris, Lilach, Lily, Podophyllum or Lime-Plant, Phlox, Narcissus, Passion-flower, Piony, Pink, Helianthus, Polyanthus, Roses, Acacia or Robina, Rudbeckia, Lychnis, Snow-ball or Viburnum, Sowberry or Symphoria, Spice-wood, Spider-wort or Tradescantia, Spiræa, Syringa or Mock Orange, Burning Bush or Strawberry-tree (Euonymus), Sweet Bay or Laurus nobilis, Fringe-tree or Venetian Sumach (*Rhus*) sometimes called the Smoke-tree, Violet, and several others. Many of these may be propagated by seed, and likewise in several other ways.

109. The following *green-house* plants have been recommended by some to be propagated by *separating the roots*, by *offsets, cuttings,* &c. though several may equally well be propagated by seed, and in other ways: Anemone, White Lily, Tuberose, Persian Iris, Verbena or Sweet Vervain, Fushia coccinea, Cobæa Scandens, Camella Japonica or Japan Rose, and Myrtle.

110. In the Lily of the Valley (*Convallaria*), each crown blossoms only once in three years. The plant should not be potted until it be ascertained that there be buds, for it is uncertain whether *one quarter* of the plants will flower. They should be placed thickly in the pots or boxes, and kept moderately moist. This potting is done from January to March, and after the flower-buds appear. After the blossoming is over, they may be planted out in borders, or plunged in the ground in pots.

111. *Ranuncules* may be planted in pots, eight or ten inches deep. The Scarlet Turban in November. The root is to be placed half an inch under the surface of a fresh loamy soil, and the pot plunged in the ground in a warm sunny situation, but not under glasses. They are covered with *mats*, if the frost be severe ; these must be frequently removed when the sun shines. They must be potted when the flowers begin to expand, three or four roots in a pot, placed under glasses; and copiously watered every day.

112. The *Anemone* is raised from seed with facility. It is planted in October, November, and sometimes in March. It is to be potted and managed in all respects as the Scarlet Turban Ranunculus. Double

varieties are multiplied by parting the roots or tubers. These separate very naturally when old, as they become hollow.

113. *Jonquils* are planted from October to January, six or eight in a pot, if pots or boxes be used. If they have grown in bunches, take them up so : If they were planted in autumn, take them up singly. They should be plentifully watered. Many let them remain in the ground *three years* before taking them up, as they will then rise in large bunches for potting, and bloom much stronger.

114. The Martagon or Turk's-Cap, and White Lilies, are all propagated by dividing offsets from old roots, and planting them in borders. The best time for potting is in January or February. They must be plentifully supplied with water, and kept in a warm sunny situation. After the flowering is over, they may be planted in the borders again, each root separately. They will bear forcing tolerably well.

115. The Provence and Moss Roses all do well for forcing, in pots. They will flower in rooms and hot-houses, and should be potted in autumn when the leaves are off. They should not be forced till the second year. The roses are increased by layers and suckers from the old roots. They may be placed in a room in December or January, and plentifully watered. The *Green Fly*, that so often infests the young shoots and flower-buds of Roses, may be destroyed by fumigating the plants with tobacco smoke for two or three hours. Other plants infested with insects may be served in this way. After this fumigation, plants are to be copiously watered, from the nose of a watering-pot, over their whole surface, to cleanse them of the smoke. The China or Monthly Roses are in flower a great part of the winter. They may be propagated by cuttings, and covered with a glass. This should be done in autumn.

116. The Double and Single Tuberose are planted in pots in April and May, one in each pot. They thrive well in hot-beds. They must be kept moderately moist, especially after the foliage on the top is grown two or three inches in length, air is to be frequently admitted. Those grown in hot-beds or hot-houses may be removed to any warm sunny apartment, when the flower-stems are five or six inches in length. They are propagated by offsets, taken after the plants are done flowering, and the green dried.

117. The Persian Iris will flower in glasses or small pots of sand. These plants are propagated by dividing the offsets from old roots, and

managed exactly, in culture, as the Hyacinths. It is common to put **3** early plants in each pot or box.

118. The Mignonette is sown at almost any time in the year.   It should be often watered, and may be successfully transplanted into pots, previous to flower, and placed in a sunny window during cold weather.

119. The *Verbena*, or Vervain, generally loses its foliage in December. It should not be thrown away as dead at this season, for if it be cut back rather short and shifted into a larger pot, as soon as the leaves fall, it will soon break again, and form a fine green plant, retaining its leaves for a considerable time. It is propagated by slips and cuttings from the young wood in summer. They will strike root in about three weeks, when they may be potted singly.

120. The *Fushia coccinea* is propagated by cuttings, that are planted in the summer. If *by the seeds*, it may be sown in April or May, and the plants will then flower in autumn. When potted, the pots should be large, and be placed in a shady situation. The earth must be kept moist.

121. The *Cobæa Scandens*, a fine creeper, is planted in April or May, and plentifully watered. It is easily propagated by seeds or by cuttings, that may be planted in pots, during the summer. Glasses are to be placed over them, the pots to be plunged, and the shoots copiously watered. The plant may be forced in a hot-house or hot-bed, so as to bloom much sooner.

122. The *Camella Japonica* is propagated by seed, layers, cuttings, and inarching. When from seed from China, they may be sown in the spring. The pots require to be large, as the plant is large. The plants require the protection of a green-house or hot-house. It is customary to wash them once a month with clean water from a watering-pot, and to wipe their leaves with a sponge. The pots must be plunged. *Inarching* is generally performed in April.

123. The *Myrtles* most commonly cultivated are the Venus, Roman, Box-leaved, Italian, Nutmeg, Orange-leaved, Gold-striped, Silver-striped, Broad-leaved Dutch, Thyme or Rosemary-leaved, and Double-Flowering. Several of them are very hardy, but sometimes killed to the ground by the frost. To keep them dwarf and bushy, the tops of the young leading shoots are to be pinched off as they advance. The myrtles are propagated by cuttings of the younger shoots in summer. They are to be treated as the Vervain or Verbena.

BB

GREEN-HOUSE PLANTS.

124. Green-house plants must be properly furnished with water, poured from watering-pots upon their tops. They should not be allowed to remain long in the water-pans under the pots, especially in the winter. They must be cleansed of their dead leaves, and have a good share of fresh air in fine warm weather.

125 It is customary to open the top windows where no plants are located. If they be exposed to the draft, they will receive injury. It is recommended to shift *Green-House Plants* every year, in April or May, into other pots, and renew the soil. A compost, such as has been recommended for bulbous roots, will be found to do well for many of these plants.

126. The Carnation is so tender, as to require cover in our climate in winter. The plant may be put into large pots, and kept in a green-house or warm room. They should be placed where they may have air and light during winter.

127. The Indian Chrysanthemums may stand in open ground till August or September, after which they must be placed in pots and housed. If covered with glasses, they will flower in the garden. After flowering, the roots may be placed in a cellar or the open ground.

128. The *Convolvulus Major*, or Morning-Glory, and *Convolvulus Minor*, or Beauty-of-the-Night, so called because opening its blossoms at evening, are propagated by seed, that must be sown in early spring.

129. The Dahlia, a native of Mexico, sometimes called Georgiana, from Georgi, a Russian traveller, has tuberous roots, resembling a sweet potato. It was named after Andrew Dahl, a Swedish botanist. It was introduced into Britain in 1804, by Lady Holland, who sent the seeds from Madrid. It was little cultivated in England till 1814, and has recently received attention in this country.

130. The seeds of the Dahlia may be sown in pots in March, and the pots placed in a hot-bed or green-house. In May, they may be taken out and placed in borders, and, as they advance in height, be supported by sticks.

131. The roots may be taken up in October or November, and preserved in boxes filled with dry sand, during the winter. In April, when they begin to sprout, the roots may be divided, and placed where they

are designed to stand. Those only that have the *bud* should be planted.

132. The *Lonicera*, or Climbing Honey-Suckle, is propagated by seed, cuttings, or layers. It climbs upon houses, over hedges, and forms arbours and bowers. It flowers in clusters. Three varieties are common. The Italian, *L. Italiana*, flowering early in the season,—the Variegated, *Lonicera caprifolia*, which blossoms monthly,—and the Scarlet Trumpet, *Caprifolium sempervirens*, that bears fine scarlet flowers which also appear every month.

133. The White and Purple Lilachs, *Syringa vulgaris*, may be budded or grafted into each other. When thus managed, bearing both white and purple flowers, the plant appears very finely. These, as likewise the Persian Lilach (*Syringa persica*), are propagated by suckers.

134. All the Lilies are bulbous-rooted, and are propagated by off-sets. The *Lilium candidum*, or White Lily, often grows four or five feet high, having large, white, fragrant flowers. The Tiger Lily, *L. tigridum*, frequently grows to the height of 6 feet, producing many flowers, spotted like a tiger. The Martagon Lily has flowers much like this, except that they are smaller and more delicate. The Asphodel, *Lilium luteum*, grows a foot or two high, and bears beautiful *yellow flowers*. These, and the other Lilies, as likewise the *Convallaria*, or Lily of the Valley, are propagated by seeds as well as by offsets.

135. The Sweet Pea, *Lathyrus odoratus*, is an annual, and should be planted in early spring. The Everlasting Pea, *Lathyrus latifolius*, a species of this genus, is sometimes cultivated as ornamental.

136. Though Roses may be propagated by cuttings, many of them are almost equally well raised from seed. As several of these afford suckers, that come out near the old stems in summer, they are often multiplied by *suckers*. The suckers, when planted, must be cut down within four or five inches of the ground. The time for planting is either in October and November, or April.

137. The soil is to be frequently stirred, and the plants kept cut down to a certain height, according to their natural size. When they get long stems and branches, they produce few flowers, and these often small.

138. The *Yellow Rose* will best flourish in an airy situation and gravelly soil. Every autumn one half of the old wood may be cut down within four or five inches of the ground. By this means, a succession of

thrifty blossoming shoots will be kept up.   China Roses require the protection of a green-house.

139.   The Tulip is found in a great variety of colours.   Mr. Prince is said to have more than *Six Hundred Varieties*, cultivated at his Linnean Gardens on Long-Island.   In Holland, about the middle of the seventeenth century, a very great passion prevailed for these flowers. One named the *Viceroy* was said to have been sold at that time for *ten thousand dollars*.

140.   This rage in Holland for flowers also extended to the Hyacinth. In 1771, *four thousand dollars* are said to have been refused for a *single bulb* of the Hyacinth.

———

ORNAMENTAL PLANTS.

141.   A due proportion of *ornamental plants* is considered an indispensable requisite to every handsome garden.   Its avenues and borders would be deemed imperfect without them.   In regard to their disposition in borders and avenues, it has been customary to range them in 4 ranks, according to their respective heights.

142.   They are to be disposed on both sides of walks and avenues. The *first* range, nearest the avenue or walk, embraces plants of the lowest kinds, as Roses, Pinks, the smallest shrubs and herbaceous flowering plants.

143.   The *second* range consists of larger plants and shrubs, from *six* to *ten feet* in height.   The *third* consists of small-sized *trees* that never attain a very great height.   The *fourth* and outer rank includes those trees only that attain the greatest elevation.   By this arrangement, avenues and borders are rendered at once impressive and delightful.

144.   The avenue or border thus lined, in order to produce its full effect, should be broad and extended, and the respective ranks or ranges at proportionate distances asunder.

145.   The *shrubs* recommended for the inner rank do not generally exceed from *two* to *five* feet in height.   Among others are often planted China and other Roses, the Snowberry (*Symphoria*), Scotch Broom (*Spartium*), St. John's Wort (*Hypericum*), Pæonia, Mezereon (*Daphne*), Japan Globe-flower (*Corchorus Japonicus*), *Camella*, or Japan Rose, Arcadian or Yellow Honeysuckle (*Diervilla*), and the Dwarf Double-Flowering Almond.

146. The *second* Range, consisting of shrubs of from *six* to *ten* or *twelve* feet in height, embraces the Acacia, *Robinia*, the Althæa, *Hibiscus*, White or Pink Honeysuckle, *Azalea*, Calycanthus, Alspice, Weeping Cherry, Colutea, Currant, *Ribes*, Leather-wood, *Dirca*, Bloody Dog-wood, *Cornus*, English Honeysuckle, *Lonicera*, Dwarf-flower, Horse Chestnut, *Æsculus*, Silver-bell or Snow-drop Tree, *Halesia*, Hawthorn, *Cretægus*, Lilach, *Syringa*, Indigo Shrub, *Amorpha*, *Magnolia Glauca*, Mountain Laurel, *Kalmia*, Mountain Rose, *Rubus*, Pomegranate, Prim or Privet *Ligustrum*, Quince, *Cydonia*, Rose Bay, *Rhododendron*, Pontic Rose Bay, Guelder Rose or Snow-ball, *Viburnum*, different species of *Spiræa*, Syringa, *Philadelphus*, Sophora japonica, and several others.

147. The *third* Range among others often includes the Venetian Sumach, *Rhus*, Willows, *Salix*, Swedish Juniper, *Juniperus*, Chinese Mulberry, *Morus*, Mountain Snow-drop, *Chionanthus*, Magnolia, Laburnum, *Cytissus*, Ash, *Fraxinus*, Mountain Ash, *Sorbus*, Red Cedar, *Juniperus*, Franklinia, *Gordonia*, Hercules Club, *Angelica*, Judas-tree, *Cercis*, Siberian-Crab, Double Flowering Almond, *Amygdalus*, and Purple-Flowering Acacia, *Robinia*.

148. The *fourth*, outer, or last Range, embraces trees of the loftiest kinds. Among others are often included the Silver-leaved Poplar, *Populus*, Catalpas, *Bignonia*, Alianthus, Beech, *Fagus*, Button-Wood or Plane, *Plantanus*, Horse-chestnut, *Æsculus*, Cypress, *Cupressus*, Elm, *Ulmus*, Lime or Linden, *Tillia*, Hemlock, *Pinus*, Larch, Hacmateck, Locust, *Robinia*, Honey Locust, *Gladitschia*, Scarlet Maple, *Acer*, Sugar Maple, White or Silver Pines, *Pinus*, Norway and Black Spruce, Sycamore, Tulip-Tree, *Liriodendron*, and Weeping Willow, *Salix*.

149. Those flowers that are cultivated in beds by themselves, and in pots, as ornamental, are distinguished by the name of *Florists' Flowers*. The Crocus, Polyanthus Narcissus, Hyacinth, Auricula, Polyanthos, Carnation Pink, Dahlia, Iris, Anemone, Tulip, Ranunculus, and the like, are of this description.

150. The *shrubbery* of a border or avenue is often mixed with tall-growing, showy, herbaceous, flowering plants, for the purpose of effect. Among others, recommended for this purpose, are the Lily of the Valley, *Convallaria*, Wood Anemone, *Anemone nemorosa*, Hollyhock, *Althæa*, Goats-beard Spiræa, *Spiræa*, Fox Glove, *Digitalis*, Monks'-Hood, *Aconitum*, Larkspur, *Delphinium*, Columbine, *Aquilegia*, Willow Herb,

Epilobium, Double Fever-few, *Pyrethrum*, Tall Asters, Golden Rods, *Solidago*, Sunflowers, *Helianthus, Rudbeckia*, Tiger Lily, *Lilium*, Sweet Woodruff, *Asperula*, and *Yucca filamentosa*.

151.　The borders for perennial flowers are often made from three to six feet wide, and the soil suitably prepared for the reception of the plant.　Among other plants often used in borders are the Coreopsis, Phlox, Willow Herb, *Epilobium*, Speedwell, *Veronica*, Wolfs-bane, *Aconitum*, Rudbeckia, Liatris, Acanthus, Spiræa, Dropwort, Bell-Flowers, *Campanula*, Sage, *Salvia*, Scarlet Lychnis, *Lychnis*, Hyssop-leaved Dragon's Head, *Drococephalum*, Silver Rod or Asphodel, *Asphodelus*, Verbascum, Lathyrum, Centaurea, and Double Siberian Larkspur, *Delphinium*.

152.　The front of borders are often decorated with the Gentians, *Gentiana*, Pasque Flowers, *Anemone pulsalilla*, Star Anemone, *Anemone hortensis*, Purple Jacobea, *Senecio*, Phlox, Lychnidea, Siberian Fumitory, *Fumaria*, Cranes-Bill Geranium, Chili Monkey Flower, *Mimulus*, Evening Primrose, *Œnothera*, Marsh Marygold, *Caltha*, Feather Grass, *Stipa*, Canadian and Sweet or March Violet, *Viola*.

153.　Among ornamental plants of a middling size are the Rose Campion, *Agrostemma*, Perennial Flax, *Linum*, Adonis, Sweet Maudlin, Sneeze-wort, *Achillea*, Rampion, *Phyteuma*, Sweet William, *Dianthus*, Fraxinella, *Dictamnus*, Cardinal Flower, *Lobelia*, Catananche, Canadian Columbine, *Aquilegia*, Garden Wall-Flower, *Cheiranthus*, Scarlet Chelone, German Goldilocks, *Chrysocoma*, Tritoma, Monarda, Perenneal Lupin, *Lupinus*, Perennial or Oriental Poppies, Red Valerian, *Valeriana*, Pæonia, Smooth-leaved Bell Flower, *Campanula*, Italian and Alpine Asters, Ragged Robin, *Lychnis*, Bachelor's Button, White-flowered Crowfoot, *Ranunculus*, Garden Rocket, *Hesperis*, Spider Wort, *Tradescantia*, Asiatic Globe Flower, *Trollius*, American Cowslip, *Dodecantheon*, Chinese Chrysanthemums, and Day Lily, *Hemerocallis*.

AQUATIC PLANTS AND ROCK WORK.

154.　In a complete flower garden, in addition to the Green-House and Hot-House, there is often a small *Pond*, for the cultivation of MARSH and AQUATIC PLANTS, and a little elevation or hillock of stones and earth, thrown together for the accommodation of such plants as require a stony and rocky locality.

155. Plants and flowers best suited for the ROCK WORK, as the latter is often termed by gardeners, are the various kinds of Lichens, Cotyledon, Cob-web House-Leek, *Sempervivum*, Stone Crop, *Sedum*, Soapwort, *Saponaria*, Primula nivalis and Marginata, Alpine Lychnis, Verbascum, Saxifrage, Soldanella Alpina, Gentian, *Gentiana*, Cyclamen, Erigeron Alpinum, Cerastium, Madwort, *Alyssum*, *Erinus Alpinus*, Red Valerian, *Valeriana*, Dianthus deltoides, Prickly Pear, *Cactus oppuntia*, and many of the *Alpine plants*, or such as grow naturally in lofty and rocky situations.

156. The AQUATIC PLANTS most used for the AQUARIUM, as the pond is sometimes termed by gardeners, are the White and Yellow Water Lily, *Nymphœa alba* and *N. lutea*, the Chinese Lily or *Nymphœa nelumbium*, Flowering Rush, *Botomus umbellatus*, Water Violet, *Huttonia palustris*, Cats-Tail, *Typha latifolia*, Yellow and Fringed Bog-Bean, *Menyanthes nymphoides*, Marsh Calla, *Calla palustris*, and many others of our native tribe of *aquaticks*, that are of great beauty.

BIENNIAL AND ANNUAL FLOWERS.

157. Among *biennials* of the ornamental kind are the *Œnothera* or Evening Primrose, *Verbascum* or Moth-Mullein, *Gloucium luteum* or Yellow Horned Poppy, *Hedysarum coronarium* or French Honeysuckle, Honesty or Satin Flower, *Lunaria*, and several others.

158. The *annuals*, that are often cultivated as such, are the Ice-Plants, Mimosa, Egg-Plant, Amaranthus, Chrysanthemum, Ipomœa or Cypress Vine, Cock's-comb, *Celosia*, Globe Amaranth, *Gomphrœna*, Mignonette, Pinks, Tunbergia, Coreopsis, Clarkea, Candy Tuft, *Iberis*, Catch-fly, *Silene*, Venus' Looking Glass, *Campanula*, Convolvulus, African Marygold, Love in a Mist, *Nigella*, Scabious, Balsam, Sweet Pea, *Lathyrus*, Eternal Flower, *Xeranthemum*, Poppy, and Purple-eyed Crepius.

INFLORESCENCE, OR MODE OF FLOWERING.

159. Flowers are sometimes *solitary*, sometimes *in pairs*, and sometimes in large collections or *aggregations*, forming a very striking feature in the appearance and habit of the plant. This is particularly in-

teresting to botanists, as forming the most invariable and most elegant of all specific distinctions.

160. The flower is generally a little elevated upon a small stalk of its own, that it may be more advantageously exposed to the action of *light* and *air*. This is *lateral* when springing from the side of the stem, *terminal* from the summit, *axillary* from the axil, between the stem and leaf or branch. It is *one-flowered* in the Tulip, *two-flowered* in the Linnæa, and *many-flowered* in the Cowslip and Lilach. In the latter it is branched. This arrangement of flowers on their respective plants is termed the *Inflorescence*.

161. When the flower-stalk springs from the stem or its branches, it is termed a *peduncle*. If it arise immediately from the earth, or rather the root, as in the Dandelion, it is called a *scape*. In the Dandelion it is hollow or *tubular*, in the Hyacinth *naked*, in the Colts-foot *scaly*, in the Sweet-flag *leafy*.

162. The positions that flowers assume on their footstalks, and in relation to plants on which they grow, have received different appellations, such as the *Cyme*, the *Corymb*, the *Fascicle*, the *Spike*, the *Raceme, Head, Whorl, Panicle, Thyrse, Spadix, Ament* or *Catkin*, and the like.

163. When a number of flower-stalks issue from a common centre and diverge like rays, bearing flowers on their summits, they are collectively termed an *Umbel*, from the Latin *umbella*, an umbrella. If the rays be undivided, as in the Silk-weed, it is termed a *simple Umbel* ; if subdivided, *compound* one.

164. If flower-stalks issue from a common centre, and rise to the same height with irregular intermediate subdivisions, supporting flowers on their summits, they are collectively called a *Cyme*. Examples are furnished us in the Elder and Sumach.

165. If rising from a common stem, the rays become proportionately shorter as they originate nearer its extremity, so that the blossoms are disposed on a level with each other, they form what is termed the *Corymb*, from the Latin *corymbus*, the head of a thistle. In the last named mode, the *rays* proceed from *different points* : in the former, from the *same point*. The Apple and Pear furnish examples of the *corymb* and *umbel*, the former of the *umbel* and the latter of the *corymb*.

166. If an assemblage of flowers be more densely disposed than in the *corymb*, but otherwise similarly arranged, they form the *Fascicle*, as

in the Sweet William. This mode of disposition in the flowers of the Sweet William has by some been termed *corymbose*.

167. A *Spike* is an assemblage of flowers arising from a common stem. It generally grows erect. Its flowers are *sessile* in the Herds-Grass, and stand on short stalks in the common Lavender.

168. This mode of expression is generally more progressive than that of the *Raceme*. A long period often elapses between the fading of the lowest flowers and the appearing of the upper ones. The flowers are commonly crowded closely together. If otherwise, they sometimes form separate groups, sometimes *whirls*, when the *spike* is called an *interrupted* or *whirled* Spike. The spike may be *simple*, as in Agrimony, or *compound*, as in Lavender.

169. The term *spikelet* is applied to Grasses, when there are many florets in one calyx. The *filiform* receptacle, to which these florets are attached, is termed the *Rachis*.

170. When flowers are assembled on the extremity of the stalk in a globular, oval, or cylindrical form, the aggregation is termed a *Head*, as in the Clover or Trefoil. If they surround the stalk or branch in the form of a ring, they form the *Whorl*, as in the Mints and Labiate flowers.

171. The *Raceme* differs from the *Spike* only in the length of its individual flower-stalks. The Currant affords a fine example of the former. If flowers be variously arranged on their stalk, which is repeatedly subdivided, their inflorescence constitutes the *Panicle*, as in the Oat. In the Grasses, the branches of the Panicle are somewhat *verticillate*.

172. The flowers in the *Thyrse* are arranged like those in the Panicle, except the branches of the peduncle being short and the flowers more compact, as in the *Syringa*, or Lilach.

173. In the *Catkin*, as in the Spike, the flowers are arranged along a common filiform receptacle, as in the Walnut and Birch. The flowers stand on *chaffy scales*, which are sometimes *deciduous*, as in the Birch, sometimes *persistent*, as in the Pine. In the latter, they form what is termed the *Cone*, in the former the *Ament*.

174. American forest trees present numerous examples of this mode of inflorescence. The *Catkin* is most common among forest-trees, and the *Spike* among herbaceous plants. In the Hop its form is *oval*, in the Birch *cylindrical*, and in the Plane-tree *globular*.

cc

175. The *Spadix* is a columnar receptacle usually rising from a sheath, and supporting a number of *sessile* flowers. In the Arum, the flowers are attached only to its base. In Pothos or Skunk's Cabbage, they crown the summit of the column. In each of these, the *Spadix* rises from the bosom of a single *spatha*. In the Indian-Corn, it is enclosed by leaves, called husks, and in Sweet Flag, *Acorus*, naked. It is branched in the Palms.

176. The peculiar calyx of Grasses is termed the *Glume*, and the pieces of which it is composed are called *valves*. In some instances, the calyx is a mere *scale*. If several scales be attached to a common filiform receptacle, they form the Catkin.

177. The calyx, that surrounds the corolla of flowers, is *double* in the Sunflower, *cylindrical* in the Garden Pink, *prismatic* in the Monkey-Flower, *urlceolate* in the Rose, *ventricose* in the Catch-fly, *turbinate* in the Syringa, *imbricate* in the Aster, *scarious* in Gnaphallum, *hooked* in Burdock, and *spinous* in the Thistle. It is *persistent*, *deciduous*, and *caducous* in different flowers.

178. The Spathe is a floral leaf, issuing from the scape, enveloping one or more flowers, by the convolution of its edges. In the Narcissus, it encloses a solitary flower ; in the Jonquil, several ; and in the Arum, it contains an assemblage of sessile florets, surrounding the base of the *Spadix*. The husks of Indian-Corn are a kind of Spathe.

179. The Bract is that leaf-like appendage to the peduncle, that often closely envelopes the flower, and assumes somewhat the appearance of a calyx. It is variously coloured, as *green, yellow, purple, scarlet,* &c. In spring, it is often mistaken for the blossom itself.

180. If the petals of the corolla be inserted into the receptacle under the germen, as in Digitalis, they are said to be *hypogynous*, if inserted upon the germen, as in the Trumpet Honeysuckle, *epigynous*.

181. The filaments, that sustain the anther in flowers, are usually *smooth*, sometimes *downy*. They are sometimes so expanded, as to resemble petals, and have occasionally been mistaken for them in the Clematis. When embraced within the corolla, they are said to be *inserted* ; when passing beyond it, *exserted* ; when converging towards its inferior part, *declinate*.

182. The anther is usually of a membraneous texture, furnished with two cells that open laterally, as in the Lily. In the Heath they some-

times open at the top. The number of anthera is usually one to each filament, sometimes *two, three, four, five,* &c.

183. The dust of the anthers, so light as to be wafted on the air in dry weather, in wet weather bursts with great force, emitting a most subtle vapour. This fine meal, or pollen, is collected by the busy, flying bee, during his excursions in the sunny days of spring, and, by some secret process, formed into that singular species of vegetable oil, termed bees-wax, rendered concrete by a peculiar acid in the insect.

184. There has been fancied a close resemblance between flowers and the butterfly and bee, those flower-loving creatures that sport among them, and feed upon their nectar, during their brief but apparently joyous existence.

185. We use the words of Rousseau, when, in speaking of flowers, he says :—" These seem destined by nature to unite the vegetable and animal kingdoms, and to make them circulate from one to the other. A flower and an insect have a great resemblance to each other. The painted butterfly, that wantons from flower to flower and delights in the summer sunshine, seems not less joyous nor greatly unlike the gay and gaudy blossom that dances in the breezes of spring. Insects are nourished by honey, and may not flowers require it also for perfecting the fructification ? They adhere to the young fruit, seemingly for the purpose of nourishment."

HOT AND GREEN HOUSES.

186. The Hot-House is a building for the production of plants, either exotic or indigenous, that will not grow in the open air of the country where they are cultivated. It is designed to force, or excite into a state of vegetation, indigenous and acclimated plants, and to accelerate their maturation at an extraordinary season, and to protect exotics.

187. The heat required by Hot-House plants, in addition to that afforded by the sun, is commonly produced by the ignition of carbonaceous substances. The air of the building is heated to the required temperature either *directly* by leaving the hot embers of wood in a furnace or stove, placed within the building ; or *indirectly,* by the passage of smoke, heated air, or steam, through flues and tubes.

188. Masses of brick-work, sand, gravel, rubbish, earth, tan, and even water, are sometimes heated. These afterwards slowly communicate

their acquired heat to the atmosphere of the house. The temperature is also sometimes raised to a requisite degree by the fermentation of vegetable substances, as dung, tan, leaves, weeds, and the like, applied beneath or around the whole or a part of the building, or placed within it, as in hot-beds. Steam is said to be the most convenient vehicle of heat, or caloric, that human ingenuity has yet discovered and employed. It is recommended for heating Hot-Houses, and indeed all places where large bodies of air are to be heated.

189. The GREEN-HOUSE is a building designed to protect, during winter, such exotic plants, shrubs, and trees, as will bear being exposed to the open air during summer, but are too tender for such exposure in the cold of winter, yet, being housed, require not generally the heat of a stove.

190. Mr. Watkins recommends the following plan for the construction of one. The building is to be sunk in the earth from two to four feet, in proportion to its size, and according to the nature of the soil where it is located. Clayey soil retains moisture and produces damp, and consequently will not admit of its being sunk so deep.

191. The height of the building should not exceed twelve feet from the exterior ground. Its width should not be more than sixteen or eighteen feet, as the sun's rays at a larger distance from the glass are very feeble. A south front is well known to be the best. Advantage is also to be taken by glazing as much of the eastern end of the building as possible, for the benefit of the morning sun.

192. The front may be made to decline northward from a perpendicular with the horizon, so that the angle made thereby with the horizon will bring the rays of the sun in winter at noon, to strike the glass at right angles. The roof should descend the opposite side without a break.

193. By this position, the rays of the sun are thrown upon every part of the whole inside, and the whole becomes heated by them. When the sun produces most heat during mid-day, there is no reflection of its rays, and at other parts of the day, the reflecting angle being obtuse, does not powerfully cast them off, so that more rays are thus introduced into the building, than there would be in any other position.

194. The inside of the rafters of the roof of a Green-House are to be lined with boards, and the space between that and the roof filled with a mixture of straw, sand, and clay, made into a mortar. Boards should be

used in preference to shingles, as there will be fewer breaks in the roof, and consequently less space for the admission of cold air.

195. Other parts of the building may be made of stone or brick work, or there may be a framed building filled in with bricks. There ought to be no flooring of any kind upon the ground. Shutters on the outside are sufficient, and it is most convenient to have them hung upon hinges. They are less troublesome in opening, than the common sliding ones. They should be made to fold into the spaces between the windows.

196. The bottom of the building is to be covered with bark from a tan-vat to the depth of about a foot, according as the building is sunk more or less in the earth. The plants may then be introduced for protection and culture.

197. The advantages gained by *thus* constructing a building for this purpose, are, 1st. The lessening the expense of building. 2d. Gaining sufficient heat from the *sun* to warm the house, and thereby saving the expense of fire and the trouble of warming it by the stove. 3d. Avoiding injury, often received by plants from too much heat, when such rooms are warmed by stoves and furnaces. 4th. Obviating the disadvantages that plants often experience from the escape of smoke through flues and pipes, when stoves are used for the purpose of warming.

198. Many persons make arrangements, when constructing a Green-House, for the introduction of a stove. They thereby gain the advantages both of a Green-House and Hot-House in the same building. Besides, in case of a long succession of cold, cloudy days, when the sun is obscured, the temperature of the building may be so reduced, as to be below that degree necessary for the preservation of the life of these plants. Under such circumstances, (which will, however, seldom occur,) a stove is necessary even for the Green-House. One clear sunny day, however, will generally warm the house sufficiently to admit of its being closed for several successive days.

199. Plants in Green-Houses of the construction described require less water than in a hot-house, and do not suffer so much for want of a pure atmospheric air. Heat, generated by the fermentation of vegetable substances and bark, free access to the plants of the electric fluid of the earth, together with such a supply of atmospheric air as will find admission from time to time, all conspire to supply the quantity exhausted by the daily rarefaction of the sun's heat, and to render plants healthy and fine. Thus reared, they are found remarkably thrifty in spring. Trop-

ical fruits may be ripened in such places during the winter, and even young fruit formed on the trees.

200. There is seldom occasion that a building thus constructed should be heated by fire. Plants placed in it generally require no other care than now and then a little watering, and that the windows be shut as soon as the sun has left them, to retain the warmth.

201. It is recommended, in the management of plants in the Green-House, to open the mould in which they are set occasionally. A little fresh earth may be scattered on the pots, and over this placed a small quantity of manure. The plants must be watered when their leaves begin to curl or wither, and the decayed ones plucked off. This operation should not, however, be very frequently repeated, as it will injure the plant.

202. Green-House plants should be kept out as long as possible in autumn, to render them hardy, great care being taken, however, that they be not exposed to injury from frost. If the windows and doors of a Green-House be kept open day and night as long as there is safety from the frost, the plants will be nearly as well off as in the open air, and little danger encountered by them. Precipitation in housing should on the one hand be avoided, and danger from the cold and frost on the other guarded against.

203. Some have prepared a very useful kind of Green-House, by excavating the earth on the southern side of a barn, sinking it partly under the floor of the hay apartment, to a proper depth. Glazing is then resorted to as before described. The hay above prevents the entrance of the cold. Care is to be taken that the room be not sunk so deep, or so far back under the barn, as to exclude the direct rays of the sun in the middle of the day. By placing a suitable compost at the bottom, and having tight walls and sufficient glazing, a Green-House may be constructed in this way that seldom if ever will require the heat of a stove.

———

STEM OR TRUNK OF PLANTS.

204. The part of the plant that rises upward, sustaining the leaves, flowers, and fruit, is termed the universal stalk, or stem. Contrary to the root, that plunges downward into the earth, this rises upward.

205. In the Lily, it is simple and undivided. In most plants, it is

branched. The arrangement, that branches assume, gives, in a considerable degree, to plants their peculiar form. This variety is the basis of botanical distinction.

206. If the stem be simple and hollow, rising like that of the grasses and having knots and joints, it is called a *Culm*. If simple and hollow, without leaves or branches, as that of a Dandelion flower, it is termed a *Scape*, from the Latin *scapus*, the shank of a candlestick.

207. When it is topped at the summit with a leaf, as in the Ferns, it is termed a *Stipe*, from the Latin *stipus*, a stake. If it be *soft*, like that of most weeds it is termed *herbaceous*, like herbs ; and, if hard and woody, it is called *arboreous*, from the Latin *arbor*, a tree. The former, in our latitude, are generally *annuals*, and the latter *perennials*.

208. The stem is sometimes of an almost uniformly solid substance, like the trunks of trees, and sometimes hollow, as in many of the Reeds and herbaceous plants.

209. In woody plants, it consists of several distinct parts, that are known by different names. In many trees, we find, 1. Externally, the *epidermis*, or *cuticle*, sometimes termed *scarf skin*. It is the external covering of the plant, and somewhat analagous to the skin in animals. The term *epidermis* is from the Greek *epi*, upon, *dermon*, the back, because covering the plant, as the skin covers the back of animals.

210. It varies in thickness, but is generally an exquisitely delicate film or membrane, in which, as far as we can judge, the vital principle seems to be extinct. It forms, both in the animal and vegetable, a fine but essential barrier between life and death.

211. In the Birch and Currant, it often becomes disengaged, to give place to new layers. It is less prone to decomposition than other parts. In most old trees, its texture is continually scaling off externally, and the stem supplied with new layers from within. When spread over the delicate parts of the flower, its texture must be almost inconceivably fine. On the Plane-tree or Button-wood, on the contrary, it is coarse.

212. It is supposed to admit of the passage of fluids, from within as well as from without. In many grasses, and in the Rattans, it contains a flinty substance. In succulent plants, inhabiting sandy and dry countries, it prevents transpiration, that might be so great as to destroy them.

213. Beneath the *epidermis*, or cuticle as it is commonly called, and next in order below it we find what has been termed the *Cellular Integ-*

ument. This is nothing more than a dark-green, semi-organized pulp, on which the *cuticle* reposes.

214. It appears like a distinct or separate epidermis in an incipient state, rather than a true and proper pulp. This tissue is sometimes considered under two divisions, exterior and interior, the latter being less coloured, and composed of regular hexagonal cells. The exterior layer is the seat of the colour of branches and leaves. This part may be seen very perfect in the branch of a Horse Chestnut.

215. Immediately under or rather imbedded in the Cellular Integument, we next find what has been termed the *Vascular Layer.* It consists of distinct bundles of entire vessels, each of which is so arranged as to present, in the transverse section of the stem, a semi-lunar aspect. These vessels are supposed to convey downward the proper juice (*succus proprius*) of the plant.

216. Immediately under the Vascular Bundles, we find another layer, constituting the internal boundary of the bark. This is termed the LIBER, from the Latin *liber,* a book, because anciently used as a writing material.

217. Dr. Smith makes but *three* divisions of the bark, 1st. The *Epidermis,* or *Cuticle,* externally. 2d. The *Cellular Integument* immediately under it, consisting of the succulent or pulpy substance that affords the green colouring of the leaves and bark, termed *Cellular* because contained in hexagonal *cells* ; and 3d. The *Liber,* or white bark next the wood.

218. In the *Daphne Lagetto,* or Lace-tree, this affords a very beautiful vegetable gauze or lace, that is sometimes employed as an article of dress.

219. Underneath the Liber or Bark we find next in order the white, soft wood, termed *Alburnum,* from the Latin *albus,* white, because of its colour. It consists of numerous concentric layers, that are very distinct.

220. If we cut across the trunk of a tree, we find the internal layers of a firmer texture, harder, and often of a different colour from those of the external, or *Alburnum.* This internal hard wood is termed the *Lignum,* or true wood. Enclosed in or near the centre of this, we find in many trees the medullary substance termed the *Pith.*

221. In recapitulating the respective parts of the trunk or stem of a woody plant, we may then say, that externally is, 1st. The *Epidermis,* or *Cuticle* ; 2d. The *Cellular Integument* ; 3d. The *Liber* ; 4th. The

Alburnum, or white wood; 5th. The Hard-wood, or *Lignum* ; and 6th. The *Medulla*, or *Pith*.

222. If the trunk or stem run directly upward, it is termed *straight* ; if nearly so, *erect ;* if bent considerably from a perpendicular, *oblique*. If first bent, it afterwards assumes an upright direction, it is said to be an *ascending* stem. If it have joints, and is bent so as to form angles at these joints, it is termed *geniculate*. When growing in a zig-zag direction, it is called *flexuose*.

223. Some plants descend, and bend, forming an arch, and then gradually turn upward. These are said to be *declined*. If they fall on the ground through weakness, they are termed *procumbent*. If they run along the ground horizontally, they are termed *prostrate*, and *repent* when they creep along, giving off roots like the ivy. Such stems upon the ground are called *runners*.

224. When a stem attaches itself to foreign bodies, and climbs upon them, it is said to be a *climbing* plant. If it effect this by twisting about them, like the Hop, it is called a *twining* stem.

225. The trunks of trees often attain to an immense magnitude. A Chestnut-tree grew at Tamworth, England, which was fifty-two feet in circumference. It was planted in the year 800, and in the reign of Stephen, in 1135, was made a boundary, and called the Great Chestnut-tree. In 1759, it bore nuts which produced young trees. Trees of *this species* are frequently found in Ohio of more than thirty feet in circumference.

226. Trees of the *Pine* genus are found on the Western coast of North-America, whose magnitude and height are truly astonishing. Some of them are 250 or 300 feet in height.

227. The Banyan-tree often attains to an immense magnitude. Ives tells us, that in his voyage to India he saw a Banyan, near Trevan de Parum, " sufficiently large to shelter ten thousand men." Dr. Fryer alludes to some so large as to shade " *thirty thousand horse and men*" singly.

228. On an island in the Narbudda, a few miles from Barroach, grows one said to be more remarkable than any other in India. All travellers speak of it as " the wonder of the vegetable world." It is " two thousand feet in circumference, and sufficiently large for armies to encamp under its branches."

DD

229. The stem of the Grape often extends to a great length. Vines are described of between 2,000 and 3,000 feet long, bearing 2,000 bunches of grapes, averaging more than 30 grapes to the bunch. Many of these vegetable prodigies are found in the rich valley of the Mississippi, particularly on the banks of the Ohio and Missouri.

ASCENT OF THE SAP

230. The sap, which is the nourishment of plants, is taken up from the earth by the radical fibres, and conveyed through the vessels of the *alburnum* to the leaves and flowers. It is there elaborated by the action of light, air, and moisture, into various substances. That, conveyed to the leaves, undergoing the changes wrought by various agents, returns towards the root, not through the same channel that it came, but through an appropriate set of vessels in the bark.

231. In its course downward, according to the opinion of many, it becomes exhausted in forming a new circle or layer of wood, and also one of bark. The number of these, it is believed, indicates, in most instances, the age of the tree, a new circle being formed every year.

232. Mr. Knight, and after him Dr. Smith, think that the sap undergoes a change in the *roots* previous to its entering the *leaves*, analogous to digestion in animals. The stem is by them deemed by no means an essential part, for there are many plants whose leaves and flowers grow directly from the root.

233. A part of the sap is conveyed into the flowers and fruit, where various fine and essential secretions are made from it, but by far the greatest portion of it is carried into the leaves. Of the great importance and utility of these to the plant itself, Mr. Knight's experiments have given us a very adequate and satisfactory notion.

234. In the leaves it is exposed to the action of light, air, and moisture, three very powerful agents. By them it is enabled to form various secretions. Here much superfluous matter passes off by perspiration.

235. These peculiar secretions not only give peculiar flavours and qualities to the leaf itself, but return by another set of vessels, as Mr. Knight has demonstrated, into the new layer of bark, which they nourish and enable in turn to secrete matter for a new layer of *alburnum* the ensuing year.

236. Dr. Smith thinks the peculiar secretions of plants, as the Gums, Resins, and the like, are principally secreted in the bark in an appropriate set of vessels. Among the most important substances, that are described as vegetable secretions, are *Starch, Gluten, Gum, Sugar, Acids Tannin, Extracts* of *Blue, Red, Green, Yellow, Brown,* Volatile and Fixed Oils, the Bitter Principle, the Narcotic Principle, Gum Elastic, Camphor, and the like.

237. From what has been said, we may readily perceive why the part of a branch above a leaf or leaf-bud dies when cut, as each portion receives nourishment from the leaf above it.

238. The vascular system of plants, then, it appears, is strictly annual. This is of course the case with herbaceous plants. It is true also in regard to trees.

239. The layer of *alburnum*, on the one hand, is added to the wood, and the *liber*, or inner layer of the bark, is on the other annexed to the layers formed during the preceding seasons. Neither have any share in the process of vegetation for the year ensuing.

240. Plants are said to possess the power of conveying their appropriate fluids equally well in either direction. It is indifferent, if this be true, whether a cutting of any kind be planted with its upper or lower end in the ground. Mr. Knight informs us, however, that cuttings so inverted retain so much of their original nature, in regard to their sap-vessels, as to deposit new wood *above* the leaf-buds, instead of *below* them. It is said by some writers, that *inverted* cuttings seldom succeed or grow at all.

241. Dr. Hope, of Edinburgh, in 1781 made an experiment upon *three* Willows standing in a row, by engrafting them all together. He then cut off the communication between the central one and the earth, so that it became suspended in the air, and was nourished merely through its lateral branches. Dr. Hales informs us of a similar experiment, successfully performed. The central tree, suspended between the two others, exhibited no different appearance, excepting that it came into leaf several days later in spring

242. The question may be asked, how the *sap* is known to ascend through the Alburnum of the trunk and branches, and whence its origin. During the season of its ascent, its motion is upward, and that incessantly. Its amount often exceeds in weight the substance of the whole tree through which it ascends. It evidently rises from the earth, for no other source could furnish such vast supplies.

243. A tree may be divested of its bark, and yet yield sap, and produce its usual supply of leaves and more than its usual quantity of fruit. It does not therefore rise through the *bark*.

244. Mr. Knight removed the pith from a young plant, and it continued to grow with its former luxuriance, and in due time produced fruits. The sap, it would appear then, rises not through the *pith*.

245. It does not pass through the central portion of the woody stem, for the vessels of the *lignum* are often nearly obliterated, and, even during the bleeding season, do not afford the fluid. It only remains then that the ascent of sap must be through the *alburnum*, or external soft white wood of the trunk, in *woody* plants. It ascends through parts analogous in herbaceous plants.

246. It has been observed, that the sap ascends with very great force through the trunks of several plants. It is said that the power, with which it is elevated through a Grape-vine, is so great, as to equal a force sufficient to raise a column of water 40 feet.

247. Passing from the root, through the trunk and its branches, it arrives at the leaves and flowers. It here is exposed to the action of *light* and *air*, the superfluous and watery parts passing off through the pores of the leaves, which at the same time give off, as is supposed by many, *oxygen gas*, and inhale or absorb *carbonic acid gas*. This is thought to be particularly the case during the presence of sunshine and light.

248. After undergoing the changes wrought in the leaves, it returns through an appropriate set of vessels to the bark, probably there to undergo further changes, where it is converted into a new circle or layer of wood, and into various vegetable secretions.

249. As the number of concentric circles are supposed to indicate the age of the tree, one forming every year, and during the spring and summer in our northern latitudes, recourse has been had to these for determining the age of those *tumuli* or immense mounds, so common in our western states and territories. If these can lead us to any definite conclusion in regard to their age, they prove them to be of very high antiquity.

250. The *wood* of plants is very various in regard to density and firmness. In the Oak and Lignum-Vitæ or Guaiacum tree it is exceed-

ingly compact and hard ; in the Pine and Cotton Wood, soft and yielding. This difference is probably owing to difference in density and closeness of fibre.

251. The central layers of the Lignum-Vitæ are *black*, those of the Oak and Laburnum *brown*, of the Mahogany and Log-wood, *red*. The outer layers of unripe wood, or *alburnum*, are much sooner ripened into perfect wood in vigorous trees, than in others that are not so. This change is often effected earlier on one side of the same tree than on the other, because its growth is more vigorous. The alburnum, when divested of its bark, acquires density and hardness in a single summer.

252. It is termed the *sap* by the Machinist, because often filled with this fluid, and is rejected by him where durability and strength are required. The trees of hot climates have but indistinctly-marked circles, because their growth is less interrupted by change of temperature and seasons. The alburnum was regarded by the ancients as analogous to the *fat* in animals, and was supposed to be destined, like it, for the nourishment of the plant during winter.

RINGING, PRUNING, ETC.

253. Some improvement in the cultivation of fruits has resulted from *Ringing*. The operation is performed by taking a narrow circle of bark from the body of the tree. *Girdling* is also practised in the new settlements of the United States for the purpose of clearing the land of forest-trees. It consists in taking a circle of the *alburnum* with the bark. A check is thus put to the ascent and descent of the sap. If a circle of the bark and alburnum be removed, the tree dies sooner or later. It sometimes leaves out on the ensuing summer, however, in consequence of a sort of vicarious influence exerted by the cellular substance of the trunk, but soon perishes.

254. If a ring of the *bark only* be removed, leaving the alburnum, untouched, the sap may continue to ascend, but is obstructed in its descent. This operation may be safely performed on a tree if the ring taken be sufficiently narrow, that the space may be filled with new bark from above during the same season. In some cases, according to Du Hamel, the whole trunk may be stripped with impunity, and even with advantage if the tree readily form new bark. It is often necessary to cover the trunk artificially, however, while the new bark

is forming.   Trees will often live 15 or 20 years after being thus deprived of their bark.

255.   The productiveness of plants may often be much increased by thus intersecting the bark.   It is explained on the principle, that the sap, ascending as freely as before to the branches and leaves, is there detained, being prevented from descending by the removal of the bark, and consequently accumulating, a larger supply is afforded for the nourishment and perfection of the fruit.   The operation is often practised by gardeners.   They thereby obtain larger and earlier fruits than they otherwise would do, as likewise of a richer quality.   Grapes are often much improved in this way, and where the circle is so narrow as to close up during the same season, the vines are not much injured by the operation.

256.   This at least is the opinion of many.   Some, however, believe the practice of ringing very injurious to plants.   They deny that the trunk may be stripped with impunity, however readily the tree may form new bark.

257.   Mr. Knight informs us that, having been requested by one of his customers to endeavour to preserve a favourite mulberry-tree, which for many years had flourished on her lawn, but which with the exception of one very large branch, was either dead or decaying, he waited till the sap had ascended, and then barked the branch completely round near its junction with the trunk of the tree.   Having filled three sacks with mould he tied them round that part of the branch which had been barked, and by means of one or two old watering pots, which were kept filled with water, and placed over the sacks, from which the water gradually distilled, the mould in the sacks was sufficiently moistened for his purpose.   Towards the end of the year he examined the sacks, and found them filled with numerous small fibrous roots, which the sap having no longer the bark for its conductor into the main roots of the tree, had thus expended itself in throwing out.   A hole having been prepared, the branch was sawn off below the sacks, and planted with them, the branch being propped securely.   The next summer it flourished and bore fruit, and is still in a thriving condition.

258.   Trees often acquire so much top as not to bear fruit plentifully unless pruned.   By taking away a part of the branches an additional supply of sustenance is afforded to those that remain.   The consequence is often, an additional quantity of fruit.   Pruning is very

necessary in the cultivation of the vine, as well as in various kinds of fruit trees. Care should be taken that plants be not deprived of too large a portion of their branches and leaves, lest the root should suffer for want of nourishment. Pruning should be performed by separating with a sharp instrument, those branches that appear the least flourishing, as likewise those that are dead and dry. After this operation has been carefully performed, the wound that the tree has received by dissevering the branch, should be covered over with some mixture to prevent the access of the atmosphere to the wounded part. The following paste has been recommended for covering the wounds of trees, and for the place where grafts are inserted. It consists of a mixture of clay and cow manure, diluted with water, of the consistency of paste, or common plaster. After the decayed wood is removed entirely and the edges of the bark and sound wood is made smooth by a sharp instrument, this composition is applied with a brush, until it forms a coat of from one eighth to a quarter of an inch in thickness. This adheres firmly without cracking until the wound heals. Some recommend a compost of fresh manure, ashes and slaked lime, mixed in various portions.

259. The design in pruning is not only to deprive plants of their useless branches and buds, but to lay open and expose every part to the air and light. By thus being exposed, they are enabled to mature and ripen their fruits.

260. If the branches of a young tree, issuing at and above the requisite height, be made, by pruning, to diverge from the trunk in every direction above the horizontal, and the interior of these be carefully kept from any interference with each other for a few years, little pruning will afterwards be necessary.

261. Various complicated systems of pruning the Apple, Pear, Plum, and the like, have been described by different writers. It is sufficient in pruning the Apple and other standard trees, that the points of the external branches should be rendered thin and pervious to the light, so that the internal parts be not wholly shaded. The light should penetrate deeply among the branches, but not entirely through to those on the opposite side of the tree.

262. Trees, judiciously managed in this way, will bear fruit on their inner as well as outer branches. They will sustain a larger amount of it without the danger of breaking. The weight upon a branch is in the

compound ratio of its quantity and its horizontal distance from the point of suspension.

263.   When the growth of any plant is weak and reclining, the principal stem may be trained to a considerable height, before it is allowed to produce shoots for permanent branches.   The horizontal and pendent ones, under these circumstances, should be dissevered.   The principal or leading stem should be encouraged, to prevent a division into two boughs. Thus forked, it is apt to split asunder when under the weight of the fruit.

264.   Mr. Knight thinks, large branches should seldom if ever be removed while young trees are in a nursery.   The form preferred by the French for a tree is a *pyramidial* or *sub-cylindrical* one.   This, and the *conical*, are those most esteemed by the Dutch.

265.   The best season for pruning is immediately preceding or during the rising of the sap.   Branches, taken away, ought to be cut close and even, leaving no stumps of limbs.   If pruning be done early, while the branches are small, there will seldom be occasion for amputating larger limbs at a more advanced period.

266.   Whatever operates in repressing the too vigorous growth of a plant, by obstructing the free circulation of its sap and causing it to accumulate, has a tendency to render it fruitful.   To effect this, different expedients are resorted to, such as, 1. *Ligatures*, and *ringing*, sometimes termed *decortication* and *circumcision*.   2. Different modes of *pruning*.   3. *Transplanting*, and confining the roots to a limited space.   4. Engrafting on stocks of a very slow growth.   5. *Bending the branches*, and sometimes by all these various modes united.

267.   The *alburnum*, situated above a *decorticated* space considerably exceeds in specific gravity that formed below it.   The same effect of accumulation is observed in the fruit, both in regard to its maturation and quality.   When a branch is small, or the space, from which the bark is taken, is considerable, a morbid maturity is induced, and the fruit becomes worthless.   The part below the decorticated space is likewise very scantily supplied with nutriment, and almost ceases to grow.   It sometimes perishes for want of suitable nourishment.

268.   *Decortication*, or Girdling, is sometimes performed to cause trees to produce blossoms, or as a means of making them set more freely. The ring of bark, in these cases, must be taken off in early summer, preceding the seasons at which blossoms are required.   If for the purpose of

fruit, on the contrary, the operation should be delayed until the bark will readily part from the *alburnum*.	The breadth of the decorticated space must correspond with the size of the branch.

269.	Girdling, or *Ringing*, when practised on small trees, proves almost invariably injurious.	A better practice is, to apply a tight ligature, on the preceding summer, about the branch, which answers in a great measure, the purpose of ringing.

270.	We may say, in general terms, that the operation of *Ringing*, or Girdling, consists in making two annular incisions quite round the limb through the bark, at the distance of about three-eighths of an inch asunder, more or less, according to the size and thriftiness of the tree, making a perpendicular slit, and removing the ring of bark to the wood. When done for the increase of *blossom buds*, it should be done in June or July.	When for increase and maturity of fruit, it is common to perform this operation at the time the tree is coming into leaf, in the spring.

271.	The practice of BARKING fruit trees was brought into notice in Britain, by Mr. Lyon of Edinburgh, about fifteen years since.	This operation, is now frequently performed in England upon Apple and Pear-trees, and upon Vines under glass.	It is also common in the Netherlands to perform this operation upon various fruit-trees, as likewise upon many of the ornamental flowering shrubs and trees.

272.	It consists in cutting off with a common hooked pruning-knife all the outer bark, quite down to the *liber*.	This is recommended to be performed in February at the winter pruning.	It is not common to practise it except upon *old trees* of eight or ten years of age.	If the experiment be made upon young ones, the bark must not be taken so deeply.	Mr. Loudon and others assert this to be a never-failing method of greatly improving, when properly performed, the quality and size of the fruit of the Apple and Pear, and likewise of the Vine.

273.	BENDING THE LIMBS of trees has been resorted to also for the purpose of rendering them productive of fruit.	This may be performed on every species of tree without disadvantage.	The operation consists in bending each limb or twig to a position below the horizontal one, while it is yet in a growing state.	This is generally done about the last of June or first of July, varying somewhat with the species and nature of the tree. By the operation a momentary stop is put to its growth.	The sap becomes concentrated, and forms fruit-buds for the production of numerous

EE

blossoms on the spring of the following year. If shoots burst forth from other parts of the tree, in consequence of the stoppage and accumulation of sap, these may be nipped off, all excepting a few eyes that may be allowed to remain. The Chinese have long understood and practised this method of rendering fruit-trees productive. When judiciously performed, its effects are very extraordinary upon trees in causing them to yield abundantly both fruits and flowers.

274. DWARFING, as it is termed by gardeners, consists in inoculating fruit trees of one kind upon stocks of the same or of different kinds of comparatively slow growth. The circulation of the sap is in consequence retarded, and the effect upon the plant somewhat analogous to that produced by Girdling.

275. The Apple is often *dwarfed*, by being inoculated upon the Paradise stock—the Peach, by being inserted upon a slow-growing Plum —the Pear upon the Quince-bush, and the like.   The Chinese extend the practice of dwarfing to flowering and other ornamental trees of various kinds.   Oranges, Peaches, Plums, and Grapes, are managed in this way among them.   They form their Dwarfs on the most fruitful limbs of bearing trees, as well as upon the stunted and slow-growing ones. French and English gardeners practise dwarfing, deeming it admirably adapted to large fruits, especially Pears for summer use, which they declare to be better in quality, earlier, and more abundant, than they otherwise would be.

276. As the leaves are thought to be exclusively the laboratory, in which the sap is prepared that goes to form the fruit, no change in quality is effected by a change of locality, or the engrafting of a *scion* of one variety, species, or even genus upon the *stock* of another.   Hence the Pear engrafted upon the Quince partakes in no degree of the quality of the latter.

276. The following operation is commonly performed in Spring, when trees are in full blossom. The branches selected are those found most loaded with flowers. The bark is to be removed quite round the branch, to the breadth of about half its diameter. The incision is covered with a large ball of composition similar to that of the grafting clay. For large trees, as the Elm, a covering of coarse cloth or straw is often used. In eight or ten weeks, when the roots are formed and sufficiently developed to preserve the vital energy of the plant, the branch may be

separated.   Any exuberance of growth is repressed by clipping the branches and leaves.

277.   Whether trees be for ornament or fruit, if they are to be potted, their branches must be bent and contorted by wires and other mechanical means, to accomplish the desired object.

278.   *Training* is practised in many parts of France, the object of which is, to induce plants and trees to assume particular forms in their growth.   The *pyramidal* form is most esteemed for fruit-trees, such as the Apple, Pear, Peach, Plum, Cherry, Apricot, Vine, &c.   This mode of training is called EN QUENOUILLE by the French, in allusion to a resemblance in form, of trees thus managed, to the ancient *distaff*.

279.   Some trees do not readily incline to throw out lateral or side branches.   They are induced to do so by pinching or clipping off their tops, as soon as they have attained sufficient height for the *first tier* of branches.   The main stem is again pinched off for the formation of a *second tier*, and so on successively at different periods of growth, till the tree has attained the requisite height.   The beautiful pyramidal form so much desired is thus attained, and thereby the tree better fitted for the production of blossoms and fruit.

280.   If the lateral branches incline to grow too fast, they must also be clipped, to preserve the proportion and beauty of the tree.   The operation of clipping requires much care and experience in order that it may be properly performed.   This produces a temporary suspension of the growth of the tree.   If the clipping be too near the top, only *one* vertical shoot will be produced—if a little lower, *two branches* will put forth—but if it be shortened still lower, *three* or *four* lateral shoots will put out just below, and a top or vertical one also.

PROPAGATION BY LAYERS.

281.   Plants are sometimes propagated by *layers* and *cuttings*.   The Roses, and many other flowering shrubs are extensively diffused in this way.   LAYERS are branches left on the parent stock, and bent down and fastened several inches, as the case may require, below the surface of the earth, leaving the extreme point out of ground.

282.   A flat stone is sometimes placed on the earth, immediately above the *layer*, to keep the earth cool, and retain the moisture.   The branch or shoot, thus bent, sends off numerous small roots at the part

covered by the earth. When these have become sufficiently numerous
to supply the new-formed plant with nourishment, the branch is severed
from its parent stock. It afterwards may be *transplanted*, if desired.
The suckers or limbs of trees are thus managed, for the purpose of multi-
plying individuals of *valuable* and *scarce varieties.*

283.   Some particular kinds of trees and shrubs are with extreme difficulty propagated in this way. Such must be TONGUED, as the gardeners term it. This operation consists in cutting the layer half off beneath
the surface and below an eye or bud, and splitting it up an inch or more.
The cleft is generally kept open by a small wedge. The operation should
be performed in spring, and the branch be separated from the parent stock
on the autumn or spring following.

284.   In the cultivation of *herbaceous* plants and *shrubs in pots*, the
pots should be frequently turned round to prevent the plants from growing *crooked.* They will invariably incline towards the sun or light, and
decline from their erect position, if this precaution be not taken. The
mould on the top should become dry before they are furnished with an
additional supply of water. If plants are to be kept in pots year after
year, the balls of earth should be taken out in October, and the sides and
bottom shaved off with a sharp knife to the depth of an inch, more or
less, varying with the size. They are then replaced, and the pot filled
with a fresh compost of very rich earth.

285.   Many shrubs and trees may be raised from CUTTINGS. These
are pieces *cut* from trees, shrubs, or plants of the last growth. They
should generally retain a small piece of the growth immediately preceding the last, of the ripened wood. They are taken generally from eight
to twelve inches in length—sometimes longer and sometimes shorter, according to circumstances and the size of the plant. They are commonly
taken when the sap is active, and with six or eight buds or joints. They
are cut transversely and smoothly with a sharp knife or other instrument,
near a joint or bud of the previous growth, or between the two last
growths. The cuttings should be placed in rich, moist earth, in a shady
situation, and the ground about them be kept moist by frequent watering.
Old hay, or something of a like nature, is often placed over the surface to
retain the moisture, especially if the weather be dry. CUTTINGS, taken
from *herbaceous plants*, should be taken from such parts as do not manifest a tendency to flower.

286.   If the *cutting* be planted in a flower-pot, the pot may advanta-

geously be placed in the earth, in a shady situation, and covered with an inverted glass, for a short time, to preserve a moist atmosphere about it. If it send out *roots*, *branches* will also soon appear, otherwise the cutting quickly *dies*. Two-thirds of the length of the *cutting* is generally buried beneath the earth. In some plants, if the bottom of the cutting be not squared and pressed to the bottom of the pot, it will not take root. Such plants as require artificial heat in the soil and a confined atmosphere, will receive much advantage by being covered with a bell-glass. This moderates transpiration, and raises the temperature, in some degree within.

287. Plants are sometimes propagated by transferring the bud or germ of one plant to the stock or branch of a kindred kind. Desirable and *scarce varieties* are thereby multiplied. The operation is principally practised upon small trees, and only while the sap flows freely. August and September is thought to be the most proper season for *budding*.

288. The buds or germs are taken from the ripest twigs of the year's growth, separating the leaves from the footstalk. A perpendicular incision is made into the smooth bark of the tree or shrub to be engrafted upon, an inch or an inch and a half in length, quite through the bark. At the the top of this a cross-slit is made of a similar length, or nearly, forming a cross. This also should be made quite through to the wood, a little slanting downwards. Raise the bark carefully on both sides with the handle of the knife, taking precaution not to injure the sap-wood or structure containing the *cambium*, or green sap. The bud is then to be taken from the twig by a small sharp knife. The knife is to be entered half or three quarters of an inch below the eye or bud and quite through the bark, separating the bark to the same distance above the bud. A very thin slip of wood is also taken of about one-third the length of the bud. The bud is then immediately inserted in the stock at the bottom of the slit, and between the bark and the wood. The top of the bud being squared even with the cross-cut, every part except the eye is firmly bound and covered with strong wet bass matting.

289. Some prefer making the cross-cut at the bottom instead of the top of the perpendicular slit, and to insert the bud upwards instead of downwards. Either mode generally proves successful. The string is to be taken off in about ten or fifteen days, otherwise it will press upon the bark. After the bud has united with its new stock and become a constituent member of the plant, the stock ingrafted upon may be cut off

about a quarter of an inch above the bud.   This should be done in spring
before the sap begins to rise, leaving the stock sloping down on the opposite side.

290.   *Budding* is sometimes performed by cutting from a small stock,
a thin narrow scollop of wood of about an inch in length, and taking from
a twig a piece, of like form and size.   The latter is then instantly applied and fitted perfectly at top and bottom, on one, and, if possible,
both of its sides, and firmly bound with wet bass matting.   This is done
in spring.   In case of failure, it may be repeated in July or August.
Roses are often propagated by budding in this way.   This mode is practised among the French.   It is termed SCOLLOP BUDDING.   *Thouin* has
described more than twenty different modes of budding plants.

291.   *Roses*, budded in this way in June, often grow and blossom the
same year.   The young and unripe wood is prepared by separating the
leaves, leaving only their footstalks.   In ten or fifteen days, the buds are
sufficiently developed for insertion.   The stock is cut off, six or eight inches above the insertion of the bud, at the time of inoculation.   Strings
of bass matting, previously dipped in a solution of alum and white soap,
and dried, are used for bandage.

GRAFTING.

292.   There are various modes of grafting, such as Whip or Splice
Grafting, Cleft Grafting, Saddle Grafting, Root Grafting, Side Grafting,
Grafting by Approach, and the like.   More than forty different modes
are described.

293.   Whip or Splice Grafting is principally practised on small *stocks*
of nearly equal size with the *scion.*   The *Scion*, which consists of the
young twig of the former years' growth, is cut of a length of three or
four inches.   *This*, as likewise the *stock*, is cut obliquely or sloping for
an inch or more, and *tongued.*   The *tonguing* is performed by cutting a
slit in the middle of the slope of the stock downwards, and a corresponding slit in the scion upwards.   Both are then accurately joined, that one
or both of the sides may coincide.   The parts are afterwards securely
bound with a matting string, covered as before described.   Grafting clay
is sometimes used for a covering.   When the stock and scion are united,
the string is removed.

294.   CLEFT GRAFTING is performed upon larger stocks, of one or two

inches in diameter. The head of the stock is sawed off at a part free from knots, and the top pared smooth with a sharp instrument. It is then split down with a thin knife through the centre, to the depth of two or three inches, and a wedge put in to keep it open for the reception of the scion. The scion, being prepared in the form of a wedge, with a bud if possible in the upper part to ensure success, is inserted so that the inner bark of the scion and the stock will accurately meet each other. The whole is then carefully covered with grafting clay, or composition, except two or three buds of each scion. In large stocks two scions, one on each side, are sometimes inserted, and in very large ones sometimes four—the stock being quartered. This mode of grafting may be practised on small as well as large trees.

295. Another mode of Grafting, practised by Mr. Knight and others, termed *Saddle Grafting*, is performed upon very small stocks, by preparing the upper part of the *stock* in the form of a wedge, by two sloping cuts one on each side. The *scion* is prepared by splitting it upward, and paring out the middle part on each side to a point. If the scion and stock be of equal size, the adjustment may be made perfect. If unequal, one side must at least be made to fit, and exactly meet. The whole is secured by a string and covered with clay, as before directed. This, in due time, must be removed.

296. ROOT-GRAFTING is often performed upon grape-vines, just below the level of the surface of the earth by the usual modes of *Cleft-Grafting*. *Pieces* of root may be thus grafted, where suitable stocks are scarce.

297. *Grafting by Approach* is generally practised upon trees and shrubs that succeed with difficulty if grafted in the other modes. As before remarked, it consists in uniting the branches of one growing tree with the stock of another in its immediate vicinity. The tree grafted upon must of course grow very near the tree that is ingrafted. The limbs of each tree to be united are prepared with a long sloping cut of several inches, nearly to their centre. The parts thus prepared are brought accurately together, and firmly secured by bandages, and covered as before directed. After the trees are fully united, they may be separated with a sharp knife, by dissevering them below their junction.

298. Grafting Clay is generally made one-third horse manure free from litter, one-third cow manure, one third clay. A small amount of hair is sometimes added to this composition, after being well beaten. The ingredients ought to be thoroughly mixed.

299. *Grafting Composition*, as it is sometimes termed, is generally formed of three parts rosin, three parts bees-wax, and one part tallow, melted together. When melted, it is usually poured into water, and worked up, like shoemakers-wax, by the hands. This composition is spread on slips of brown paper with a brush when soft, and applied as a wrapper.

FORMS OF STEMS, BRANCHES.

300. The trunks of plants, when round like a pillar, are termed *cylindric* ; when half-round, *semi-cylindric*, as that of the Butomus. When like a two-edged sword, they are called *ancipital*, from the Latin *anceps*, two-edged. Stems are said to be *compressed* when flattened on their sides ; *angular*, having corners. When they have *three* angles, they are termed *triquetrous*, from the Latin *triqueter*, three-cornered.

301. The branches of a stem may be *erect, horizontal, incurved, recurved, reflexed, declined, spreading, diffuse, devaricate,* or *fastigiate.*

302. Stems, branching out from their extremities, are termed *proliferous*, from the Latin *proles*, an offspring. If, like that of the Misletoe, the stem divide into two parts, it is termed *dichotomous*, from the Greek *dis*, twice, and *temno*, to split, meaning forked.

303. When the stem terminates by equal branches, so as to make a level like the roof of a house, it is said to be *fastigiate*, from the Latin *fastigium*, the roof. If it be subdivided several times, bearing numerous flowers on the branchlets, it is said to be *paniculate.*

304. If the branches spring from the stem first on one side and then on the other at nearly equal distances, they are said to be *alternate* ; and *opposite*, if they shoot out in pairs on opposite sides. They are sometimes scattered *irregularly*, without apparent order.

305. When disposed circularly around the trunk, they are said to be *verticilate*, from the Latin *verto*, to turn. The branches of the Yew-tree, and some others, are so thickly and irregularly disposed about the trunk, as almost entirely to hide it. Some stems are wholly without branches, but most are furnished with them. The branches are sometimes called the *arms* of trees.

306. Some stems are too flexible or weak to sustain their own

weight. These are often furnished with means of support. Little thread-like appendages or *claspers* arise from the branches opposite the leaves, as in the Vine. These, which are termed *tendrils*, from the Latin *teneo*, to hold, often stretch out and lay hold of objects within their reach, for the purpose of affording support to the parent stem.

307. The *tendril* sometimes springs from near the origin of the branch or leaf, and is said to be *axillary*, as in the Passion-flower. In a few instances, it arises from the leaf itself, and, *very rarely*, from the *peduncle* or flower-stalk. In the Clematis, the *peduncle* performs the office of a *tendril*, as well as that of flower-stalk.

308. In the *Annona Hexapetala* it forms a hook, which grasps the neighbouring branches, that are compelled to help sustain its very heavy fruit. The *tendril* usually proceeds in a straight direction while grow-ing, until it meets with some object to cling to. It then lays hold of it by assuming the spiral form, and *clasps* the parent plant firmly to it.

309. Some *claspers* turn from *right* to *left*, and some from *left* to *right*. There are a *few* that twine in either of these directions indif-ferently.

310. The appendages of attachment in some *creepers* and *climbers* do not twine at all, as in the Ivy. They penetrate the bark of trees, and, if denied access to these, they cling to the naked walls, old trees, fences, and whatever comes in their way. Attaching themselves firmly, as their stems elongate they often rise to the summit of the loftiest trees, and reach the tops of highest battlements, giving greenness and beauty with their foliage to ruin itself.

311. The Common Creeper has branched tendrils. Their minute extremities cling powerfully to the hardest and smoothest rocks. This is the only native Ivy that is well suited to " decorate and beautify with foliage not its own the cheerless wall." The Ivy " that poets sing" is not an American plant.

312. The whole *stem* in some plants takes upon it the office of *tendril* or *clasper*. Examples of this may be seen in the Beans, Hops, and the like. The *tendril* is termed *foliar* when springing from the leaf, *petio-lar* springing from the *petiole*, *peduncular* from the *peduncle*, *axillary* from the *axil*. It may also be *revolute*, *involute*, *simple*, or *forked*.

EPIDERMIS, OR CUTICLE.

313. This exterior covering is often distinguished for its delicacy and singular beauty. In the root it is coarse and hard like crust, forming a considerable part of the bark. In the leaves, flowers, and tender shoots, on the contrary, it is a fine colourless and transparent film not thicker than gossamer.

314. It is colourless when detached or separated. When adherent, it is always tinged with some peculiar shade. This it borrows from the part immediately beneath it. It is green in the leaf, and in fruits and flowers assumes all the beautiful variety of colours and tints imaginable.

315. In woody plants, as the Birch, it often becomes spontaneously disengaged. In herbaceous plants, on the contrary, and in the leaf, flower, and fruit of other plants, it never disengages itself spontaneously, nor is it regenerated and restored when once destroyed.

316. Saussure asserts, that, in the leaves of the Digitalis and Jasmine, it is composed of two layers, the inner one being a net-work, interspersed with numerous little glands, while the outer one is a fine, transparent membrane, destitute of organization.

317. The glands here alluded to are supposed by some to be mere pores or apertures, perforating the *epidermis* or *cuticle*. They are regarded as organs of respiration. The number and magnitude of these is very various in different plants.

318. By observing how soon the faded branch or leaf is restored, when immersed in water, or how soon the recently dissevered branch withers, we may in some measure determine the magnitude and number of these pores.

319. Aquatic plants wither in a few moments, when their branches are detached from the stock or root, because furnished with numerous large pores, through which they discharge their fluids rapidly. The *Sempervivium* and Aaron's Rod, on the contrary, have few pores, and remain green several days, and sometimes several months.

320. The *Nine Bark, Spiræ Opulifolia,* as its name implies, has at least *nine* of the cortical layers forming its *epidermis*. The epidermis of straw gives it its strength, and the silex or flinty matter in the Rush is what renders it so obnoxious to animals. This part protects the young tree from injury, preserves the fruit from decay, retains the verdure in the leaf, and the evanescent fragrance and beauty in the flower.

CELLULAR INTEGUMENT.

321. The soft, juicy coat under the Epidermis, called the Cellular Integument, consisting of numerous cells, and forming a considerable part of the covering of the plant, is discernible in *herbaceous* plants, in *pulpy fruits*, in *leaves*, and in *flowers*. In the seed-lobes or *cotyledons* it is commonly *white*, in the leaves *green*, in flowers and fruits of almost *every colour*. It receives its tinge from the contents of its cell.

322. It has been before remarked, that it is composed of an assemblage of *hexagonal* or six-sided cells, resembling those of the *honeycomb*. The partitions of these are extremely fine and transparent. They are generally perforated with small pores, forming the medium of communication between the different cells. They are also bordered with a sort of small glandular ring. The respective parts appear very distinct when under the magnifying power of good glasses.

323. Its tissue appears extremely delicate, particularly in flowers. It is destroyed by the slightest pressure or by maceration in water. When the cells are emptied of their contents, this part appears colourless and transparent ; but when filled with juices, it assumes all the various colours of *red, yellow, brown, green, white, blue,* and the like, communicating its acquired colour to the epidermis or cuticle.

324. The mere *empty* cells make the *cellular membrane.* The cells, filled with their appropriate juices, constitute the *parenchyma*, or pulp. This pulp forms the great mass of succulent plants and *pulpy* fruits. As it is the seat of operations indispensably necessary to healthy vegetation, no plant can be destitute of it.

INNER BARK.

325. Beneath the Cellular Integument, we find the *cortical layers*, concentric and in all cases constituting the most essential portion of the bark. They are supposed to correspond in number with the age of the stem or branch. In some instances, they constitute almost the entire substance of the bark.

326. In the exterior of old layers, which are coarse and loose in their texture, they exhibit a conspicuous and indurated irregular net-work. This is principally composed of bundles of fibres running longitudinally.

They do not, however, ascend the stem directly, but wind more or less around its axis.

327. As the layers recede from the circumference, the net-work becomes finer and its texture more compact. The meshes of different layers often correspond, forming an aperture in the bark as far as they coincide with each other. These openings diminish in size as they penetrate towards the centre, and, in trunks of aged Oaks, Elms, and the like, the apertures widen into large gaps and chinks, still retaining, however, visible but rough traces of the net-work of the original layers. The parts have been laid bare by the decay of the *epidermis* and *cellular integument*, which in young trees was filled with the *pulpy substance*.

328. The *Liber*, or inner layer, (to which some have restricted the term *liber*,) is more delicate and at the same time more important than the other parts, whether we consider it in relation to the economy of vegetation or as subservient to the wants of man.

329. From it books were formerly made. The natives of Otaheite, in the Pacific, manufacture garments from the *liber* of a species of the Mulberry. Some of these are of great beauty, and wrought with much ingenuity. The *liber* of the *Linum*, or common Flax, affords us our linen " fine and white." Cordage and sail-cloth are made of that of the Hemp. The Lace-Bark of Jamaica, even when unwrought, affords a fine and beautiful *lace*, at once soft, flexible, shining, fine, and strong, like silk.

330. The cellular or intervening pulp appears to contain the peculiar secretions of plants, frequently in their most perfect state. If the base of the Cinnamon be macerated in water, the woody fibres of the net-work remain uninjured, while the intervening cellular substance, that contains those exquisite flavours of the bark, is disengaged. The astringent principle of the Oak is contained within this pulp, as likewise the peculiar vegetable secretions of most plants. These are often obtained by maceration in boiling water, and likewise in other ways.

331. The Pine tribe have no net-work in the constitution of the bark. The *liber* of the bark of these trees is composed only of *harebell* adhering fibres. The outer layers appear like dried plates of cellular integument, separated from each other by an intervening *epidermis*.

MEDULLA, OR PITH.

332. The soft spongy substances of many plants, in or near the centre of the stem, that extends from the roots to the extremity of the young branches, is termed the *pith*, or *medulla*, from the Latin *medula*, morrow. In the Ash it is compact and uninterrupted, in the Gorget composed of transverse partitions intersecting the tube of the stem. In the Thistles it resembles the spiders-web, and in the Hemlock forms a fine delicate lining of great brilliancy. In the Wild Rice it forms distinct partitions, that intersect the cavity of the stem. It is usually *green* when young, and, when old, *yellow, white,* or *brown.*

333. Its texture is very similar to that of the *cellular integument.* Its cells are large and generally filled with fluid, when the plant is young, as in the Elder. In old stems and branches, the fluid disappears, leaving the cell empty.

334. In some plants this substance is interspersed with fibres of a different texture from itself. These are readily distinguished from the pith, by their colour. They are often found imbedded in it. Examples are afforded us in the old stalks of Indian Corn, and the stem of the *Sambucus,* or Elder.

335. The use of the Pith in the economy of vegetation is little known. Some suppose, that its functions are the same as those of the *Cellular Tissue.* Linnæus, at one time, regarded it as the " source of nourishment and seat of vegetable life." Knight supposed it the reservoir of moisture to supply the leaves in a drought.

336. The *pith* of a plant may be destroyed without injury to its growth. The moisture that it contains is not sufficient in many plants to supply an hour's perspiration of a single leaf. These notions, therefore, of its purposes must be without foundation in truth.

VEGETABLE FIBRE AND VESSELS OF PLANTS.

337. In a transverse section of the concentric layers of the trunk of a woody plant, as the Oak and the like, there are exhibited numerous divergent or spreading plates of singular brightness, that have been named *Silver Grain,* in allusion to their bright colour.

338. The purpose of these seems to be to bind the annual circles of the wood together. They increase the strength of the timber and prevent it from being shattered to pieces. When destroyed, as sometimes happens in the Hemlock and other trees, we frequently see the annual layers separate from each other.

339. The *Silver Grain* is found, on close inspection, to consist of minute, parallel fibres, closely crowded together. They appear somewhat analogous to compressed cellular membranes. *Wood* is, therefore, composed of *longitudinal fibres*, forming a net-work and *cellular tissue*, extending in a transverse direction, the two sets of fibres being interwoven, like the warp and woof of a web.

340. The close, strong, and large fibres, often found imbedded in the pith or medullary substance of the cornstalk, and several other plants, are found to consist of a number of slender, thread-like, elastic portions, that may be easily subdivided. No art, however, can again divide the component parts to which these may be so easily reduced.

341. The net-work fibres of the wood and those of the *silver grain* may, in like manner, be separated from one another. These fibres differ in their structure and degree of strength. Hence it is that wood may be so easily split in the direction of its longitudinal fibres, but no art can split it in the direction of its transverse plates. Though the silver grain is of a strong, tough fibre, the other is much stronger.

342. The *firmness* of wood, and consequently its value for mechanical purposes, depends upon the *number* and *density* of its longitudinal fibres. In the Mahogany and Lignum-Vitæ they are numerous and compact; in the Poplar and Pine, few and soft. These require age in most trees to gain solidity. In recent layers the fibres are soft and tender. If wounded in the *young bark*, they soon unite again ; but if the *wood* be wounded, it never heals. The bark, being external and exposed to injuries, is made capable of restoring itself ; but the wood, more secure, possesses not this power of renovation.

343. These fibres, so slender that the naked eye can scarcely detect them, are found, on close inspection, to be *tubular*, or *hollow*. They are supposed to be the channels through which the fluids of the plant pass from one organ to another. When united, they form bundles of *hollow cylinders*, that consist of tubes that are of different qualities and calibres, and have received different names.

345. Botanists have designated the several kinds of tubes found in plants by the names of, 1st. *Simple Tubes* ; 2d. *Porous Tubes* ; 3d. *Spiral Tubes* ; 4th. *False Spiral* ; and 5th. *Small Tubes.*

346. The *Simple Tubes* are larger than the other kinds, and have no lateral perforation. They are found chiefly in the *bark,* sometimes in the *alburnum,* and are occasionally met with in the stems of *herbaceous* plants, particularly those that contain thick, resinous juices. We are sometimes able to detect them by the colour of the juices they contain.

347. The *Porous Tubes* resemble the preceding in their general aspect. The membrane that forms them is not, however, entire. It is pierced with numerous small holes, arranged in parallel transverse rows. This kind occurs principally in the *woody* plants, particularly in the Oak. The purpose of these is not satisfactorily determined.

348. The *Spiral Tubes* are well seen in the fracture of the stem of the Elder and Snow-Ball. When separated by force into fragments, the parts will appear to have been connected by little transparent fibres that, on close examination, even with the naked eye, appear like the coil of a *gallows-wire.* They have been uncoiled by the separation of the parts.

349. These have, by some naturalists, been compared to the *trachea* or wind-pipe in animals, and sometimes mistaken for organs of respiration. They however bear in many respects a closer analogy to the wire of suspenders, that forms a complete tube, except when extended.

350. Of their nature and use little is known. They are found frequently in the stems of *herbaceous plants,* in *young trees* and *shrubs,* and in *leaves* of every description. The *stems of Liliaceous plants* afford them in great perfection.

351. They are seldom found in roots or in the mature wood. Some have considered them as *sap vessels,* others as *air vessels,* that accompany the sap vessels as they pass upward towards the leaf. As plants require air during growth that undoubtedly enters into the composition of their substance, the latter notion seems not altogether unreasonable. This opinion seems somewhat confirmed also by the circumstance that these *tubes* are particularly abundant in leaves and their appendages.

352. The *False Spiral Tubes* have an intermediate appearance between the two preceding. They have transverse fissures analogous to the pores of the *one,* and, between those fissures, *rings* which are not unlike the spiral coat of the *other.* They are very abundant in herbaceous

plants, and in the Vine. They are probably formed by the partial u n ion of the spiral rays.

353. The *Small Tubes* are composed of an assemblage of elongated cells, that are not greatly unlike a bundle of *tangent reeds*. Individually they appear like a straw of *wheat*, whose cavity is interrupted by the joints. The membrane forming them is generally perforated with numerous pores.

354. The solidity of plants is supposed to depend on the number of cellular or interrupted tubes. These are not discoverable in the embryo or young plant. They pervade the ramifications of broncheæ Lichens, the stems of Mosses, and surround the tubes of herbaceous plants. They also intermingle themselves with the tubes of woody plants, and constitute the ligneous layers and prominent ridges that mark the surfaces of vegetables. They pervade the fine and delicate parts of plants, and assume here a consistence resembling that of *cellular tissue*.

355. From the preceding observations it appears, then, that the structure of vegetables is entirely vascular : That they are but an assemblage of *tubes* and *cells* : That these are formed by the foldings of a membrane so *colourless, transparent,* and *fine,* that no traces of its organization have hitherto been discovered. The cells, though generally *hexagonal* or six-sided, are sometimes of other forms. Grew compared them to floating *bubbles,* that are seen to rise on the surface of fermenting liquor.

LEAVES OF PLANTS.

356. Leaves are light, membraneous, succulent organs, generally of a green colour, and attached to the branches and stem of plants, and sometimes to the root. They are regarded as the organs of respiration, and considered indispensably necessary to vegetable life. These beautiful decorations of plants, that give the green appearance to our fields in spring, and tinge with scarlet, purple, and gold, our forests in autumn, are likewise of higher importance in the economy of nature in purifying the air we breathe, and in affording subsistence to a large portion of the animal creation.

357. Leaves are generally of a flat form. Their upper surface is more even than their lower one and of a deeper green, exhibiting conspicuously the fibres and vessels that pervade it.

358. The point of attachment of a leaf is termed its *base*, the opposite extreme its *summit*, and the boundary of its expansion the *margin*. When its expanded surface is rolled outward, it is said to be *revolute* ; when inward, *involute* ; and when enveloping another on the side, *convolute*. Leaves may also be *imbricate, conduplicate, plicate, circinal, radical, cauline,* or *floral.*

359. A *sessile* leaf arises immediately from the stem, branch, or root, without any footstalk. An example of this is furnished in Solomon's-Seal. When two opposite leaves unite at their bases, as in the Boneset, they are said to be *connate.* If the stem pass through the leaf, as in the Horehound, *perfoliate.* If leaves form a *sheath* for the stem, as in the Grasses and Flags, they are termed *sheathing.* This in the former is a kind of *expanded petiole.*

360. When a leaf extends down the side of the stem forming a leafy border or wing, it is termed *decurrent.* The Mullein, Thistle, and Pea, are familiar examples.

361. Leaves are named variously, according to their forms. They are termed *deltoid, rhomboid, cuneate, spatulate, ovate, subulate, cordate, runicate, palmate, filiform, reniform, lancinate, pectinate, acerose, pinnatifid, bi-pinnatifid,* and the like, which, being translated, means that they assume the forms of the *Greek delta,* of the *rhombus,* the *wedge,* the *spatula,* the *egg,* the *awl,* the *heart,* *saw-teeth,* the *hand,* the *filament of thread,* the *kidney,* the *lance,* the *comb,* the *needle,* the *feather of a bird's wing,* and the like. Some of these terms refer to their borders, and some to their forms.

362. Their edges may be *entire* or *serrated,* or *lacerated,* or *erose,* or *thorny.* The summits *acute, acuminate, obtuse, truncated,* or *tendrilled.* The import of these, and like technical terms, must be learned from the botanical dictionary and grammar.

363. Leaves are in various ways attached to plants. Some have a small footstalk, that unites them with the trunk or branch, termed a *petiole.* The footstalk of the blossom is termed the *peduncle.* Some leaves have no *petiole.* Such are often immediately attached to the stem or branch, and are said to be *sessile,* from the Latin *sedeo,* to sit.

364. The *petiole* is sometimes *channelled* on its upper surface for the purpose of conducting water to the trunk and roots of the plant. St. Pierre, in his Studies of Nature, asserts that the capacity of this groove almost invariably indicates the degree of moisture required by different plants.

365. The *petiole* of the *Populus tremuloides*, Trembling Poplar, or American Aspen, is flattened at its sides to admit of a lateral motion in the leaf. Thus being compressed, the lightest breath of air will put it in motion. The " trembling aspen leaf," waving in the light zephyr, has not escaped the observing eye of the poet.

366. The *petiole* is generally branched out in various ramifications in the substance of the leaf. Its main branch is termed the *mid-rib*,—its ramifications, the *veins* and *nerves*.

367. The surfaces of some leaves are *smooth*, others *furrowed*, some *pubescent* or hairy, others *hirsute* or prickly, some *tomentose* or cottony, and others *thorny*. The appendages that seem destined to protect the plant, as thorns, prickles, and the like, have sometimes been called the *armature*.

368. The period that leaves remain on respective plants is called their *duration*. In reference to this, such as fall and perish every autumn are termed *deciduous*, from the Latin *de* and *cado*, to fall from. If they fall not at the end of summer but remain till spring, they are said to be *persistent*. If they remain green during several successive seasons, they are termed *ever-greens*. In tropical regions, most trees are of the latter description. Many of them are remarkable for the magnitude, as well as the duration of their leaves.

369. Many tropical plants, whose leaves remain upon the plant for eight or ten years, when removed to higher latitudes, lose their leaves every autumn. The Quince and far-famed Cydon are *evergreens* in Southern Europe, but in our latitudes lose their leaves *annually*. The Currant, on the other hand, originally an inhabitant of the North of Europe, and there annual in its foliage, when transferred to the island of St. Helena, is soon seen crowded with *perennial* leaves and becomes an evergreen.

370. Plants growing in cold countries and high latitudes, generally have small leaves. Those, on the contrary, of equatorial countries, and warm regions, are often clothed with those of a most magnificent size. The mosses of Lapland have leaves that are so small as scarcely to be discernible with the naked eye, while the Talepot of Ceylon bears a leaf so large as to be capable of affording a complete shelter to more than *twenty men*. This vegetable wonder is venerated by the traveller of

these sultry regions, who finds a comfortable retreat from the scorching sun in its friendly shade, and a kind protection from the tempests that here prevail during the changes of the *monsoons.*

371. The largest leaved plant known is said to be indigenous to Surinam in South-America. It is the *Troolie,* and has a leaf that extends on the ground to a length of more than *thirty feet.* This is from *three* to *four feet* broad. The Banana bears a very fine large leaf, and has sometimes been supposed to be the *Fig-tree,* with the leaves of which our first parents were clothed.

372. The different position or folding of leaves during the night has been termed the *Sleep* of plants, by Linnæus. Some so much change their aspect during darkness and wet weather, as scarcely to be recognized. This change of appearance is more remarkable in young than in old plants. Flowers as well as leaves are subject to it, as has already been remarked. Plants of the same species, growing in the same temperature, are very regular in their changes, at given periods.

373. In speaking of the *sleep* of plants, we may notice what has been termed the *Horologium Floræ* of Linnæus. He selected 48 flowers, of which he constituted a kind of *Vegetable Time-piece.*

374. These plants were distributed into, 1st. *Meteoric,* or such as expand their blossoms sooner or later, according as the cold, warmth, or moisture affected them. 2d. *Tropical,* or such as open in the morning and close in the evening of every day, the hour of expansion being earlier or later as the length of the day increases or decreases. 3d. *Equinoxial,* or such as open at an exact hour, and, with slight variations, close at another determinate or given hour.

375. The flowers, most conspicuous for exactness in regard to their opening, are many species of *Convolvulus* and *Campanula, Mirabilis* or Marvel-of-Peru, called also *Bel-de-nuit, Leontodon, Genista, Spartium, Calendula, Tulipa, Goats-beard, Succory, Hawk-weed, Thistle, Lettuce, Mallow, Sandwort, Cress, Hibiscus, Yellow Lily, White Water-Lily, Purslain,* and Pink or *Dianthus.* Of these and other like plants was constructed his " Floral *Time-piece.*"

376. From what has been remarked of the structure of the wood and bark, of the ascent of the sap to the leaves, and its return thence to subserve the purposes of vegetation, we may form some idea of the processes by which the sap becomes elaborated or changed into several vegetable secretions.

377. The operation of leaves in elaborating *oxygen, hydrogen,* and *carbon,* helps us to understand how the *essential oils* may be produced. *These* are known, as well as sugar, to be composed of *oxygen, hydrogen,* and *carbon,* in various proportions. Variously combined these elements also probably produce many of the other vegetable secretions.

378. Mr. Knight has proved that very little *alburnum* or new wood is deposited when leaves are not exposed to the action of light. A large portion of wood consists of *carbon.* We see, therefore, that the action of the leaves is of the highest importance in the economy of vegetation.

379. The leaf generally appears before the fruit, sometimes after it. A branch, deprived of its leaves, will not perfect its fruit. In equatorial countries the leaves of plants are of great importance in shielding the fruit from the intense rays of the sun. In culture, however, we are sometimes obliged to strip them of a part of the leaves, to let in the sun and air. By so doing, the natural rich flavour of many fruits, as the Melon, Orange, and Grape, are restored.

380. There is an almost incessant exhalation of invisible vapour rising from the leaves of plants during the daytime. This may be collected, condensed, and examined. A detached branch or leaf withers and dies from exhaustion. Want of its nourishing fluids, that have been discharged through the pores of the leaf, causes it to perish.

381. If the stem of a plant, plucked from its root, be immersed in water, the leaves remain green much longer. When partly withered, flowers may often be thus restored. Placed in a close tin box, the plant retains its verdure during a still longer period, often for weeks. Confining the air, already saturated with vapour, prevents the further escape of moisture from the leaves. Plants in these situations, though they perform none of the functions of life, exhibit the appearance of perfect health.

382. The quantity of vapour exhaled is very different in different states of the atmosphere. In dry, warm, sunny weather, plants perspire much more freely than in cloudy, cold, and wet weather. Hence the maxim of " making hay while the sun shines."

383. Succulent and juicy plants generally exhale less than others. Originally formed for inhabiting dry, sandy, and hot regions, nature designed them to be more sparing of that moisture, that they with so much difficulty procure. Plants with membranous leaves, inhabiting moist situations, generally perspire copiously.

384. A large-sized Sunflower perspires more than two pounds, or a

quart, in a day. The Cornelian Cherry, a common shrub, is said to exhale daily a quantity of vapour equal to twice its own weight. A parcel of grass, placed under an inverted tumbler, will soon cover its inside with moisture. Experiments have been made in this way which go to prove, that an acre of grass land perspires more than 2000 gallons in a single day.

385. The rapidity with which plants wither will teach us how fast their leaves exhale and their roots absorb. Knowing this we can form some opinion of the places where they will best grow, and how much moisture they will require. We also see the reason why wet and cloudy days are the best for *Transplanting*.

386. The vapour, exhaled from leaves, generally possesses no peculiar properties. Sometimes these exhalations are combined, however, with volatile and aromatic oils, that communicate to the surrounding atmosphere the peculiar fragrance of the plant. An example of this is afforded in the Geranium.

387. It is also common, as we pass the " leafy forest" or cultivated field in summer, to meet the morning breeze or evening zephyr loaded with freshness and *fragrance*, even when not surcharged with the aromatic odours of flowers.

388. If the temperature suddenly change, this insensible perspiration is sometimes condensed in the form of tears. The plants on which they are formed are denominated " Weeping Plants," as the *Salix tristis*, *Salix Babylonica*, Weeping Willows.

389. Groves of Poplar and Willow strikingly exhibit this phenomenon in England in hot, calm weather, when drops of water are often seen trickling from their leaves, like a slight shower of rain.

390. Ovid, in his Metamorphoses, has made an elegant use of the resinous exudation of the *Populus dilatata* or Lombardy Poplar, which he supposes to be the tears of Phäeton's sisters, who were transformed into these trees. " The drops that glitter on their leaves bespeak their anguish."

391. The *Yellow Impatiens*, or Touch-Me-Not, sometimes called Jewel-Weed and Ear-Drops, grows in shady swamps and is often seen moist with vapour in the form of tears, when every other plant around is dry and parched.

392. The exudations of some plants are very different from these tears. The effusion is sometimes *resinous*, as in the Cistus ; sometimes

saccharine, as in the Orange ; and sometimes *glutinous*, as in the Lime-tree. In the *Fraxinella*, or *Dictamus albus*, it is a highly *inflammable vapour*, that takes fire and explodes on the approach of a candle or other ignited body.

394. The *odorous matter* of flowers is inflammable. This arises undoubtedly from an *essential oil*, in which they abound. When plants grow in the dark, their odour is diminished, but restored on exposure to the light. It is strongest in hot climates and sunny situations.

395. The *honey-dew*, seen on the leaves of the Oak and Birch, denote an unhealthy state, and are occasioned by dampness of the atmosphere. The *manna*, found on the leaves of the Ash, *Ornus*, does not indicate disease. It is procured as we procure sugar from the Maple, and is adhesive, bitter, and in some degree inflammable. It sometimes exudes spontaneously.

396. Leaves not only exhale, but also absorb moisture. If a withering leaf be enclosed in a tight box, containing a small quantity of moisture, it will be in a degree restored. This renovation arises from the absorption of moisture. The power of absorption is different in the leaves of different plants. The leaves of *trees* absorb most on their *inferior* surfaces, those of *herbaceous plants* on their *superior* or upper surface. This is proved by letting different leaves float in water with their different sides upward, and observing the time they retain their verdure.

397. Two leaves, united together, and placed so that one may imbibe moisture and the other not, will remain green for a long time, one absorbing moisture and communicating it to the other. If leaves exhale too much, or roots absorb too little, plants droop, as in transplanting. This difficulty is in some degree obviated by watering and covering them with glasses.

398. The existence of *air-cells* in the substance of leaves is discernible by the aid of glasses. Spiral-coated vessels are also seen in them. These are supposed to act in concert in the absorption and elaboration of air. The cells receive it, and the vessels convey it to every part of the plant. The theory seems somewhat confirmed from the circumstance, that leaves copiously evolve air when placed under the exhausted receiver of an air-pump.

399. The experiments of Priestley have already been noticed, which go to show that the leaves of plants give out *oxygen gas*, and absorb *carbonic acid gas*, thus purifying and rendering salubrious the atmospheric air. This becomes contaminated by the respiration of *millions of animals*, and is again restored to purity by *millions of plants*.

400. Plants lose their green colour, natural elasticity, and strength, if deprived of light. Their fluids are retained. No oxygen escapes. The quantity of *alkali*, on which their green colour depends, is diminished.

401. The upper side of leaves is the part principally influenced by the action of light. Hence they expand in the morning and turn towards the light and sunshine at all times of the day. Hence flowers, as well as leaves, close at night and in cloudy weather, and expand in clear weather and in the day time.

402. The economy of the *Sarracenia*, an American genus, of which we know only *four* species, and of the *Nepenthes distillatoria*, an Indian plant, deserve particular mention. Both grow in bogs, though not absolutely in the water, and both are endowed with very curiously formed leaves.

403. The former (*Sarracenia*) has *tubular* leaves like a funnel, which catch the rain, and retain it. This is particularly the case with the *Sarracenia purpurea*, the margin of the leaves of which seems dilated expressly for this purpose, while the orifice of the tubular part just below it is contracted, to restrain evaporation.

404. Linnæus supposed this plant required more than an ordinary supply of water, which its leaves were calculated to catch and retain, so as to enable it to live without being immersed in a river or pond. The truth of this hypothesis, says Dr. Smith, is very doubtful.

405. For the *Sarracenia flava* and especially the *Sarracenia adunca* are so constructed that rain is nearly excluded from the hollow of their leaves. Yet that cavity contains water that seems to be secreted by the base of each leaf. What then is the purpose of this unusual construction ?

406. The mystery seems to be, says Dr. Smith, that an insect of the *Sphex* or *Ichneumon* kind, as far as we can learn, is oftentimes seen dragging large flies and other insects to this cavity, and, with some apparent difficulty, forcing them under the *lid* or cover of the leaf, to deposit them in the tubular part that is half filled with water. All the leaves, on being examined, are found crammed with dead or drowning flies.

407. The *Sarracenia purpurea* is usually observed to be stored with putrifying insects, whose scent is perceptible at a considerable distance as we pass the plant in a garden. The margins of its leaves are beset with inverted hairs, which, like the wires of a *mouse-trap* render it very difficult for any unfortunate fly that has fallen into the *watery tube* to crawl out again. Here he finds his tomb.

408. It is probable that the air evolved by the dead insect may subserve the purposes of vegetation. This curious construction seems designed to entrap them, and while the water is provided to tempt them, it at the same time seems designed to drown them.

409. The *Sphex* or *Ichneumon*, an insect of prey, stores up insects in this cavity, unquestionably for its food or for the sustenance of its progeny, depositing its eggs in their carcasses, as others of the same tribe do their eggs in various caterpillars, sometimes burying them afterwards in the ground.

410. Thus a double purpose is answered, nor is it the least curious circumstance of the whole that an European insect should find out an American plant in a hot-house, in order to fulfil that purpose.

411. The *Nepenthes distillatoria* is not less curious than the *Sarracenia*. Each leaf terminates in a sort of close-shut tube, like a tankard, often holding an ounce or two of water. This is undoubtedly secreted through the footstalks of the leaf, whose spiral-coated vessels are uncommonly large and numerous.

412. The lid of its tube either opens spontaneously, or is easily lifted by small worms and insects, who are supposed to resort to it in search of a purer beverage than the surrounding swamps afford. Rumphius says, " various little worms and insects crawl into the orifice and die in the tube, except a small *Squilla* or Shrimp with a protuberant back, sometimes met with, which lives there."

413. I have no doubt, says Dr. Smith, that this shrimp feeds on other insects and worms, and that the same purposes are answered in this instance as in the *Sarracenia*. Probably the leaves of the *Dionæa Muscipula* as well as of the *Droseræ* and other CATCH-FLIES, intrap and destroy insects for a similar purpose.

414. From what has been said in the preceding pages of the structure of the wood and the agency of the leaves, it would appear that the latter are the medium of communication between the *tubes* of the *alburnum* and those of the *bark*. It follows of consequence, that, if a tree be deprived of its leaves, this communication will be cut off and the plant perish.

415. The vascular system of plants must then be coexistent with the leaf, *annual* in *deciduous* plants, and *perennial* in others.

416. Having attended to the functions of the *leaves* and *roots*, and the structure of the trunk, we are enabled to understand why the following rules have been adopted by gardeners in shifting the localities of plants.

TRANSPLANTING.

417. Transplanting is the changing of the localities of entire plants. It is effected by disengaging the roots from the soil, and placing them in new situations favourable to the growth and developement of the plant.

418. To accomplish this successfully it is desirable that the roots be preserved fresh and entire.

419. The proper seasons for transplanting ornamental and other trees and shrubs, are the spring and fall. Generally in October and November of the latter period, and March and April, of the former. It is commonly best in colder latitudes to remove the more delicate shrubs and trees in spring, but where the climate is not so severe the autumn is preferable. In the latter case, the winter is not so likely to prove injurious to them.

420. Those which are natives of countries equally cold and rigorous, with the one to which they are removed, may be transplanted either in the spring or autumn, indiscriminately. Such as are natives of warmer climates, and have become acclimated, by culture, to higher latitudes, may be transplanted in spring. They ought to have every advantage that the warm season can afford, previous to their exposure to the rigours of winter.

421. Plants transferred to a less favourable climate, should be removed at a period most favourable for them to support the change without injury. Delicate trees, when transplanted in spring, form new roots, that take firm hold of the earth during summer. Their roots become established in their position, so that there is far less prospect of injury, from the severities of winter. It is a matter of little consequence, however, at which of these seasons the hardy kinds are removed.

422. Plants, when taken from the earth to be transferred, should be removed with much care. Should any injury be sustained by loss or mutilation of a part of the roots, the whole body of the plant, together with the roots, may be immersed in fresh water during a period of twenty or thirty hours, previous to setting it in the earth again.

423. The top is to be lessened in proportion to the loss the roots may have sustained. Otherwise the plant will perish from a loss of its wonted nourishment. The ordinary quantity of root being diminished, the ex-

H H

haustion from *evaporation* will be greater than the *absorption* of the remaining portion of root, so that the plant will die by transpiration.

424. October and November, after the first frosts have arrested the progress of vegetation in woody *perennials*, is recommended as a proper season for *Transplanting* them. Some are of the opinion, that the Peach, Plum, Cherry, and most ever-greens, succeed best when transplanted in Spring.

425. Any trees, even the most delicate, may be successfully transplanted in autumn, if a little protection be afforded them by covering the root during the first and most trying winter. Where complete success is hoped, it is best to shift their locality in the fall, if possible.

426. The protection of most trees, shrubs, and woody plants, may consist in spreading a few inches of litter from the stable around the trunk and over the roots.

427. Moss from the meadow and ever-green boughs are highly recommended for the protection of delicate plants. They are not liable to undergo decomposition during the winter, and thereby injure and destroy what they were designed to protect.

428. Delicate plants are sometimes supposed to be destroyed by too much protection after being transplanted, when, in fact, they perish for want of it, being killed by the alternate freezing and thawing of the earth at its surface. This difficulty might have been easily obviated by covering them with evergreen boughs or meadow moss.

429. When trees or shrubs are transplanted in *autumn*, the earth becomes consolidated at their roots, so that the radical fibres soon take firm footing in the earth, and the plant is prepared to vegetate with the earliest advances of spring.

430. The excavations in the earth for the reception of the roots of trees and shrubs should bear some proportion to their size. They may generally be made from four to six feet in diameter, and of about eighteen or twenty inches in depth. Large trees will require a larger opening than this, and small ones not so large.

431. The yellow or sub-soil where they are to be located may be thrown out, and replaced at bottom with a fine mould, intermixed with a portion of good manure.

432. Trees transplanted should stand two or three inches deeper in the earth than they stood previous to their removal. In no cases should the extra depth exceed this.

433. The radical fibres are to be spread horizontally in their natural position, and the soil intimately blended with them and compactly pressed about the trunk and over the roots.

434. No manure should be permitted to come in immediate contact with the roots, though it should be plentifully placed about them on all sides. Should it touch them, they will be likely to sustain injury and rot.

435. The ground, before being trodden very hard about the roots, is to to be plentifully moistened by pouring water about the plant. The necessity for this has been explained in a previous page.

436. In transplanting Evergreens, it is generally recommended, previous to treading the earth about their roots, to pour several gallons of water about the trunk, and, after filling in with earth, to finish by treading it as hard as possible for the space of half an hour or more. This would be a good rule to follow in regard to all trees of whatever kind.

437. June has been considered by many as the best month for transplanting *annuals* that are cultivated as Florists' Flowers, and September most suitable for transplanting *biennials.*

438. In transplanting plants of every description it is desirable that as much earth as possible be removed with the roots. If this be done, there will be less danger of their suffering by the change of situation.

439. Though moist, cloudy weather is generally best for transplanting, it should not be done when the ground is very wet. The earth should be only moderately moist, otherwise it will be clammy and heavy.

440. The operation of Transplanting is most successfully performed in cloudy days, and a little before evening previous to a shower. The reasons for this are obvious. If it be done when the earth is dry and in the middle of the day, plants require watering and shading for a considerable time afterwards.

441. If the root be small, or injured, or destitute of earth when taken up, it will require that the earth which is placed about it be made finer, and pressed more firmly, and that the plant be more plentifully watered. It will also require to be longer shaded.

442. Plants, transferred to pots and boxes, after having the soil pressed firmly about them on all sides, should also be plentifully watered and for some time shaded. Care is to be taken that the shell be placed over the aperture at the bottom of the vessel, otherwise the plant will perish through a superabundance of moisture. Saturation of the earth, without an outlet at the bottom, will rot the root, and destroy the plant.

VEGETABLE SECRETIONS.

443. The ascent of the sap has been attributed to the *capillary attraction* of the *tubes* of the trunk, to change in their *calibre* from change in *temperature*, to *motion* from the winds, causing them alternately to contract and dilate, and to an *inherent irritability* in the vessels themselves. The last appears the most rational hypothesis.

444. Whatever may be the cause of its ascent, it is certain, that, after undergoing various important changes in the leaf, it descends to the bark. Here it assumes a new aspect, and has received the name *Cambium.* This seems to be a secretion, wrought in some degree in the *cellular* and *vascular* tissue of the bark. It is *green* in the Periwinkle, *white* in the Poppy, and of other colours in other plants. It is oftentimes the seat of their *medicinal virtues.*

445. It has been said, that, among the most important *vegetable secretions*, are enumerated Starch, Gluten, Gum, Sugar, Acid, Tannin, Extracts of Blue, Yellow, Red, Brown, Volatile and Fixed Oils, Resin, the Narcotic and Bitter principles, Camphor, and the like.

446. STARCH is a well-known vegetable production, obtained from Potatoes and many kinds of Grain. That obtained from the *pith* of East-Indian Palms is termed *Sago.* When procured from the roots of various kinds of Orchis, it is called *Salep.* It is abundant in many kinds of roots, and is found in flour. After it has been extracted from the latter, there remains a darkish, adhesive substance called *Gluten*, or Vegetable Glue. This yields large quantities of *fixed air* when exposed to moderate heat, which makes bread light and porous. *Yeast* contains it, and being tenacious, retains the fixed air evolved by its decomposition.

447. GUM is commonly obtained from trees and shrubs that, in an uncultivated state, abound in *thorns.* They are supposed originally to have been designed to protect the tree from the depredations of animals, that often wound them in obtaining it. The *Mimosas*, Plums, Tragacanth, and several other trees, yield it abundantly. It is also obtained from the Mosses, Lichens, the leaves of the Mallows, and the seeds of Quinces. That from the Lichens is often substituted for the more costly gums of Crete and Arabia.

448. SUGAR in tropical countries is usually obtained from the expressed juice of the *Saccharum officinarum* or Sugar Cane. In higher latitudes and colder countries, is is obtained from the *Acer* or Sugar Maple,

Cornstalks, Virginia Aloe, and several kinds of roots, as those of the *Beta* or Beet. The aboriginal Americans formerly obtained it from the *Agave* or American Aloe, and other plants. Large quantities of it were found stored in several of the Mexican cities, at the time of their discovery. The Chinese have long known and employed it. It was not known in western Europe until about the *fifth* century.

449. ACIDS are found in the leaves and fruits of many plants, as in the leaves of the *Oxalis* or Wood Sorrel, and the fruit of the Lemon. *Prussic Acid*, a deadly poison, may be obtained from the distilled leaves of the Cherry and Peach. *Tartaric Acid* exists in the juice of the Grape ; and *Malic Acid* in that of the Apple, Plum, Currant, and Strawberry. *Jellies* contain the peculiar acids of the fruits of which they are made, united with sugar, mucilage, and starch.

450. TANNIN is afforded by nut-galls pulverized, and by bruised Grape-seed, which communicate it to water. It exists also in the bark of the Hemlock, in the Peruvian, and various other bitter and astringent barks. It is used in making leather, and for medicinal purposes. United with sulphate of iron, it forms ink. It is of a yellowish colour, astringent, brittle, and very soluble in water or alcohol. United with gelatine, it forms an insoluble compound, as in leather.

451. Many of the vegetable *Extracts* are used in Medicine and the Arts. They have commonly a strong affinity for the fibres of linen, cotton, and the like, to which they may be made to communicate an almost indelible tinge. The most common colours are *blue, yellow,* and *brown. Indigo* presents us with a fine example of the *blue* ; and the *Woad,* used by the ancient Britons for staining their bodies, affords this colour in nearly equal perfection.

452. *Red* is obtained from several plants. The dried roots and stems of the *Rubia Tinctoria* affords the *Madder* of commerce. A species of Lichen yields the same colour. Saffron affords a *red*, which, united with powdered *talc*, forms the cosmetic termed by the French, *Rouge.* The Brazil and Campeachy woods also afford this colour in great abundance.

453. *Yellow* is obtained from the bark of the *Rhus*, Sumach, and Quercitron, and likewise from the *Bixa orellana* of South America. This tree yields its fruit twice a year, from the seeds of which is manufactured a *yellow lake.* The *Brown* is found in the bark of the Butter-nut, Walnut, and Oak, as likewise in the leaves of several plants.

454. Two kinds of *Oils* are obtained from plants and fruits, *essential*

or *volatile*, and *fixed* oils. The latter are usually extracted from seeds, sometimes from pulpy fruits. They are used in food, medicine, and the arts, or in the preparation of the most durable paints. The *Olive* and *Almond*, two well-known shrubs of Southern Europe, afford the oils that are known by these names. The seeds of the Poppy yield an oil that partakes very little of the narcotic nature of the plant itself.

455. The *Essential Oils*, called also *Volatile*, because of their tendency to fly off, are obtained from several plants. They are found in the bark of the Cinnamon, in the leaves of the Partridge-berry and Geranium, and in the flowers of the *Clethra*, Jessamine, and Rose. They are often obtained by distillation. The odour of the Jassmine flowers may be preserved by steeping them in *fixed oil*, until it has acquired their rich fragrance. Both *volatile* and *fixed oils* become concrete by absorbing *oxygen*.

456. From the *Pine* genus exudes a *Terebinthinate* substance, that, by distillation, yields the *Spirits of Turpentine*, and the residuum is called *Rosin*. *Tar* is obtained by burning the wood of Pines in a confined situation, and collecting the *Turpentine* as it escapes. The *resin* of a kind of *Sumach* is called *Copal*; that of the Pistacea, *Mastic*; of the Juniper, *Sandarach*. The Balm-of-Gilead yields a kind of resinous balsam, famed for its healing virtues.

457. The *Bitter principle* is found in the Gentian, the Coptis, and many of the large forest trees in great abundance, and the *Narcotic principle* in such plants as are recognized by their *lurid aspect*. The Henbane, the Night-shade, the Poppy, the Stramonium, and many other plants, afford it. The famed Upas of Java is supposed to owe its poisonous qualities to this principle.

458. Camphor is obtained from the wood of a species of *Laurel*, by distillation. It is also found in the Marjorum, Sassafras, Sage, and some other plants.

459. The *Gum Elastic*, called India Rubber, is the concrete milky juice of *Urceola jatropha*. This is also afforded by several other plants, as the *Asclepias*, or Milk-Weed.

— — —

FRUIT AND SEEDS.

460. The term *fruit* is understood by botanists to imply seed-vessels of every description, together with the seeds themselves, whether naked

or enclosed in a *pericarpium*. The latter may be a thin *epidermis*, as in the skin of the Apple, or a *bark*, as the Orange-peel, or a *shell*, as that of the Filbert.

461. After the fading of the blossom, the germ continues to expand until it forms the mature fruit. The part that contains the seed, it has been said, is called the *Pericarpium*. Its supposed purpose is to protect and convey nourishment to the seed, and, when ripe, to assist in scattering it at a distance.

462. The *pericarpium* frequently separates into several distinct portions, called *valves*. Their number varies in different fruits. If they be torn away, leaving the central *column*, this portion is termed the *axis* of *the fruit*. These valves, when united, may form *one cavity*, as in the Pink ; or *several*, as in the Stramonium. The partition of the cells may arise from the *margin* of the *valves*, from their inner surface, from the central column,or may be formed by the inflection of the borders of the valves themselves. The seed vessel may be *monospermous*, having one seed, *dispermous*, having two seeds, or *polyspermous*, having many seeds.

463. If the *Pericarpium* be a dry, membranous, woody covering, separating when ripe into a determinate number of parts, it is called a *Capsule*, from the Latin *capsula*, a little box. A long, dry seed-vessel, formed of two valves, separated by an intervening membranous partition to which the seeds are attached, is called a *Silique*, from the Latin *siliqua*, a pod.

464. If the seed-vessel consist of two oblong valves, without an intervening partition, with seeds attached to one of the margins, it is called a *Legume*. A pulpy seed-vessel, enclosing a *capsule*, is termed a *Pome* or apple, as the Apple and Pear. If the pulp contain one or more seeds, inveloped in it without a capsule, it is called a Berry. This generally grows soft as it ripens, whereas the capsule hardens. The Orange and Lemon are considered as *berries*, as likewise the Melon, Cucumber, Gourd, and the like, though the latter are distinguished by botanists by the name of *Pepo*. The *berry* and *apple* differ in the enclosure of the seed, one having *capsules* for them, and the other having them imbedded in the pulpy substance of the fruit.

465. When several berries are united, each having a single seed, as in the Raspberry, they constitute what is termed the *Compound Berry*. The Mulberry has a *calyx*, that becomes juicy ; the Strawberry, a pulpy receptacle, studded with naked seeds ; and the Fig is only a juicy calyx, filled with its seeds.

466. The *Nut* is distinguished by its firm, hard texture, that rarely separates into valves and never spontaneously into more than two. The Filbert, Walnut, and Chestnut, are familiar examples of the *Nut*. The Filbert is enclosed in a leaf-like calyx, and the Chestnut in a prickery one.

467. If the *nut* be enclosed in a pulp, forming a seed-vessel externally, like the berry, it is termed a *Drupe*, as in the Cherry and Peach. If the *pericarp* be wanting, as sometimes happens, the seed is said to be *naked*. A prominent *calyx* sometimes supplies the place of a *capsule*.

STRUCTURE OF SEEDS.

468. The unripe seed is attached to the receptacle, whose small vessels convey to it nourishment. When matured, these little tubes are broken and the seed becomes detached. The place of attachment becomes visible on the surface, and is called the *Hilum*, or Scar. Near this may often be seen a small orifice, where water is absorbed during the process of germination.

469. The seed is usually covered with a firm, hard coat, called *testa*, from the Latin *testa*, a shell. This is of various colours; in the Apple, *brown*, in the Bean, *white*, in Indian Corn, *yellow*, and in the Fumitory, *black*. It is often lined with a delicate membrane, differing in colour from the external coat. The *testa*, or shell, bursts at the period of germination, from an enlargement of its contents.

470. Within the *testa* or shell of many seeds we find two *lobes*, called *cotyledons*, as in the Bean, Squash, and the like. Packed carefully and closely between these or upon their sides may be seen the *embryo* of the future plant, sometimes called the *corcle*. This is the rudiment of the future plant, or rather the *future plant in miniature*, and exists in all seeds. It is, however, not always easily discernible. It is *central* in umbelliferous plants, *eccentric* in Coffee, *external* in Grasses, *straight* in the Apple, *curved* in the Kidney Bean, *erect* in the Dandelion, *recurved* in the Parsnip, *oblique* in the Parsimmon, and *horizontal* in the Palm.

471. The *embryo* is composed of two portions, the *radicle*, or root, which first makes its appearance during germination, and the *plumula* (from the Latin diminutive *plumula*, a little plume) that afterwards rises from the earth, and forms the stem and herbage of the plant.

472. Seeds are furnished with various appendages to assist in their *dispersion* over the face of the earth. Among these may be enumerated the *tail*, the *beak*, the *wing*, the *down*, the *arillus*, and the *pellicle*.

473. The *tail* is a prominent *style* that remains attached to the seed, and assumes a feathery or hairy appearance, as in the *Clematis*. The *beak* is an elongation of the seed-vessel, as in the *Geraniums*, or of the summit of a naked seed, as in the Sweet Sicily. The *wing* is a membranous appendage, attached to seeds or their capsules, as in the Ash, Maple, Catalpa, and the like. The seeds of the Bignonia present us with a very perfect example of *winged seeds* enclosed in a *capsule*.

474. The *pappus*, or down, is the chaffy, feathery, or hairy crown, arising from the partial calyx of many naked seeds, and remaining till the blossom is faded. In the Dandelion it is elevated on a small stalk and is said to be *stipitate*. In the Thistle it is *sessile*,—in the Cacalia, *pilose*,—in Salsify, *plumose*,—and in the Bur-Marygold, or Tick-weed, formed of several *barbed bristles*, that lay hold of objects within their reach.

475. The use of these appendages is evidently to transport seeds to a distance. This is accomplished by committing the *winged ones* to the power of the winds, and attaching the *hooked, beaked*, and the like, to the shaggy coats of animals. Light masses of Thistle and other *down* are often seen traversing the air, and spreading over wide-extended tracts of country. The Milk-weed has seeds with a *feathery crown*, enclosed in a *capsule*. The Cotton Grass, Willows, and Cotton itself, are furnished with these downy appendages to facilitate the dispersion of their seeds.

476. The *awn* is usually an appendage to the flower and seeds of grasses. This term is sometimes also applied to the *beak* of naked seeds. It is usually attached to the corolla, arising from its base, as in the *Alopecurus*, or Fox-tail Grass. It sometimes arises from its extremity, as in the Rye. It is *straight* in the Herds-grass, *contorted* in the Oat, and *plumose* in the Feather Grass. The *contorted awn* possesses the properties of a *Hygrometer*, curling up in dry weather and extending in moist.

477. The *pellicle* often adheres closely to the surface of seeds, concealing their colour, as in the Convolvulus. The *arillus* is a partial or entire covering of the seed, attached only to its base. It is soft and *pulpy* in Euonymous, *membranous* and *elastic* in Sorrel, *coriacious* and *divided* in the Nut, and *papery* in the Coffee. The *Mace*, the envelope or

II

rind of the Nutmeg, forms a *partial arillus.* The small seeds of the Orchis are completely invested with this coat. The loose, husky coat of the *Carex* has sometimes been called an *arillus.* Seeds have generally a smooth surface, to permit of an easy passage into the earth ; sometimes a rough and bearded one, to prevent their being withdrawn by the feathery appendage that breaks off and flies away.

478.   *Water* is a vehicle for the dispersion of seeds. By currents of the ocean the seeds of Indian plants are often conveyed to Norway. Plants of Germany find their way to England and Sweden by this means, and those of Spain and France to Northern Europe, Africa, and the seashore of the Mediterranean.

479.   Plants have thus migrated from one continent to another, and, where the climate or soil is not so different as to prevent their growth, have taken root and flourished.   Rivers often bring in their currents seeds from thousands of miles.   These become deposited in the soil of their banks, and are eventually spread over a wide extent of country.

480.   The *winds* waft them through the air on their " wings that never tire."   Instead of being impeded by the tempests, they are hurried on to their places of deposit, often on the summit of the loftiest mountains, or the depths of the most remote vallies.

481.   This *feathery crown,* often found on the seeds of compound flowers, is of curious construction, enabling the *Leontodon Asclepias,* and other silk weeds, to become disseminated widely over almost every country. The *Staphylea* has seeds, as likewise some other plants, enclosed in an inflated *cup* or *calyx,* resembling a *balloon,* that enables them to sail through the air.   The Maple and Oak have their winged *capsules,* the Catalpa and Pine their winged *seeds,* and the Erigeron of Canada on its *feathery crown* has travelled to the Eastern continent, and become disseminated all over Europe.

482.   The *Walking* or *Animated Oat,* (*Avena sterilis,*) not being endowed with an appendage for *flying,* or prepared for *swimming,* is possessed of an *awn* that is made to move by the slightest variation of atmospheric vapour.   Thus stimulated, it frequently " *marches off at a distance*" from its original place of habitancy, and penetrates the earth, where its seeds germinate.

483.   The *Erodium Moschatum,*'or Musk Geranium, possesses a *beak* equally alive to the vicissitudes of dryness and moisture.   Straight when

the plant is growing, it becomes coiled when the seed is mature, but, on being exposed to moisture, regains its original form.

484. *Animals* assist in the dispersion of seeds. The squirrel fills his winter storehouse with *nuts*, and the jay deposits various small seeds and grains in the bark-chinks of old trees. The *birds* disseminated the *Nutmeg* over the Spice Islands, when an attempt was made by the Hollanders to destroy it, after losing possession of these islands. The seeds of some *Aquatics* adhere to the *feathers* of *birds*, that visit the places of their growth, and are thus transported to distant ponds or lakes. There is no place, however remote, where the Water Lily gains not access, though it can neither *fly* nor *crawl*.

485. *Man* himself contributes more particularly to the dissemination of seeds. He visits every shore and ransacks every country, that he may gather around his habitation and render subservient to his wants various plants. In his *kitchen, flower* and *fruit garden*, and *tilled fields*, he has collected the natives of almost every region of the globe.

486. The *Peach* is said to be a native of Persia, the *Apricot* of Armenia, the *Apple* of Northern Europe, the *Quince* of Southern Europe, the *Damson Plum* of Syria, the *Almond* of Morocco, the *Pomegranate* of Carthage, the *Cherry* of Cerasonte, the *Potato* of Peru, *Buck-Wheat* and various kinds of *Grain* of Southern Asia, the *Stramonium* of Central Africa, *Rice* of Madagascar, *Tulips, Lilies, Roses* and *Asters* of various kinds, found in our gardens, of Persia and Southern Asia, and our garden *Nasturtion* of Peru.

487. Medicinal and flowering shrubs and plants and various kinds of useful seeds and grains are thus accumulated by man from every region of the globe and made to subserve his wants.

488. Plants, though having no eyes to see, and no voluntary power to avoid danger, are well provided with the means of perpetuating their *various species.* Their seeds are often so numerous as to render it nearly impossible that the species should by any accident become extinct.

489. The *seeds* of a single *Tobacco plant* often amount to more than 300,000, and Didort informs us that those of the Elm exceed 500,000. These plants seem barren and unproductive, however, compared with the common Puff-Ball, or even with the Mosses and Ferns. The seeds of a single leaf of Moss exceed almost the power of man to enumerate, and the *fine, impalpable, blue powder* of the *Licoperdon Tuber* or Puff-Ball are all supposed to be seeds of the plant, each capable, in proper situations, of giving rise to a new race of plants.

IMPERFECT PLANTS.

FERNS, MOSSES, SEAWEEDS, AND MUSHROOMS.

490. There is an extensive tribe of plants, belonging to the 24th Class of Linnæus, that have been denominated IMPERFECT PLANTS. Linnæus, finding their flowers invisible, or incapable of being seen by the naked eye, named them *Craptogamia,* from the Greek *kruptos,* hidden, and *gamos,* nuptials. Other botanists, considering their simple and often defective organization, have called them IMPERFECT PLANTS.

491. They were distributed by Linnæus into *four* orders, 1st. *Filices,* or Ferns ; 2d. *Musci,* or Mosses ; 3d. *Algæ,* or Seaweeds ; and 4th. *Fungi,* or Mushrooms. Dr. Smith makes of these plants five orders, 1st. *Felices* or Ferns ; 2d. *Musci* or Mosses ; 3d. *Hepaticæ* or Liverworts ; 4th. *Algæ* or Seaweeds ; and 5th. *Fungi* or Mushrooms. These are not plants of great importance ; but, as they constitute a *numerous* class, it will be proper to give them a passing notice.

FERNS.

492. The *Ferns* are usually distinguished with ease from the more perfect plants. They have their *leaves, branches,* and *stems,* so united as to contitute one organ. Their fructification or fruit is usually on the back of the leaf. That part, analogous to the stem of other plants or to the petiole of a common leaf, is called a *stipe.* The various parts united, whether in a *Fern* or other plant, are called a *Frond.*

493. The floral or flowering organs are very small. They are entirely unlike those gay blossoms, that adorn the landscape and beautify the shrubs that bear them. We should hardly be able to determine that these plants had any flowers, was not the existence of these organs established by the production of seeds, which are found growing in the back of the leaf or *frond,* or is a *separate spike,* or at the *base of the stem,* and sometimes in the *axils* of the leaves.

494. When the seed organs or fructification are in scattered patches on the back of the leaf as in the *Polypodium,* the Fern is said to be *dorsiferous,* from the Latin *dorsum,* the back, and *fero,* to bear, in allusion to their mode of bearing seeds.

495. When examined with a microscope, the fruit of *Ferns* is found to consist of a capsule, usually surrounded by an elastic transverse ring. These capsules open, when ripe, for the discharge of the seed. The

capsules are usually accompanied by an additional integument, named *Indusium.* This is nothing more than a thin membrane enclosing the unripe fruit. It originates sometimes from the veins, and sometimes from the margin of the leaf. The presence or absence of the *Indusium* or involucrum, and the mode in which it bursts, affords means of determining the *genera* of *Ferns.*

496. The floral organs of Ferns are not always confined to the back of the *frond*, or leaf. The leaves and stem are not always thus intimately incorporated. In *Equisetum*, or Horse-tail, the fruit is attached to peltate receptacles. These are collected into a spike, and terminate or top-off the stem. The numerous seeds are enfolded by *four* pollen-bearing filaments. Those Ferns having their capsules bound with an elastic transverse ring are called *annulatæ*, annulated, or ringed ; and those wanting the ring, or having only a vestige of it, *exannulatæ*, and sometimes *thecatæ.*

497. Among Ferns may be named the *Polypodium, Aphioglossum, Botrychium, Osmunda, Scolopendrium, Isoetes*, and several others. These afford examples of some of the different kinds.

498. The *Lycopodium*, or Ground Pine, from the Greek *lukos*, a wolf, and *pous*, a foot, so called from its supposed resemblance, is generally known by the name of Club-Moss. Its capsules are sometimes in the axils of the leaves, and sometimes at the summit of the stem. The Mosses are essentially unlike the Ferns, whose herbage constitutes a *frond*, and they rank with them only because no one has been able to detect those organs which serve to characterize the more perfect plants. In most of the Floras which have been published in the United States, Ferns alone of the *Cryptogamic* plants are included.

499. Their herbage is frequently very beautiful. The polished *stipe* or stem of the Maidens-hair, *Adiantum*, presents a glittering surface, which is not surpassed in beauty by any of the more perfect plants. The *Lycopodium rupestre*, or Festoon Pine, is an interesting trailing vine, growing on gravelly banks and rocks. The *L. complanatum*, Ground Pine, *L. dendroideum*, Tree-Weed, and *L. clavatum*, Club-Moss, are all found growing in woods in New-England.

500. The *Ophioglossum*, from the Greek *Ophis*, a serpent, and *glossa*, tongue, so called from the resemblance of its fruit, is generally known by the name of Adder's-Tongue. The *Batrychium* was so named from the Greek *Batrachos*, a frog, because of the likeness of its

fruit ; and the *Scolopendrium*, from *skolopendra*, an earwig. The latter is called Hearts-Tongue.

501. The term *Polypodium* is from the Greek *polus*, many, and *pous*, feet. From a fancied resemblance to the polypus, it is in English termed Polypod. The *Osmunda* is so named from Osmund, who first used it ; and the *Equisetum* from the Latin *equus*, a horse, and *seta*, a bristle, from its resemblance to a horse's tail. Hence its name Horse-tail and Mares-tail.

MOSSES.

502. The Mosses, *musci*, constitute a second order. They are too minute to attract the notice of the passing observer. Yet, when examined with attention, they exhibit a beauty of structure that we cannot fail to admire. They are furnished with *leaves* and *stems*, presenting a miniature of the lofty forest trees. Like them too they usually have their floral organs distinct.

503. Sometimes, however, the stem is wanting. Sometimes it sinks into the soil, and, as the *old root* decays and becomes converted into mould, the old stem also sinks annually with it, to emit radical fibres and be converted into a root.

504. The *leaves* of *Mosses* are very minute. They are often transparent, arising from every side of the stem. They are *linear, oval, lanceolate, pointed,* and *imbricate.* They are very like other leaves, and their different forms are designated by the same terms.

505. The *floral organs* of Mosses usually occur on separate plants. In some cases, however, they are *Monœcious,* having *barren* and *fertile* flowers, distinct, but on the same plant. The former are the stars that terminate the branches, or the buds that sit on the bosom of the leaves. The latter are the urn-shaped capsules, that are usually elevated above the rest of the plant. They are concealed, when young, by an exterior membrane.

506. The *fertile* flowers of Mosses are not furnished with any integument that can decidedly be called a *calyx,* though the leaves immediately surrounding them are generally different, both in size and structure from the other leaves of the plant.

507. In the genus *Hypnum* they are so obviously different, as to have obtained the appellation of *perichœtium,* a *fence,* being an assemblage of loose imbricated scales, rather than leaves. If they are not regarded as a *real calyx* or a part of the real leaves, they may be considered as floral leaves. Like the floral leaves, they are contiguous to the flower and analogous to them.

508. In the original distribution of mosses, they form a peculiar bud, from the centre of which the flower is seen. It presents, when first visible, the appearance of a fine and minute point, projecting from the bosom of the leaves. As the process of fructification advances, the parts of the flower assume a different appearance.

509. The fine and pointed subdivisions, expanding into a cone, invested by a thin membrane, that adheres to the summit and base, finally separate into two distinct portions. The under portion remains attached to the base of the fructification. This is called a *sheath*. The upper portion adheres to the top of the *capsule*, and invests it in the form of a *light extinguisher*. In this state, it is called the *clyptra* or veil, from the Greek *kalupto*, to hide, because it hides the urn-like capsule of the Moss.

510. This *capsule* is sometimes *sessile*, sometimes elevated on a slender stalk. It is said to be *erect, drooping, smooth, or striated*. In the young plant it is *green*, or *white*,—in the old *yellow, red, or brown*. The mouth of the capsule is covered with a lid.

511. When this lid is removed, the mouth of the capsule is seen, invested with a fringe. The number of the teeth of this fringe is uniform in the same genus. This number is in all cases a multiple of 4—being 4 : 8 : 16 : 32 : 64 : et cet.

512. In the urn there is a slender *column*, passing through its whole extent and perforating the *lid* or *veil*. As the urn and column are concentric, there is an intermediate and cylindrical cavity, filled with a powder, usually brown or yellow, sometimes dotted.

513. Hedwig sowed this powder, and reared from it a crop of young Mosses. These were like the parent plants. It would appear, therefore, that this dust was the seed of the plant. Mosses are therefore formed with all the organs necessary for the constitution of a flower, and the production of perfect seeds.

514. These plants are very tenacious of life. They flourish in the coldest climates and at the coldest seasons of the year. It is said, that, after they have been preserved a hundred years, their freshness may be restored by the mere application of water.

515. Their real use, though seemingly small, is very great. The seeds are wafted to the naked rocks, where they vegetate, deriving their nourishment from the atmosphere. They clothe their barren summits, and thus prepare the way for plants of greater magnitude. When these appear, they retire, giving place to more serviceable plants.

516. Mosses, in lofty situations, abstract moisture from the clouds, prevent evaporation from the sun's heat, and thus contribute to the formation of fountains and rivulets, that at length unite into majestic streams. They improve and enrich the soil, protect the trunks of trees from the cold of winter and the parching heat of summer, and are of great use in covering the roots of shrubs and trees that are to be removed to a distance.

517. Many plants grow luxuriantly when nourished merely by moss. Many an impenetrable morass has been converted, through the agency of the "grey moss," into a fertile soil, where the yellow corn and waving grain are seen in lieu of a barrenness that had previously existed for ages.

518. The *Andræa, Tetraphis, Hypnum, Splachnum, Tortula, Barbula, Fissidens, Dicranum, Orthotrichum,* and *Polytrichum* or Hair Moss, are among those kinds often noticed, and referred to by writers.

HEPATICÆ, OR LIVERWORTS.

519. Besides the *Ferns* and *Mosses,* there is another order of *Imperfect* plants, called *Hepaticæ* or Liverworts. They were so named from the Greek *hepar,* the liver, because thought to be highly useful in liver complaints. They are small herbaceous plants, whose herbage constitutes a frond, and whose fruit, like that of the Mosses, is enclosed in a capsule.

520. The veil of the capsule usually opens at the summit. It is not furnished with a *lid,* like the one in the Mosses. These plants form a small and uninteresting tribe. The common Brook Liverwort is a good specimen for the student's inspection. The *peltate* receptacle of this kind, however, is very different from the capsules of the other genera. In the *Jungermannia* the capsule is four-valved.

521. Among others are named the *Athoceros* and *Marchantia,* with their different species. These are often alluded to by different writers. The plants of this order are not of much utility in medicine or the arts. They were formerly, as their name imports, held in high repute in the treatment of liver complaints.

ALGÆ, OR SEAWEEDS.

522. This term, applied originally to marine or sea-plants, has recently been employed in a more extended signification. It has been made to embrace many of the *Lichens* that cling to the rocks, and the *Byssi* which seem chiefly to delight in the damp atmosphere of the cellar.

523. The *Lichens,* that constitute a very extensive order, have nothing analogous to a root, except the fibres that issue from the inferior sur-

face of the frond. In many cases even these are superseded by a cement, that attaches the plant so closely to the smooth rock that we can separate it only with great difficulty.

524. The *Algæ* proper, or Seaweeds, have leather-like, olivaceous fronds, with the *Sporæ* inclosed in bubble-like, or inflated portions of the frond. The frond of *Lichens* may be either a leaf-like expansion, or branched and like a shrub in miniature. It may be a mere crust or powder consisting of gelatine and mucilage.

525. The organ of fructification of *Lichens* seems to be a peculiar kind of germ, called by some *propago*, without leaves of a regular form, sometimes naked, and sometimes covered with an envelope, that separates from the parent plant and is dispersed like seeds.

526. The *Lichens* seem to form a natural order, distinct from the other imperfect plants. The whole body seems to perform the office of a universal receptacle, without distinct root or stem. The vegetative organs abound in this substance, and on their surface. They are sometimes collected into nests, and called *saucers*, *shields*, and *cups*.

527. The aquatic or submarine *Algæ* abound both in salt and fresh water. They form a distinct tribe, more properly termed Sea-Weeds. In the *Ulva* the seed-organs are dispersed under the cuticle throughout the surface of the frond. The *Fucus* has its seeds collected together in tubercles, or swellings of various forms and sizes ; and the *Conferva* is commonly known by its capillary and jointed frond. The *Submersed Algæ* are often fixed merely by the roots, and imbibe their nourishment solely through the pores of their surfaces. Many of them float about without any attachment.

528. The Branched Coralline Lichen affords subsistence to the reindeer of the North of Europe ; and the inhabitants of Iceland, Lapland, and Norway, use a species of Lichen as an article of diet. Lichens are also useful in the arts, and have had much repute for their medicinal virtues. They yield a mucilage that is said to be a tolerable substitute for Gum Arabic, and valuable medicine in diseases of the lungs.

FUNGI, OR MUSHROOMS.

529. The last order of *Imperfect plants*, which we shall have occasion to mention, is the *Fungi* or Mushrooms, sometimes called Toad-stools. They are destitute of leaves and flowers. They appear to want almost

KK

every property that would entitle them to rank with other vegetables. In taste they approach near to the lower tribe of animals.

530.   By some writers they have indeed been arranged with *zöophytes*, and regarded as animated beings.   Enlightened observation, however, has pointed out their analogy to some of the preceding orders.

531.   Hedwig, Persoon, and others, have demonstrated that Mushrooms are organized vegetables, that consist of fibres, vessels, and roots ; that they have organs appropriated to the formation of seeds or gems ; and that, without these, no production can take place.   In short, they spring up, flourish, and decay, like other organized vegetable beings, and after they have transmitted their principles of vitality to a new race exactly similar to themselves, they perish.

532.   In examining some kinds of Fungi, we find what has been termed the *wrapper* that envelopes the young plant, but, in its mature state, remains close to the earth.   There is also the *pileus* or hut, called sometimes the *cap* or summit, supported on its peculiar stem or *stipe*.

533.   The inferior surface of the cap is beset with *gills* in the *Agaracus*, pierced with *holes* in the *Boletus*, and beset with prickles in the *Hydnum*.   These *gills*, *prickles*, and *pores*, are supposed to be the seat of the reproductive organs.   The stipe or stem may be either *central*, *lateral*, *solid*, or *hollow*.   It is sometimes connected with the gills, and sometimes separate.

534.   In one kind of Mushroom, the seeds or germs are *internal*, as in the common Puff-Ball, *Licoperdon* ; in another, they are imbedded in an appropriate membrane.

535.   These plants, notwithstanding their simple organization, have been converted to useful purposes.   The powder of the Puff-Ball is employed as a styptic.   It is remarkable for its property of repelling moisture.   If a vessel be filled with water, and a small quantity of the powder be sprinkled upon the surface, the hand may be plunged to the bottom without coming in contact with the liquid.

536.   Varieties of Mushrooms are employed as articles of diet, and with safety, unless gathered with unskilful hands.   The Subterranean Tuber of the Southern States, the *Sclerotium Cocos* of Schweinitz, is esteemed as an article of food.   It is said to be as large as the human head, and exactly of the form of a cocoa-nut.

537.   It is covered with a ligneous, fibrously scaly, hard brown bark, and internally filled with a somewhat fleshy, cork-like matter.   When in

perfection, this approaches to a flesh colour. It is scarcely acted upon by any re-agent and remains unaltered for months, having when macerated in water no fermentable substance.

538. The *Tuber Cibarium* is a native of Europe and the United States, and is often collected for food. It grows above the earth, is solid, globular, destitute of a root, and in decay becomes of a dark colour.

539. Among the Mushrooms are the *Agaricus, Boletus, Phallus, Licoperdon, Tuber, Sclerotium,* and many others. These vegetable anomalies have been examined by Sowerby, Bulliard, Schæffer, Dryander, Hedwig, Munchausen, and several others.

TEMPERATURE.

540. The mean temperature of any country is found, by daily noting down the degree, as indicated by the mercury of the thermometer, and dividing the sum of the observations, by the number of observations noted. The result will show the mean temperature of the place for the period during which they were made.

541. The result of observations of this nature made in several places show, that the Mean Temperature between the tropics, a space of 23 degrees on each side of the equator, ranges from 78 to 81 degrees of Fahrenheit. Within these limits grow the *Theobroma,* or Chocolate-tree, (from the Greek *Theos,* God, and *broma,* food,) the Pepper, Pimento, Sugar-Cane, Coffee-Tree, Palms, Rice, Cotton, Fig, Plantain, Banana, Yam, Pine-apple, Tamarind, Cocoa-nut, Orange, and Lemon. These all require a constant heat of nearly 80 degrees, in order to grow and flourish.

542. Such may be considered the limits of the growth of the finest Spices. The Sugar-Cane, however, and some of the other species named, are found in tolerable perfection, without the tropics. The limit of growth of the Sugar Cane, may be considered to be, where the mean annual Temperature falls below 68. That of the Cotton-tree and Olive, where it falls below 60 ; of the Wine Grape and Peach below 50, that of Wheat below 38, and finally of cultivation, when it falls below 32. This seems to be the limit of cultivation of Barley and Oats.

543. There can be little or no cultivation of Grain, beyond 61 or 62 degrees of latitude. The Potato, Turnip, Plum, Cherry, Peach, Apple,

Pear, Rye, Oats, Barley, Wheat, Flax, Pine, Fir, and many of the Berries, flourish and thrive best, where the mean temperature ranges from 30 or 34 to 68 or 70 degrees. These observations are of importance, in regulating the temperature, where foreign plants are cultivated in Green-Houses and Hot-Houses.

544. The mean annual temperature of New Holland is about 67 degrees ; of the western coast of South America, in Peru, 81 : of the West Indies 77 or 80 : of Alabama, Mississippi, and Louisiana, 64 : of the Carolinas, and Virginia, from 56 to 59 : and that of the New England and Middle States, from 48 to 53 deg. The Sugar Maple flourishes and thrives well, in a mean temperature of 45 degrees, and the Birch as low as 38.

545. The Eastern Continent is much warmer, in the same parallels of latitude, than the Western. The mean annual temperature of Italy, Spain, and France, ranges from 55 to 63 degrees : of Sweden and Norway, from 42 to 43 : England, Scotland, and Ireland from 45 to 50 : and the Cape Verd Islands have a mean temperature of about 74 or 75 deg. The temperature at Cape Horn is 67 deg. : Madagascar and Borneo, 80 : Hindostan, and the Indies, generally from 75 to 81 or 82 degrees. In all these cases, however, due allowance is to be made for the elevation of places above the sea, and for other causes operating to produce a difference of temperature.

546. In determining the degree, therefore, which will be required to rear any given plant, it will be necessary to understand the temperature of the climate of its native growth. Within the Polar Circles, or 23 degrees of the poles, vegetation is found nearly the same in both hemispheres. The mean temperature here is very low. Lapland, Greenland, and the shores of Hudson's-Bay, afford but a scanty vegetation. The mean temperature there ranges from 25 to 33 or 34 degrees. The mercury often falls in these countries as low as 24 deg. below zero.

———

POISONOUS PLANTS.

547. Though animals feed on plants and find them essential to their well-being, there are many of them, that, externally applied, or taken into the system, uniformly effect such a derangement in the animal economy, as to produce disease. These are termed POISONOUS PLANTS.

548. The most active *poisons*, so deleterious in certain doses, however, form, in small doses, the most valuable *Medicines*. Thus many plants affect the animal system very powerfully, but at the same time are doubtless intended for the wise purpose of checking any morbid action that may arise in the sytem.

549. The skilful phytologist readily recognizes such as are POISONOUS, 1st. By the *dull, lurid colour of the corolla* and *nauseous, sickly smell*, particularly when they have five stamens and one pistil, as the *Datura, Solanum, Hyoscydamus, Nicotiana,* and the like. In these plants, if the colour of the corolla is tolerably bright, and the smell less nauseous, the degree of poison is considerably diminished. An example is afforded in the Potato.

550. The *Umbelliferous* plants of a nauseous scent and aquatic kind are almost invariably poisonous, as the *Cicuta virosa* or Water Hemlock, Cow-Parsley, and the like. If the smell be pleasant, and they grow in the dry upland, they are *not* poisonous, as the Fennel, Dill, Caraway, and the like.

551. Plants with *labiate corols* and *seeds in capsules* are frequently poisonous, as *Digitalis* or Foxglove, *Antirrhinum* or Snap-Dragon, sometimes called *Three-Birds* and *Toad-Flax.*

552. Plants, from which issues *a milky juice on being broken*, are generally poisonous, particularly if they bear not compound flowers, as the *Asclepias* or Milkweed, *Apocynum* or Dog-Bane, and the like.

553. Plants, having *an appendage* of any kind to their corolla and *twelve* or more *stamens*, are generally poisonous in some degree. Examples are afforded us in the *Aquilegia* or Columbine, *Ranunculus* or Crows-Foot, and several other plants.

PLANTS NOT POISONOUS.

554. Plants with a *Glume calyx* are *never poisonous*, as *Zea Mays* or Indian Corn, *Triticum* or Wheat, *Avena* or Oats, *Alopecurus* or Fox-tail Grass, and the like. Such plants as have their *stamens standing on the calyx*, are never poisonous, as the Apple, Currant, Strawberry, and Peach.

555. Plants with *Cruciform Flowers* are seldom if ever poisonous, as the Cabbage, Mustard, Turnip, Water-Cress, and the like. If the plant have *Papilionaceous Flowers*, we may be almost equally sure that it is *not poisonous.* Examples are seen in the Bean, Pea, Locust, Clover, Wild Indigo, and several other plants.

556. Such plants, as have *Labiate corols* and bear seeds *without pericarps*, are almost invariably *not poisonous*, as the Catnep, Mints, Hyssop, Marjorum, Mother-Wort, and the like. We may be nearly as certain also, that plants bearing *Compound Flowers* are *not* poisonous. Such are the Dandelion, Sunflower, Lettuce, Burdock, and several others.

557. Finally, as a GENERAL RULE in avoiding *poisonous plants*, we may say : That those with *few stamens* are not often poisonous, unless the number be *five.* If the number be *twelve* or *more*, and the smell be nauseous, heavy, and sickly, such plants are very generally *poisonous.* The *narcotic* principle is, however, sometimes possessed in a slight degree.

LINNEAN CLASSIFICATION.

558. Linnæus, to test the truth of his system, made an experiment, that may be easily repeated and understood by any one. He removed the *anthers* from the flower of the *Glaucium Phœniceum*, stripping off the rest of that day's blossoms. Another morning he repeated the same experiment, only sprinkling the stigma of that blossom, which he had last deprived of its own stamens, with the pollen from another. The flower first mutilated produced no fruit, but the second afforded very perfect seeds.

559. Gardeners formerly attempted to assist nature, by stripping off the barren flowers of Melons and Cucumbers, which, having no germen they found came not to fruit. They supposed these *male flowers* an unnecessary appendage to the plant. But finding they obtained no fruit at all by thus doing, they soon learned the wiser practice of admitting air as often as possible to the flowering plants, for the purpose of blowing the *pollen* from one blossom to the other. They even gather the barren kinds and place them over those destined to bear fruit. These facts with numerous others of a similar nature, have established beyond doubt, the truth of the *Sexual relations* among flowers. The Squash, Cucumber, and Melon, are examples of *Androgynous* plants, where the male and female flowers are separate, yet both on the same stem ; this is the case also with the Walnut, Chestnut, and the like.

560. It may be proper to make an additional remark upon the alterations that have been made in the Linnæan system. It has undergone

several modifications and changes since the time of its author, according to the fancies of different writers. Scarcely any two have entirely agreed in their arrangement.

561. The pupil of Linnæus, Tunberg, abolished the 20th,21st,22d,and 23d Classes. Gemlin, professor at Gottingen, abolished the 22d, and Dr. Thornton, with the "approbation of Professor Martyn," as he informs us, *has "attempted almost an entire New System"* out of the *ashes* of the *old.* Others have been more modest, and have discarded only a few of the Linnæan classes. Eaton makes only 22 Classes, merging in the others the *Polyadelphia* and *Polygamia* as "too uncertain and variable to be longer retained."

562. Professor Nuttall also, in his able and valuable work recently published, makes but 22 or rather 21 Classes, esteeming the *Cryptogamous* Plants (and very justly) as not properly coming within an *artificial,* but *natural* arrangement. Dr. Thornton, in his " *Reformed Sexual System"* makes but 13 Classes, retaining the remaining 11 Classes as *Orders* to these classes. For this alteration, he assigns his reasons, which however have not been sufficiently cogent to induce others to follow *his* method of classing. The arrangement followed by Eaton and Nuttall seems to be as rational as any, if we depart from that of Linnæus.

563. Nuttall assigns as a reason for the abolition of *Dodecandria* or 11th Class, " that as there are scarcely any plants in existence with exactly *twelve stamens,* and as this is made to embrace flowers possessing from *eleven* to *nineteen* inclusive, this slender distinction of number, irregular and inconstant, *and more than ten,* does not deserve to form the basis of any particular Class, and all the plants of *Dodecandria,* according to the insertion of the stamens, may be distributed in one or other of the two following clases: for without this generalizing, species of one *natural* Genus might be dispersed into two different Classes, as in *Hudsonia,* where some species are *Dodecandrous* and others *Icosandrous* !"

564. Speaking in regard to abolishing the *Polyadelphia,* or 18th class, he says, " In the St. John's Wort (*Hypericum*) there are Species with filaments in bundles, and others with stamens simply *Polyandrous.* In the beautiful examples of *Melaleuca,* this character can be nothing more than *generic,* as it is in fact the principal distinction which separates it from the *Icosandrous* Metrosideros."

565. The class *Dodecandria,* abolished by several late writers, has the plants formerly belonging to it transferred to other classes. Some

still retain it.   The class *Polyadelphia*, as before observed, has been rejected by many, and most of the plants that it embraced have been
arranged under the 12th and 13th Linnæan classes.   Some have pro-
posed to abolish only the classes *Monoecia, Diaæcia,* and *Polygamia.*
Dr. Smith proposes to unite the *Polygamia* class with the two preceding
ones, and Prush has united all three of them into one, under the
appellation of *Diclinia*, in allusion to their separate flowers.   There
are numerous anomalies, which nature ever presents to baffle our feeble
systems, and to assert her predilection for endless variety.   We meet in
nature (says Nuttall) with none of those broad, abrupt distinctions, which
System makers are fond of seeing.

565. Botanical writers have also made several alterations in the *Orders* of
the Linnæan classes, abolishing some, and adding others.   It will be unnecessary to notice in this place these alterations.   It should be remarked
however, that several new orders of plants have been discovered, and added to the Linnæan system.   The new *Orders* for the Northern and
Middle States may be seen by comparing Eaton's ' *System of Genera*'
for these States with the *Synopsis*.   New *Genera* and *Species* are occasionally coming to light.

566. The exact number of stamens will not *always* be found in flowers,
as is indicated by the signification of the name of the class to which
they are referred.   This at least is the case in several of the classes.
Thus, in class 9, or *Enneandria*, which is a very small class, the number of *stamens* is not always 9, but is very variable in all the flowers
found in it.   The number is sometimes more than 9, and sometimes less.

567.   In Class 10, or *Decandria*, some flowers have but half the number of stamens required, in part of the *species* of a *genus*.   In *Dodecandria* or 11th Class, as before remarked, there may be from 12 to 19 inclusive.   In *Icosandria*, or 12th Class, the number of stamens is said to
be 20 or more, growing on the calyx or cup.   Some flowers in this class
have but *half* this number of stamens.

568.   In class *Polyandria*, or 13th Class, the *stamens are more numerous* than in any other class ; growing on the receptacle.   Though they
are said to be *more than twenty*, as in the Pond Lily, St. John's Wort,
&c. if the number of stamens does not exceed 20, provided they are not
placed on the calyx or cup, still the plant belongs to this class.   The
number of stamens is more variable in this extensive class than in all others.   When several flowers in the same plant, as the *American* Cows-

lip, have a *variable number* of *stamens placed on the receptacle*, we may generally presume that it belongs to this class, even if none are found with so many as *twenty stamens*.

569. The *Monadelphia*, or 16th Class, includes such flowers as have their stamens united laterally by their filaments into one group or set, as the Hollyhock. If the flowers are Papilionaceous or butterfly-shaped, they belong to the next class, even if the stamens are so united, as in the Lupine. Some species of genera that belong to this class, have stamens not attached at all, but broad and membranaceous at the base, as in some of the Geraniums. They generally recede from the base of the petals, approaching the pistil in the form of a column.

570. The 17th, or *Diadelphous* Class, has been said to have the stamens of its flowers united into *two groups* or *sets*, laterally by their filaments. In most cases, *nine stamens* are united into one set, and *one stamen* stands alone. In some flowers however, all the stamina are united into one set. If the flower be *Papilionaceous*, the plant is referred to this class, though it might seem otherwise to belong to the preceding one. If the stamens are not united at all, though the corol be *papilionaceous*, the plant does not belong this class, as the *wild* Indigo and Cassia, which belong to the 10th Class.

571. The *Syngenesia*, or 19th Class, consisting wholly of plants with compound flowers, is composed of plants with flowers having perfect staminate, pistilate, and neutral florets, in which those having anthers have them united laterally, so as to form a hollow cylinder, as the Sunflower, Dandelion, &c. The Violet, Lobelia, Jewel-weed, and the like, have been separated from this, and united with the 5th Class, though their anthers are united. The *Gynandria*, or 20th Class, includes those perfect flowers whose stamens stand on the pistil, or grow out of it. These stamens are inserted at a distance from the place where the calyx and corolla are inserted. In the *Syngenesia* Class the stamens are inserted on the germ of the pistil, in all its plants, but they are inserted in connexion with the corol.

572. The *artificial* Linnæan sexual system has been explained. Other methods of classing have been adopted. Jussieu and Linnæus himself have both attempted a *natural* arrangement. The design of this is to bring together into the same *Natural Order* such plants as agree in habit, and mostly in medicinal properties. They may possess

those common properties, however, or the qualities of the order to which they belong often in a very feeble and scarcely perceptible degree.

573. The *Genera Plantarum* of Jussieu, arranged in *Natural Orders*, is really of the highest and most important use in the study of plants. This, as likewise the *Species Plantarum* of Linnæus, cannot be too highly prized by the student, who wishes to acquire a knowledge of the *natural affinities* of plants.

574. Tournefort, a learned botanist, attempted a classification of plants founded on the *different forms* of the *corolla* or *blossom*. This system is truly an ingenious and beautiful one, but unhappily for it, the various forms of flowers are not sufficiently distinct to indicate in all cases under which of the classes a plant should be arranged. The system therefore soon fell into disrepute. From its ruins Linnæus formed his *natural* System, and from both these Jussieu formed his. The last, about 40 years since, was approved of by the Royal Academy at Paris.

575. The number of *Genera*, yet described as native of North America, both Cryptogamous and Phenogamous, is only about 1045. There are probably not 50 *species* of Phenogamous plants (says Prof. Eaton) in the United States, undescribed—perhaps not one east of the Mississippi.

576. The single *genus*, *Oak*, is said to comprehend within the United States, more *species* than Europe reckons in the whole amount of its trees. The celebrated Schweinitz has compared 2000 species of American *Fungi* with European species, and found them to agree in most of their characteristics. The Fungi are very numerous in America. In his opinion they are nearly the same in all countries.

577. The 3d Linnean Class contains chiefly the *natural* tribe of *Grasses*,—the 5th, the *Lurid plants*, a *poisonous tribe*, also the *Umbelliferæ*—the 6th, the *Lilies* :—the 12th, the *Edible fruits*—the 13th, poisonous plants,—14th, the ringent or gaping flowers,—the 15th, natural tribe of *Cruciform Flowers*, which are *antiscorbutic*,—the 16th, the *Mallow tribe*,—the 17th, the *Papilionaceous tribe*, which produce mostly *edible seeds* :—the 18th, the *Compound flowers* :—the Cryptogamia Class comprehends the natural tribes of *Ferns*, *Mosses*, *Seaweeds*, and *Mushrooms*. These remarks apply particularly to the improved arrangement of Eaton and Nuttall.

578. It will be seen, by inspecting the Synopsis at the close of the volume, that only 110 Orders are there enumerated. Several new Or-

ders, as before observed, have been discovered since the time of Linnæus, and it is probable there are others still existing that have not been described, which may be added to the system at some future time. New *Genera* are, from time to time, coming to light, and still more frequently new *Species* of the different *genera*, and new *varieties* of the *species*. Authors disagree as to the number of existing *genera*, as likewise the number of described *species*. Some make as many as 60 or 70 thousand species, while others make as few as 40,000. There are probably more than 50,000 at present described. Nuttall proposes 18 new genera for our district.

GENERA EMBRACED IN DIFFERENT CLASSES.

579.   The 1st Linnæan Class has 2 Orders, and embraces the Glasswort, Samphire or Salicornia, Water Star-wort or Callitriche, Valerian or Valeriana, Blitum, Cardamums, Ginger, Turmerick, and a few plants besides.

580.   The 2d Class has 3 Orders, and includes the elegant and fragrant Jasmine, and Lilach, the Olive, Veronica, Salvia, Rosemary, Anthoxanthum, Piper, and a few of the Labiate flowers with naked seeds. Of the latter we have examples in the Cunila or Penny-Royal, Monarda or Oswego Tea, and Lycopus or Water Horehound.

581.   The 3d Class has 3 Orders, and embraces the Iris, Gladiolus, Ixia, and several others of the *sword-leaved* plants, that have been termed ENSATÆ, from the Latin *ensis*, a sword.   They constitute a very beautiful *Natural Order*, having sword-shaped leaves and *liliaceous* flowers.   The Crocus, Lolium, Scirpus, Cyperus, Schœnus, Tillæa Muscosa, and many of the little pink-like plants, also belong to this class.

582.   The 4th Class has 3 Orders, and contains the Protea, Banskia, Lambertia, Scabiosa, Embothrium, Plantago, Rubia, Epimedium, Buffonia, Ilex, Potamogeton, Ruppia, Centunaclus, and many others.   Many of the AGGREGATÆ or Aggregate flowers and splendid exotics belong to this class.   The Button-Bush or Cephelanthus, from the Greek *kephelon*, the head, and *anthos*, flower, because of its round form, is an American example.

583.   The 5th Class is very large, having 6 Orders, and embraces the Borago, Lycopsis, Echium, Primula, Cyclamon, Aretia, a charming Alpine plant, Huttonia, Lysimachia, Convolvulus, Campanula, Lobelia,

Impatiens, Viola, Datura, Hyoscyamus, Atropa, Nicotiana, Vinca, Garde-
nia, Chenopodium, Gentiana, Beta, Eryngium, Cicuta, Rhus, Viburnum,
Corrigiola, Tamarix, Evolvulus, Parnassia, Statice, Linum, Aldrovanda,
Drosera, Crassula, Sibbaldia, Myosurus, and several other genera. It
embraces the Asperifoliæ, or rough-leaved plants, the Preciæ, or elegant
tribe of spring plants, Rotaceæ plants, bearing a wheel-shaped corolla, Lu-
ridæ, or lurid plants, noted for their dark, gloomy aspect, indicative of their
narcotic and dangerous qualities, and the tribe called Contortæ, from the
Latin con, with, and torqueo, to twist, because of their oblique or twisted
corolla. The natural assemblage of Umbelliferæ, belongs also to this
Class.

584. The 6th Class has 6 Orders, and embraces the Liliaceous family
with or without a *spatha*, called by Linnæus " the nobles of the vegetable
kingdom." The Juncus or Rush also belongs to this class, the Oryza or
Rice, Rumex, Colchicum, Petiveria, Wendlandia, Alisma, and many
others.

585. The 7th Class has 4 Orders, and includes the Trientalis, Æsculus,
Limeum, Saururus, Aponogeton, Septas, and some other genera. Many
of the genera of this Class are exotics. The class is probably the smallest
in the Linnæan System.

586. The 8th Class has 4 Orders, and embraces the Tropæolum, Epilobium, Fuchsia, Gaura, Rhexia, Vaccinium, Erica, Daphne, Acer, Ga-
lenia, Mœhringia, Polygonum, Adoxa, Paris, Poullinia, Cardiospermum,
and several other genera.

587. The 9th Class has 3 Orders, and embraces among its genera the
noble and precious Lurus or Laurel, including the Cinnamon, Camphor,
Sassafras, Bay, Fever-bush, and many other fine plants, besides the
Rheum or Rhubarb, and Butomus, so ornamental to rivers and pools.

588. The 10th Class has 5 Orders, and includes among others a tribe
of flowers, that are more or less correctly termed *Papilionaceous* and
Leguminous. These differ very materially from the rest of the natural
order in having ten stout, firm, separate stamens, as in the Cassia, Sophora, and the like. The Ruta, Dictamus or Fraxinella, Dionæa, Muscipula, Kalmia, Rhododendron, Andromeda, Arbutus, Pyrola, Saxifragia, Dianthus, Cucubalus, Silene, Arenaria, Malpighia, Banisteria, Lychnis,
Cerastium, Cotyledon, Sedum, Oxalis, Neurada, Phytolacca, and Stellaria, are also of this class.

589. The 11th Class has 6 Orders, and embraces in its different Or-

ders the Asarum, Lathyrum, Salicaria, Halesia or American Snow-drop tree, Sterculia, Heliocarpus, Agrimonia, Reseda, Euphorbia, Punicea, Calligonum, Aponogeton, Glinus, Blackwellia, and Sempervivum or House-leek, whose styles vary from 12 to 18 or 20.

590. The 12th Class has 3 Orders, and includes among the other genera of its different Orders the Peach, Apple, Plum, Cherry, and the like ; also the *natural* tribe of Myrtles, the Spiræa, Mesembryanthemum, Calycanthus, Rosa, Rubus, Fragaria, Potentilla, Tormentilla, Geum, Dryas, and Comarum. The Rose, Bramble, Strawberry, Cinquefoil or Potentilla, and the like, were termed by Linnæus, SENTICOSÆ, from the Latin, meaning like Briers or Brambles ; the whole natural tribe of which are elegant plants, and agree in the astringent qualities of their roots, bark, and foliage, and in their generally eatable, always innocent fruit.

591. The 13th Class has 7 Orders, and embraces the Papaver, Sanguinaria, Cistus, Nymphæa, Cleome, Pæonia, Fothergillia Alnifolia an American shrub, Delphinium, Aconitum, Tetracera, Caryocar, Aquilegia, Nigella, Raumuria, Stratiotes, Brasenia, Dillenia, Liriodendron, Magnolia, Anemone, Atragena, Clematis, Thalictrum, Adonis,Ranunculus, Trollius, Helleborus, Caltha, and many other genera. The *first* Order of this Class forms a numerous and various assemblage of handsome plants, but many of them are of a suspected quality. The beautiful genus Cistus of this Order is remarkable for its copious, but short-lived flowers, some of which have *irritable stamens*, like those of the Barberis vulgaris or Barberry-bush.

592. The 14th Class has 2 Orders very *natural*, and includes the Mentha, Perilla, Phryma, Lavandula, Westringia, Teucrium, Ajuga, Lamium, Prunella, Cleonia, Parsium, Bignonia, Antirrhinum, Linaria, and several other genera. Plants of the *first Order*, Gymnospermia, of this Class, are mostly *aromatic*, and none, I believe, are poisonous. They have their flowers commonly in *whorls*, and form the *Natural Order* termed by Linnæus, VERTICILLATÆ, from the Latin *verto*, to turn. Jussieu termed them LABIATÆ, from the Latin *labium*, a lip. Examples are afforded us in the Mints, Germander, Balm, Cat-mint, Ground-Ivy, and the like. The flowers of the *Trichostema* and some other genera of this assemblage are not *verticillate*. The PERSONATE, or masked flowers, are chiefly found in the 2d Order of this class, as Mimulus, Chelone, Antirrhinum, and the like.

593. The 15th Class has 2 Orders, perfectly *Natural*, and embraces

the Draba, Lunaria, Thlaspi, Iberis, Crambe, Isatis, Bunias, Raphanus, Cheiranthus, Hesperis, Brassica, Cardamine, Sysimbrium, Sinapis, and others. Scarcely any plants belonging to this Class are remarkably *noxious*. The *Cruciform* plants are vulgarly called *antiscorbutic*, and supposed to be of an *alkalescent* nature. Their *essential oil*, obtained in very small quantities by distillation, is very acrid, and smells like *volatile alkali*. Hence the fœtid scent of water, in which Cabbages and the like have been boiled.

594. The 16th Class has 8 Orders, and embraces, according to Dr. Smith, the Sisyrinchium, Ferraria, Aphyteia, Tamarindus, Erodium, Hermannia, Linum, Pelargonium, Aitonia, Pistia, Geranium, some species of Oxalis, Brownea, Petrospermum, Pentapetes, Althæa, Malva, Hibiscus, Alcea, Carolinea, Gustavia, (from Gustavus, late king of Sweden,) Camella, Stuartia, Barringtonia, and many other genera. The Geranium, Oxalis, and others of this Class, having a *five-petalled* corolla, and the fruit surmounted by a *beak*, were called by Linnæus, GRUINALES, from the Latin *Grus*, a crane, from a supposed resemblance to the *beak* of a crane. The *Malvaceous* plants were called COLUMNIFERÆ, or column-bearing, because their tube of stamens rises like a *column* in the centre of the flower.

595. The 17th Class has 4 Orders, and embraces such plants as have flowers almost universally *Papilionaceous*. Among other genera belonging to its different Orders are the Monieria, Saraca, Fumaria, Polygala, Dalbergia, Orbus, Pisum, Lathyrus, Vicia, Ervum, Biserrula, Phaca, Astragalus, Psoralea, Stylosanthes, Trifolium, Melilotus, Hedysarum, Hippocrepis, Ornithopus, Scorpiurus, Smithia, Indigofera, Robinia, Cystisius, Clitora, Lotus, and Medicago. Linnæus asserts that, " among all the *Leguminous* or *Papilionaceous* tribe, there is no deleterious plant to be found." Dr. Smith thinks this assertion " rather too absolute." *Papilionaceous* plants are rarely noxious to the larger animals, though some species of Galega intoxicate *fish*. The seeds of the Cytisus Laburnum are said to be violently *emetic*, and those of the Lathyrus Sativus are supposed at Florence, to soften the bones and cause death. The Negroes have a notion that the beautiful little *scarlet and black* seeds of the Abrus Precatorius, that are frequently used for necklaces, are extremely *poisonous*. They suppose them so deleterious, that *half of one* is sufficient to kill a man. This is probably not the fact.

596. The 18th Class has 3 Orders, and embraces the Theobroma or Chocolate-tree, Bubroma, Guazuma, Abroma, Monsonia, Citrus, Melaleu-

ca, Hypericum, Thea, and other genera. Willdenow made several improvements in the arrangement of the *Orders* of this Class, and Smith has ventured to propose several modifications of the Linnæan distribution, asserting that "no part of the Linnean system has been less accurately defined or understood than the Orders of the 18th Class."

597. The 19th Class has 5 Orders, is truly a *natural one*, and its different Orders embrace the Leontodon, Tragopogon, Hieracium, Cichorium, Carduus, Onopordum, Arctium, Carlina, Santolina, Bidens, Eupatorium, Artemisia, Tanacetum, Conyza, Gnaphalium, Perdicium, Bellis, Aster, Chrysanthemum, Inula, Anthemis, Sigesbeckia, Tussilago, Coreopsis, Gorteria, Athanasia, Centaurea, Rudbeckia, Helianthus, Calendula, Othonna, Arctotis, Asteospermum, Silphium, Filago, Echinops, Stœbe, Corymbium, Jungia, Elephantopus, and other genera. Its *first Order* consists of three sections. 1st. Of such plants as have their florets *all linguate* or strap-shaped, called by Tournefort SEMIFLOSCULOUS. These flowers are generally *yellow*, sometimes *blue*, and very rarely *reddish*. They expand in the morning and close towards noon in cloudy weather. Their herbage is usually *milky* and *bitter*, as the Leontodon, Tragopogon, Hieracium, Cichorium, and the like. The 2d section of *this* Order embraces flowers generally *globose*, uniform, and regular, having florets *all tubular*, 5-cleft and spreading, as in the Carduus, Onopordum, and Arctium. The 3d section has flowers *discoid*, with florets *all tubular*, *regular*, *crowded*, and *parallel*, forming a *surface nearly flat*, or *exactly conical*, as the Santolinum, Eupatorium, Bidens, and the like. The colour of these flowers is most generally *yellow*, in some cases *pink*.

598. The 2d Order of the 19th Class is also sometimes distinguished into three sections. 1st. The *Discoid* flowers, the *florets* of the margin being obsolete or inconspicuous, from the smallness or peculiar form of the corolla, as in the Artemesia or Worm-wood, Tanacetum or Tansy, and Gnaphalium or Life-everlasting. 2d. The *Linguate*, 2-lipped florets, as in the Perdicium, an exotic genus; and 3d. The *Radiant* flowers, with marginal florets linguate, forming spreading and conspicuous *rays*, as in the Aster, Bellis or Daisy, Anthemis or Chamomile, Chrysanthemum Leucanthemum or Ox-eye-Daisy, sometimes called May-Weed and White-Weed, Inula or Elecampane, and the like. Such are called *double flowers* in this Class, and very properly.

599. The 3d Order of the 19th Class embraces the genus Coreopsis, which Smith says is the very same as that of Bidens, only furnished with

unproductive radiant florets. Some *species* of Coreopsis indeed have never been found *without rays*. The Coreopsis bidens of Linnæus is the same species as his Bidens cernua. C. coronata is his B. frondosa, and C. leucantha his Bidens pilosa. " I should be much inclined," says Smith, " to abolish this Order."

600. The 20th Class has 3 Linnean Orders, and is one of those that have been abolished by the celebrated Thunberg, and by several less intelligent writers. Smith thinks it should be retained. " The character of this Class," says he, " is as evident, constant, and genuine, as any other in the system." No doubt can arise, if we be careful to observe that the *stamens actually grow out of the germen or style.* To this Class belong the beautiful and curious *natural family* of ORCHIDEÆ, or the Orchis tribe, the Cypripedium, Ophrys, Diuris, Malaxis, Dendrobium, Stelis, Thelymitra, Forstera, Stylidium, Salacia, Rhopium, Strumpfia, Nepenthes, (placed here by Linnæus, but removed by Dr. Smith to class Diæcia,) Ayenia, Gluta, Passiflora, (all since removed to 5th Class,) Aristolochia, Scopolia, Cytinus, and other genera. The Orders Decandria and Dodecandria of this Class have been abolished by Smith and others. Polyandria has also shared the same fate. Smith says, "I am not aware of any *genus* that can be admitted into this Order." The organs of impregnation in the Arum, Calla, Ambrosinia, Ayenia, Passiflora, and the like, are merely elevated on a common stalk, and are justly removed by Schreber to Class Monœcia. Dracontium and Pathos, of the same *natural* family, having perfect or united flowers, the former with 7, and the latter with 4 stamens, are conveniently referred to their corresponding Classes, Heptandria and Tetrandria.

601. The 21st Class, having 9 or 10 Orders, by several " *reformers of the Linnean system*" has been abolished. This has also happened to the *two following* Classes. Smith assigns very substantial reasons for retaining the Monœcia Class. Among other genera, embraced in the different *Orders* of this Class, are the Ægopricon, Artocarpus, the celebrated Bread-fruit, Anguria, Carex, Sparganium, probably Typha, Tragia, Hernandia, Phyllanthus, Littorella, Betula, Buxus, Urtica, Morus, Empleurum, Xanthium, Ambrosia, Nephelium, Parthenium, Iva, Clibadium, Cucumis, Bryonia, Pharus, Epibaterium, Pometia, Ceratophyllum, Myriophyllum, Sagittaria, Begonia, Quercus, Coryles, Carpinus, Juglans, Plantanus, Arum, Clalla, Ambrosinia, Pinus, Acalypha, Croton, Jatropha, Ricinus, and several others of the *natural* order EUPHORBIÆ, which are acrid,

milky plants. They were so named from Euphorbus, physician of king Juba. The *Gourd* tribe, including the Melon, Cucumber, Pumpkin, Passion-Flower, and the like, form a *natural Order*, termed by Linnæus, Cu-CURBITACEÆ, from the Latin *a curvitate*, in allusion to their often crooked form. The AMENTACEÆ also, another *natural Order*, the genera of which mostly belong to this Class, embracing the Oak, Walnut, Poplar, Willow, Alder, and the like, were so named because their fruit constitutes *an Ament* or catkin. The Pine, Larch, Cypress, and the like, form a separate *natural Order*, called CONIFERÆ, because they bear fruit in the *form of a Cone* or *strobile.*

602. The 22d Class has 8 Orders, and embraces the Brosimum, Najas, Phelypæa, the wonderful Valisneria, Cecropia, Salix, Elegia, Restio, Empetrum, Ruscus, Osyris, Maba, Caturus, Trophis, Batis, Viscum, Humulus, Spinacia, Cannabis, Populus, Hydrocharis, Mercurialis, Corica, Taxus, Juniperus, Ephedra, and several other genera, some of which may perhaps with more propriety be referred to other Classes.

603. The 23d Class has 3 Orders, and embraces in them the Atriplex, perhaps Hippophæ, Ficus or Fig, and a few other doubtful genera. Speaking of this Class, Smith says : " All things considered, it may be scarcely worth retaining." Yet, as we know two or three genera, entitled to a place in it, upon principles which the analogy of the two preceding Classes shows to be sound, we *cannot tell but others may exist in the unexplored parts of the globe.* For this reason, and for the uniformity of the System, I would venture to *preserve it.*" He proposes to have the system reformed, however, " by some judicious and experienced hand," by retaining, in the 21st and 22d Classes only such *genera* as have a permanent difference in the accessory as well as essential parts of their flowers, or uniting *all three* (this and the *two preceding*) into *one Class*, terming it Diclinia ; in allusion to the two distinct stations of the organs of fructification.

604. The 24th and last Class has, according to Dr. Smith, 5 Orders, and embraces plants whose stamens and pistils are either not well ascertained, or cannot be numbered with any certainty. Some of the *genera*, embraced in its different *Orders*, have already been enumerated under the head of *Imperfect Plants*. The reader is therefore referred to the brief notice of them there given.

605. It should be remembered that many of the *Genera*, enumerated under the different *Classes* in the preceding pages, are by some writers

referred to *other Classes* ; that even the most experienced and judicious naturalists are often at a loss where to arrange particular plants. Names of high repute can be brought to show, that plants, of the *same genus and species*, are often placed in different Classes. Probably no two have entirely agreed in their arrangement.

606. Nor is this to be wondered at, when we consider the endless diversity in which nature presents herself to our inspection. She will not conform to our " *arbitrary systems*," nor are we able entirely to adapt our feeble systems to her diversified manifestations.

607. The *Violet*, for example, might seem at sight to be a *Syngenecious* plant, because its 5 *anthers are united into a tube*, as in the *Compound Flowers*. Its corol, however, is totally unlike those of this *very natural tribe*, and it has therefore been removed from the 19th *Syngenesia* Class, where Linnæus arranged it, to the 5th *Pentandria*, because supposed to bear a closer analogy to the latter than the former Class. ·The same may be said of the *Impatiens* or Touch-me-not, *Lobelia* or Cardinal-flower, and several others. Some writers refer them to one of these Classes and some to the other.

608. The Passion-flower, *Passiflora*, has often been referred to different Classes by different writers. Likewise the genera Ayenia and Gluta, some making them *Gynandria* and *Pentandria*, or 20th Class, 5th Order,—and others, with more propriety perhaps, referring them to the 5th Class.

609. So the Calla, Arum, and Ambrosinia, have been removed from *Gynandria Polyandria*, 20th Class, 10th Order, to *Monœcia*, and the Xylopia and Annona from the same to the *Polyandria* and *Polygynia* or 13th Class, 7th Order of Smith's arrangement.

610. The Dracontium and Pathos, of the same *natural family*, and formerly of Class *Monœcia*, have been transferred by Dr. Smith, the *one* to the 7th or *Heptandria*, and the *other* to the 4th or *Tetrandria* Class.

611. It is not always easy to determine what is a *style* or a *stigma*, these parts often seeming to run into each other. The *receptacles* in the Arum, Calla and Pathos are somewhat analogous to *a single pistil*. This part, which is here termed a *Spadix*, however, sustains the parts necessary for the perpetuation of the species, and, whether we call it a *pistil* or *receptacle*, it is quite unlike either.

612. These remarks are made, that the inquirer may not be at a loss to understand, when, in consulting books on botany, he finds that differ-

ent writers have referred the *same plants to different Classes and Orders*.

613. The *genera* in the preceding pages have been brought together under the different Classes for the purpose only of enabling the student, in consulting more systematic works, to choose from a larger range both of *indigenous* and *exotic* specimens.

614. Many of the genera enumerated are not *indigenous* to the United States. Some of them are rare. Yet *exotics* are so generally cultivated, and the taste for flowering plants and foreign fruits become so general within a few years, that it is often easier for the botanist to obtain *specimens* of *exotic plants* than those that are native.

615. The particular *Orders* to which the different genera should be referred have not been put down for want of room. The genera enumerated under the respective Classes, however, will generally be found to afford specimens of *all the Orders*. They will be found to correspond in most instances with the Orders themselves in regard to the order of their arrangement.

616. It should be remarked, that *species* of the same *genus* are sometimes referred to different *Orders*, though rarely. Where species of the *same genus* are separated into two *different Orders* by this " artificial system," we are made strikingly to feel its defects. It should be remembered also that the same genera are occasionally referred to different *natural Orders*, by different writers. These remarks only show that *all Systems*, both ARTIFICIAL and NATURAL, are imperfect in their nature.

CHARACTERISTICS

OF THE PRECEDING GENERA.

Page 22. ŒNOTHERA, *Scabish* or *Tree-Primrose*. Calyx four-cleft; tubular, caducous, divisions deflected : petals four, inserted on the calyx : stigma four-cleft : capsule four-celled, four-valved, seeds not feathered.

P. 24. NARCISSUS, *Jonquil, Daffodil*. Corol bell-form, spreading, six-parted or six-petalled, equal, superior : nectary bell-form, one-leafed, enclosing the stamens.

POLYANTHES, *Tuberose*. Corol funnel-form, incurved : filaments inserted in the throat : stigma three-cleft : germ within the bottom of the corol.

P. 26. PASSIFLORA, *Passion Flower*. Calyx five-parted, coloured : corol five-petalled, on the calyx : nectary a triple filamentous crown within the petals : berry pedicelled.

P. 28. VIOLA, *Violet, Pansy.* Calyx five-leaved : corol irregular, with a horn behind (sometimes the horn is wanting :) anthers attached by a membranous tip : capsule one-celled, three-valved.

P. 30. CISTUS, *Rock-Rose, Frost-Plant.* Calyx five-leaved, two of them smaller, corol five-petalled : capsule three-valved, opening at the top.

P. 32. GALANTHUS, *Snow-drop.* Petals three, concave, superior : nectaries (or inner petals) three, small, emarginate : stigma simple.

P. 34. ROSA, *Rose.* Calyx urn-form, inferior, five-cleft, fleshy, contracted towards the top : petals five : seeds numerous, bristly, fixed to the sides of the calyx within.

P. 36. SILENE, *Catch-fly.* Calyx one-leafed, inferior, cylindric, prismatic or conic : petals five, with claws appendaged at the mouth : capsule imperfectly three-celled.

P. 38. PAPAVER, *Poppy.* Calyx two-leaved, caducous : corol four-petalled : stigma with radiating lines : capsule one-celled, dehiscent by pores under the permanent stigma.

P. 40. LAURUS, *Laurel, Sassafras, Spice-bush.* Calyx four-to-six-parted : corol none : nectaries three, each a two-bristled or two-lobed gland, surrounding the germ : drupe one-seeded (stamens vary from 3 to 14—often diœcious. The calyx may be taken for a corol.)

P. 42. HYACINTHUS, *Hyacinth.* Corol roundish or bell-form, equal, six-cleft : three nectariferous pores at the top of the germ : stamens inserted in the middle of the corol : cells somewhat two-seeded. Exotic.

P. 44. PRIMULA, *Primrose, Cowslip.* Umbellets involucred : tube of corol cylindric, throat open, divisions of corol emarginate : capsule one-celled with a ten-cleft mouth : stigma globular.

P. 46. CHIRANTHUS, *Stock-july-flower, Wall-flower.* Calyx closed, two of the leaflets gibbous at the base : petals dilated : silique when young with a glandular tooth each side : stigma two-lobed : seed flat.

P. 48. ANEMONE, *Wind-flower, Rue Anemone.* Petals five to nine : seeds numerous, naked.

P. 50. ROSA, *Rose.* Described, No. 34.

P. 52. AMARANTHUS, *Amaranth,* Red *Cocks-comb.* Staminate flowers—calyx three or five-leaved : corol none : stamens three or five. Pistillate flowers—calyx and corol as the staminate : styles three : capsule one-celled, opening transversely : seed one.

P. 54. TULIPA, *Tulip.* Coral six-petalled, liliaceous : style none : stigma thick : capsule oblong, three-sided. Exotic.

P. 56. VINCA, *Periwinkle.* Coral salver-form, twisted, border five-cleft, with oblique divisions ; throat five-angled : seed naked, oblong : follicles two, erect, terete, narrow.

P. 58. DIANTHUS, *Pink, Sweet-William.* Calyx inferior, cylindrical, one-leafed, with four to eight scales at the base : petals five with claws : capsule cylindrical, one-celled, dehiscent at the top.

P. 60. RANUNCULUS, *Crowfoot.* Calyx five-leaved : petals five with claws, and a nectariferous pore or scale on the inside of each : seeds naked, numerous.

P. 62. CALLA, *Water Arum.* Spathe ovate, becoming expanded : spadix covered with the fructification : stamens intermixed. Staminate flowers—calyx and corol none ; anthers sessile. Pistillate flowers—calyx and corol, none : berries one-celled, crowned with the short style.

P. 64. MESEMBRYANTHEMUM, *Ice Plant.* Calyx superior, five-cleft : petals numerous, linear, cohering at the base : capsules fleshy, many-seeded, turbinate. Exotic.

P. 66. DIANTHUS, *Pink.* Described, No. 58.

P. 68. PRIMULA, *Primrose.* Described, No. 44.

P. 70. ROSA, *Rose.* Described, No. 34.

P. 72. RANUNCULUS, *King-cup, Butter-cups.* Described, No. 60:

P. 74. LOBELIA, *Cardinal Flower, Wild Tobacco.* Coral irregular, often irregularly slitted : anthers cohering, and somewhat curved : stigma two-lobed : capsule two or three-celled.

P. 76. AQUILEGIA, *Columbine.* Calyx none ; petals five : nectaries five, alternating with the petals and ending in horns beneath : capsules fine, distinct.

P. 78. RESEDA, *Mignonette, Dyers-Weed.* Calyx one-leaved, four to six parted : petals in many divisions : capsule one-celled, dehiscent at the top : seed reniform ; stamens 11 to 15 : styles three, five, or none.

P. 80. TULIPA, *Tulip.* Described, No. 54.

P. 82. CHRYSANTHEMUM, *Chrysanthemum, Oxeye-Daisy, Fever-few.* Calyx hemispherical, imbricate, with the scales membranous at the margin : egret none, or a narrow margin.

P. 84. HYACINTHUS, *Hyacinth, Jacinth.* Described, No. 42.

P. 86. CONVOLVULUS, *Bind-weed, Morning Glory.* Coral funnel-form, plaited : stigma two-cleft or double : cells of the capsule two or three ; each two-seeded.

P. 88. ALTHÆA, *Hollyhock.* Calyx double, outer one six or nine-cleft : capsules many, one-seeded. Exotic.

P. 90. NARCISSUS, *Jonquil, Daffodil.* Corol bell-form, spreading, six-parted or six-petalled, equal, superior : nectary bell-form, one-leafed, enclosing the stamens. Exotic.

P. 92. CAMPANULA, *Bell-Flower.* Corol bell-form, closed at the bottom by valves bearing the stamens : stigma three to five-cleft : capsules three to five-celled, opening by lateral pores.

P. 94. GERANIUM, *Geranium, Cranesbill, Herb Robert, False Crow-foot.* Calyx five-leaved : corol five-petalled, regular : nectiferous glands five, adhering to the base of the long filaments : arils five, one-seeded, awned, beaked at the head of the receptacle : awn naked, straight.

P. 96. ROSA, *Rose.* Described, No. 34.

P. 98. PRIMULA, *Auricula Primrose.* Described, No. 44.

P. 100. ALTHÆA, *Althæa.* Described, No. 88.

P. 102. TAGETES, *French Marygold.* Calyx simple, one-leafed, five-toothed, tubular : florets of the ray about five, permanent : egret five erect awns. Exotic.

P. 104. ANEMONE, *Anemone, Wind Rose.* Described, No. 48.

P. 106. LILIUM, *Lily.* Corol inferior, liliaceous, six-petalled : petals with a longitudinal line from the middle to the base : stamens shorter than the style : stigma undivided : capsules with the valves connected by hairs crossing as in a sieve.

P. 108. MELISSA, *Balm.* Calyx dry, flattish above, with the upper lip sub-fastigiate : corol with the upper lip somewhat vaulted, two-cleft ; lower lip with the middle lobe cordate.

P. 110. JASMINIUM, *Jasmine.* Corol salver-form, five to eight-cleft : berry two-seeded, each seed solitary, arilled. Exotic.

P. 112. ACONITUM, *Monks-Hood.* Calyx none : petals five, upper one vaulted : nectaries two, hooded, peduncled, recurved : capsules three or five, pod-like. Exotic.

P. 114. DIGITALIS, *Fox-glove.* Calyx five-parted : corol bell-form, ventricose, five-cleft : stigma simple or bilamellate : capsule ovate, two-celled. Flowers racemed.

P. 116. AMARANTHUS, *Amaranth.* Described, No. 52.

P. 118. COREOPSIS, *Tick-seed-Sunflower.* Calyx double, both many-leaved (8 to 12) : seed compressed emarginate : receptacle chaffy : egret two-horned.

P. 120. HYPERICUM, *St. John's-Wort.* Calyx five-parted, divisions sub-ovate : corol five-petalled : filaments often united at the base in three or five sets : styles two to five : capsules roundish, with a number of cells equal to the number of styles.

P. 122. NYMPHÆA, *Pond Lily.* Calyx four to seven-leaved, corol many-petalled, petals about equalling the length of the calyx leaves, attached to the germ beneath the stamens : stigma marked with radiated lines : berry many-celled, many-seeded.

NUPHAR, *Yellow Pond-Lily, Water-Lily, Toad-Lily.* Calyx five or six-leaved, petals many, minute, inserted on the receptacle with the stamens, nectariferous on their backs : stigma with radiate furrows, sessile : berry many-celled, many-seeded.

P. 124. HELIANTHUS, *Sunflower, Jerusalem Artichoke.* Calyx imbricate, sub-squarrose, leafy : receptacle flat, chaffy : egret two-leaved, chaff-like, caducous.

P. 126. AGAVE, *American Aloe, Agave.* Corol erect, superior, tubular or funnel-form : filaments erect, longer than the corol : capsule triangular, many-seeded.

128. HOUSTONIA, *Venus's Pride.* Calyx half-superior : corol salver-form : capsule two-celled, two-seeded.

130. ASTER, *Star-flower.* Calyx imbricate, inferior scales spreading : egret simple, pilose : receptacle scorbiculate. (Florets of the ray more than ten, except in solidaginoides and a few other species, colour purple or white.)

P. 132. CONVOLVULUS, *Bind-weed, Morning Glory.* Described, No. 86.

P. 134. DIANTHUS, *Pink.* Described. No. 58.

P. 136. SOLANUM, *Night-shade, Bitter-sweet, Potato.* Calyx permanent : corol bell or wheel-form, five-lobed, plaited : anthers thickened, partly united, with two pores at the top : berry containing many seeds.

P. 138. TROPÆOLUM, *Nasturtion, Indian Cress.* Calyx four or five-cleft, coloured, spurred : petals four or five, unequal : nuts leathery, sulcate. Exotic.

P. 140. OXALIS, *Wood Sorrel.* Calyx five-leaved, inferior : petals five, cohering by the claws : capsule five-celled, five-cornered, dehiscent at the corners : stamens with 5 shorter, outer ones adhering at their bases.

P. 142. CROCUS, *Saffron.* Spathe radical : corol funnel-form, with a long slender tube : stigma deep-gashed, crested. Exotic.

CARTHAMUS, *False Saffron, Safflower.* Calyx ovate, imbricate with scales, ovatish-leafy at the apex : egret chaff—hairy or none : receptacle chaff-bristly. Exotic.

P. 144. NUPHAR, *Water Lily*. Described, No. 122.

P. 148. LEONTODON, *Dandelion*. Calyx double : receptacle naked : egret plumose, stiped.

P. 150. PÆONIA, *Peony, Piny, Piony*. Calyx five-leaved : petals five : styles none : stigmas two or three : capsules pod-like, many-seeded. Exotic.

P. 152. BELLIS, *Garden Daisy*. Calyx hemispherical, scales equal : egret none : receptacle conical : seed obovate. Introduced.

P. 154. ASTER, *Starwort, Star-flower*. Described, No. 130.

P. 156. DELPHINIUM, *Larkspur*. Calyx none : corol five-petalled, unequal : nectary two-cleft : horned behind : capsules one or three, pod-like. Exotic.

P. 158. SPARTIUM, *Spanish Broom*. Calyx extended downwards : keel generally pendant : filaments adhering to the germ : stigma villose lengthwise on the upper side : legume oblong,one or many-seeded. Exotic.

GENISTA. *Dyers' Broom, Kneed-grass*. Calyx two-lipped, two upper teeth very short : banner oblong, reflexed back from the pistil and stamens. Exotic.

P. 160. CONVALLARIA, *Lily-of-the-Valley, Solomon's Seal*. Corol inferior, six-cleft, bellfunnel-form : stamens inserted on or attached to the inder side of the base or tube of the corol : berry three-celled, spotted before ripening.

P. 162. MIMOSA, *Sensitive Plant*. Calyx five-toothed : coral five-cleft, five-petalled, or none : stamens capillary, very long, four to ten or more, sometimes not united : legume sometimes jointed. Exotic.

P. 164. DIANTHUS, *Pink*. Described, No. 58.

NUTTALL'S TABULAR VIEW

OF THE

CLASSES OF THE SYSTEM OF LINNÆUS.

---

1. PHÆNOGAMOUS PLANTS, OR WITH CONSPICUOUS FLOWERS.

Classes dependent on the *number* of stamens only.

I.	MONANDRIA.	One stamen.
II.	DIANDRIA.	Two stamens.
III.	TRIANDRIA.	Three stamens.
IV.	TETRANDRIA.	Four equal stamens.
V.	PENTANDRIA.	Five stamens.
VI.	HEXANDRIA.	Six equal stamens.
VII.	HEPTANDRIA.	Seven stamens.
VIII.	OCTANDRIA.	Eight stamens.
IX.	ENNEANDRIA.	Nine stamens.
X.	DECANDRIA.	Ten stamens.

Stamens many, indefinite in number, and in which the *situation* is essential.

XI.	ICOSANDRIA.	15 or more stamens on the calyx.
XII.	POLYANDRIA.	15 or more stamens on the receptacle.

Stamens definite, but of *unequal* length.

XIII.	DIDYNAMIA.	4 stamens ; 2 longer. Corolla irregular.
XIV.	TETRADYNAMIA.	6 stamens ; 4 longer. Corolla cruciform.

Stamens with the *filaments* united.

XV.	MONADELPHIA.	Filaments united in one bundle.
XVI.	DIADELPHIA.	Filaments in two bodies. Corolla papiliona- ceous.

Stamens with the *anthers* united.

XVII.	SYNGENESIA.	Flowers compound.

Stamens attached to the pistillum.

XVIII.	GYNANDRIA.	Stamens generally one or two.

Flowers of *two kinds*, on the same or on different plants.

XIX.	MONŒCIA.	Two kinds of flowers on the same plant.
XX.	DIŒCIA.	Two kinds of flowers on two different plants.

II. CRYPTOGAMOUS PLANTS, OR WITH INCONSPICUOUS OR HETEROMORPHOUS FLOWERS.

XXI.	CRYPTOGAMIA.	No proper flowers ; and spora for seed.

DISTINGUISHED BOTANISTS.

Previous to the sixteenth century few plants only were described. Theophrastus is by some considered the father of botanical science. Pliny and a few other ancient writers have described a small number of plants. Fuschius of Germany and Lobel of England published works on this subject about 1650. Clusius also wrote about this time, and likewise Gesner of Switzerland. Cæsalpinus soon after following the proposal of Gesner to divide plants into classes, formed his system. About two centuries since, flourished the two brothers John and Casper Bauhin, who wrote very ably. After this, wrote Morrison of Scotland. He was soon followed by Rivinus of Germany, who founded his system upon the number and regularity of the *petals*. Ray, a clergyman of the English church, about the beginning of 1700, published a ' General History of Plants,' embracing nearly 20,000 species and varieties. Tournefort of France lived about this time, and wrote his ' *Institutions*,' which became the " torch that illumined the early path of Linnæus" himself. Kæmpfer, Dillenius, and Vaillant, were also distinguished writers on this subject. Charles Linnæus was born in Sweden, on the 3d of May, 1707—at the age of 40 created " Knight of the Polar Star." Tunberg was his successor as botanical professor at the college in Upsal, and Vahl his favourite pupil. Gemlin, and Pallas, were distinguished Russian botanists, and Wildenow a very distinguished Professor at Berlin. Murray and Hoffman of Germany,—and Curtis, Withering, and Smith, of England,—Decandolle of Geneva,—Jussieu, Lamark, and Desfontaines, of France, have all been distinguished botanical writers. Much credit is due them for their zeal in promoting the advancement of this science. The names of Lœfling, Jacquin, and Swartz, as well as those of Brown, Humboldt and Bonpland should also be remembered.

Among botanists of our own country, or those who have investigated its botanical riches, are Bertram, of Philadelphia,—Bannister, of Virginia,—Clayton, author of the Flora of Virginia,—Houston,—Kalm, a Swedish divine,—Cutler, an enumerator of New-England plants,—and

NN

Walter and Fraser, describers of the plants of the South and West. The intrepid Michaux explored the forests of the United States from Maine to Georgia. He informs us, for the first time, that the " single family of the Oak comprehends within its limits more species, than the whole amount of forest trees in Europe." He enumerates 140 forest trees of our country, of which 95 are employed in the arts ; while France, he tells us, contains less than 20, only 7 of which have been used for building.

Dr. Muhlenburgh of Lancaster, and Professor Barton of Philadelphia, have both written ably on this subject.

Grew of England, and Malpighi of Italy, were succeeded by Dr. Hales, an English clergyman, and Duhamel of Paris,—as likewise Bonnet of Geneva, Gærtner, a German physician, Mirbel, professor at Paris, and Knight, a worthy Englishman, who were all distinguished. Bigelow of Boston, Torrey of New-York, Eaton of Albany, and Nuttall of Cambridge, Elliot, Barton, Locke, Waterhouse, Smith, Ives, Dewey, and many others, have become distinguished in this department.

Professor Nuttall, in his Introductory work, recommends to students the perusal of the works of Grew, Malpighi, Kieser, Mirbel, Senebier, Du Hamel, Hill, Bauer, Riechel, Keith, Thompson, Knight, and the supplement to the Encyclopædia Britannica.

There is probably no work that affords so large an amount of pleasing and useful information in so short a compass as the abridgment of Dr. Smith, with notes by Dr. Bigelow of Boston. The work is written in an easy and familiar style, and has the advantage of coming from the hands of one of the most learned and talented naturalists that Great-Britain has had.

DICTIONARY

OF

BOTANICAL TERMS.

Acuminate. Ending in a long, produced, sharp point, more than *acute,* as in the leaf of the Elm.

Acute. Ending in a sharp point.

Abrupt. Terminating suddenly as if cut off.

Axil. The angle between the leaf and stem on the upper side.

Axillary. Springing from the axil.

Aril. The exterior coat of a seed that falls off spontaneously.

Awn. The beard or stiff bristle of corn or Grasses.

Bract. A Floral leaf. They are of different shape and colour from the other leaves.

Brachiate. A stem, branching in pairs, and each pair standing at right angles with those above and below.

Bi-pinnate. Twice pinnate.

Bi-glandular. Having two glands.

Bi-ternate. Twice ternate.

Bi-fid. Twice cleft.

Bi-valve. Two-valved.

Bi-locular. Having two cells.

Carinate. Keeled. Like the keel of a ship.

Cauline. Growing on the stem.

Caulescent. Having a stem different from the one that produces the flower.

Caducous. Falling off very early. When applied to the calyx, falling at the opening of the flower. Before the end of summer, in leaves.

Corol or *Corolla.* The petals of the flower collectively taken : whether there be *one* or more.

Cordate. Shaped like a *heart.*

Capsule. A hollow seed-vessel, that opens and becomes dry when ripe.

Cannate. Two opposite leaves, uniting at their base, so as to have the appearance of a-single leaf, as in Honeysuckle.

Cilliate. Fringed with parallel *hairs.*

Crenate. Scolloped.

Crenulate. Finely scolloped.

Deciduous. Falling off. Opposed to *persistent* and *evergreen.* Later than *caducous.*

Deflected. Bent off. Bent downward.

Dehiscent. Gaping or cracking open.

Decompound. Twice compounded.

Denticulate. Minutely toothed.

Declined. Curvature toward the earth.

Digitate. Five leaflets coming off from a petiole, like the *fingers* of the hand, as in Horse-Chestnut.

Diffuse. Branches spreading different ways.

Disk. The surface or top, in distinction from the edge.

Discoid. Having a *disk* covered with florets, but no ray.

Drupe. A fleshy fruit, enclosing a stone : like the Cherry.

Emarginate. Having a *notch* in the end.

Entire. Even and whole at the edge.

Erect. Upright. Perpendicular.

Egret. The *downy* or *feathery* crown of some seeds.

Fascicled. Collected into bundles.

Fastigiate. Flat-topped. Like a house roof.

Follicle. A seed-vessel opening at *one* side.

Flexuose. Zig-zag. Serpentine.

Filiform. Thread-like. Very slender.

Glomerule. A small roundish *head* of flowers.

Glabrous. Having a smooth or slippery surface.

Glaucous. Pale-bluish green or sea-green.

Germ. The lower part of the pistil that eventually becomes the fruit.

Gibbous. Swelled out on one side.

Glandular. Having glands.

Hispid. Covered with *stiff hairs* or *bristles.*

Hirsute. Rough with hairs.

Horn. A spur, as in Columbine.

Hooded. Rolled or folded inward like a *cowl,* as in Arum Triphyllum.

Imbricate. Tiled. Like shingles on a roof.

Involucre. The *general* calyx of Umbelliferous plants at some distance from the flowers.

Inflexed. Leaves bending inward toward the stem.

Incrassate. Increasing in thickness upward as the footstalk approaches the flower.

Incurved. Bent inwards.

Inferior. Lowermost. Calyx and corolla below the germ, when applied to flowers.

Inflated. Apparently blown up like a bladder.

Keel. The under petal of a papilionaceous flower.

Keeled. Shaped like the *keel* of a vessel.

Lanceolate. Spear or lance-shaped. Narrow and tapering towards both extremities, as in leaves of Persian Lilach.

Lyrate. Shaped like a *lyre* or *harp.*

Lobe. A large division of a leaf or petal.

Lip. The *upper* or *under side* of a *labiate* corolla.

Linear. Like a line. Long and narrow with parallel sides.

Lamina. The border or flat end of a petal, in distinction from the *claw.* Also a thin membrane or plate of any kind.

Lamellated. In thin plates.

Liliaceous. Resembling the Lily.

Mucronate. Dagger-like. A leaf, terminating in a sharp point.

Membranous. Very thin and delicate.

Muricate. Covered with *sharp spines.*

Nectary. The part of the corolla containing the honey. Also sometimes the internal, supernumerary part of the calyx or corolla.

Nectariferous. Bearing *honey,*

Nerves. Parallel veins.

Ovate. Egg-shaped. *Oval,* with the lower end the largest, as in the leaf of the Pear.

Ob-ovate. The *ob* prefixed to another term denotes the inversion of the usual position, as *ob-ovate, inversely ovate,* and the like.

Obtuse. Blunt. Rounded, *not acute.*

Orbicular. Circular. Like an orb.

Obsolete. Indistinct. Scarcely discernible.

Palmate. Hand-shaped. Leaf, shaped like an *open hand.*

Plicate. Folded *like a fan.*

Punctate. Appearing as if pricked full of *small holes* or *dots.*

Pinnatifid. Cut in a *pinnate form.*

Pinnate. Winged-leaf. A kind of *compound leaf,* where the leaflets are fixed on a common stalk, opposite each other.

Pedicel. The ultimate branch of a *peduncle.*

Pubescent. Hairy or downy.

Papillose. Covered with *fleshy excrescences,* like nipples.

Panicle. A loose spike. A loose, irregular bunch of flowers, with subdivided branches.

Petal. A *single* flower-leaf.

Pod. A dry seed-vessel.

Radical. Growing directly *from the root.*

Rugose. Wrinkled, like Sage-leaves.

Rhomboid. -Having four sides with unequal angles, like the rhombus.

Retuse. Having a superficial or slight notch in the end.

Reflexed. Bent backwards toward the trunk.

Raceme. A *cluster,* like a bunch of Grapes or Currants or Barberries. Applied to flowers also.

Reniform. Shaped like a *kidney.* Kidney-form.

Receptacle. The basis on which the parts of fructification are connected.

Sessile. Seated immediately on the stem without a footstalk.

Scabrous. Rough. Rugged.

Scape. A stalk springing from the root and sustaining the flower, but no leaves.

Subulate. Awl-shaped. Sharp-pointed.

Serrate. Toothed like a saw, as in the leaf of the Rose and Strawberry.

Sub-crenate. The particle *sub* prefixed to a term implies that the qualities are diminished, or belong to it in an inferior degree.

Truncate. Terminating squarely, as if cut off.

Tomentose. Downy, Cottony.

Terminal. Situated at the extreme, or end.

Terete. Round. Cylindrical.

Turbinate. Top-shaped. Pear-shaped.

Ternate. In *threes,* as leaves of Red Clover, and the like.

Throat. Passage into the tube of a corolla.

Turgid. Swoln. Puffed out.

Umbel. Flower-stalks, diverging from a centre, like rays in an *umbrella,* as in Parsnip and the like.

Umbelliferous. Bearing umbels.

Urceolate. Pitcher-shaped.

Ventricose. A spike, narrowing at each extremity and bellying out in the middle.

Villose. Covered with soft hairs.

Viscid. Clammy. Glutinous. Moist.

Whirled. Turned around the stem.

Woolly. Covered with a soft coat like wool.

SYNOPSIS OF ARTIFICIAL ORDERS,

ACCORDING TO THE MODERN METHOD OF ARRANGEMENT.

ORDERS OF EACH CLASS.

Class	1ST.	2D.	3D.	4TH.	5TH.	6TH.	7TH.	8TH.	10TH.	13TH.	16TH.
„ 1	Mon.	Dig.	—	—	—	—	—	—	—	—	—
„ 2	Mon.	Dig.	Tri.	—	—	—	—	—	—	—	—
„ 3	Mon.	Dig.	Tri.	—	—	—	—	—	—	—	—
„ 4	Mon.	Dig.	—	Tet.	—	—	—	—	—	—	—
„ 5	Mon.	Dig.	Tri.	Tet.	Pen.	—	—	—	—	Pol.	—
„ 6	Mon.	Dig.	Tri.	Tet.	—	Hex.	—	—	—	Pol.	—
„ 7	Mon.	Dig.	—	Tet.	—	—	Hep.	—	—	—	—
„ 8	Mon.	Dig.	Tri.	Tet.	—	—	—	—	—	—	—
„ 9	Mon.	—	Tri.	—	—	Hex.	—	—	—	—	—
„ 10	Mon.	Dig.	Tri.	—	Pen.	—	—	—	Dec.	—	—
„ 11	Mon.	Dig.	Tri.	Tet.	Pen.	Hex.	—	—	—	—	—
„ 12	Mon.	Dig.	Tri.	—	Pen.	—	—	—	—	Pol.	—
„ 13	Mon.	Dig.	Tri.	Tet.	Pen.	Hex.	—	—	—	Pol.	—
„ 14	Gym.	Ang.	—	—	—	—	—	—	—	—	—
„ 15	Silic.	Siliq.	—	—	—	—	—	—	—	—	—
„ 16	—	—	Tri.	—	Pen.	—	Hep.	—	Dec.	Pol.	—
„ 17	—	—	—	—	Pen.	Hex.	—	Oct.	Dec.	—	—
„ 18	Æq.	Sup.	Frus.	Nec.	Pen.	—	—	—	—	—	—
„ 19	Mon.	Dia.	Tri.	Tet.	Pen.	Hex.	—	—	—	Pol.	Mon.
„ 20	Mon.	Dia.	Tri.	Tet.	Pen.	Hex.	—	Oct.	—	Pol.	Mon.
„ 21	—	Dia.	Tri.	Tet.	Pen.	Hex.	—	Oct.	—	Pol.	—
„ 22	Filices.	Musci.	Hipaticæ.	Algæ.	Lichenes.	Fungi.	—	—	—	—	—

The numbers at the head of each column are used to express the Orders directly under them.

SYNOPSIS

OF

ALL THE CLASSES AND ORDERS

OF THE

LINNÆAN SYSTEM,

Scientifically arranged.

———

Class I.
MONANDRIA.

Order		Order*
1.	Monogynia	1.
2.	Digynia	2.

Class II.
DIANDRIA.

1.	Monogynia	1.
2.	Digynia	2.
3.	Trigynia	3.

Class III.
TRIANDRIA.

1.	Monogynia	1.
2.	Digynia	2.
3.	Trigynia	3.

Class IV.
TETRANDRIA.

1.	Monogynia	1.
2.	Digynia	2.
3.	Tetragynia.	4.

Class V.
PENTANDRIA.

1.	Monogynia	1.
2.	Digynia	2.
3.	Trigynia	3.
4.	Tetragynia	4.
5.	Pentagynia	5.
6.	Hexagynia	6.
7.	Polygynia	13.

Class VI.
HEXANDRIA.

1.	Monogynia	1.
2.	Digynia	2.
3.	Trigynia	3.
4.	Tetragynia	4.

Order		Order
5.	Hexagynia	6.
6.	Polygynia	13.

Class VII.
HEPTANDRIA.

1.	Monogynia	1.
2.	Digynia	2.
3.	Tetragynia	4.
4.	Heptagynia	7.

Class VIII.
OCTANDRIA.

1.	Monogynia	1.
2.	Digynia	2.
3.	Trigynia	3.
4.	Tetragynia	4.

Class IX.
ENNEANDRIA.

1.	Monogynia	1.
2.	Trigynia	3.
3.	Hexagynia	6.

Class X.
DECANDRIA.

1.	Monogynia	1.
2.	Digynia	2.
3.	Trigynia	3.
4.	Pentagynia	5.
5.	Decagynia	10.

Class XI.
DODECANDRIA.

1.	Monogynia	1.
2.	Digynia	2.
3.	Trigynia	3.
4.	Tetragynia	4.
5.	Pentagynia	5.
6.	Dodecagynia	12.

* The figures on the left denote the *Number* of the *Orders*, according to Smith, Thornton, and several others. Those on the right designate the *number* according to Eaton and the more modern method of munmbering them.

Class XII.
ICOSANDRIA.

Order		Order
1.	Monogynia	1.
2.	Pentagynia	5.
3.	Polygynia	13.

Class XIII.
POLYANDRIA.

1.	Monogynia	1.
2.	Digynia	2.
3.	Trigynia	3.
4.	Tetragynia	4.
5.	Pentagynia	5.
6.	Hexagynia	6.
7.	Polygynia	13.

Class XIV.
DIDYNAMIA.

1.	Gymnospermia	1.
2.	Angiospermia	2.

Class XV.
TETRADYNAMIA.

1.	Siliculosa	1.
2.	Siliquosa	2.

Class XVI.
MONADELPHIA.

1.	Triandria	3.
2.	Pentandria	5.
3.	Heptandria	7.
4.	Octandria	8.
5.	Decandria	10.
6.	Endecandria	11.
7.	Dodecandria	12.
8.	Polyandria	13.

Class XVII.
DIADELPHIA.

1.	Pentandria	5.
2.	Hexandria	6.
3.	Octandria	8.
4.	Decandria	10.

Class XVIII.
POLYADELPHIA.

1.	Dodecandria	11.
2.	Icosandria	12.
3.	Polyandria	13.

Class XIX.
SYNGENESIA.

Order		Order
1.	Polygamia æqualis	1.
2.	Polygamia superflua	2.
3.	Polygamia frustranea	3.
4.	Polygamia necessaria	4.
5.	Polygamia segregata	5.

Class XX.
GYNANDRIA.

1.	Monandria	1.
2.	Diandria	2.
3.	Triandria	3.
4.	Tetrandria	4.
5.	Pentandria	5.
6.	Hexandria	6.
7.	Octandria	8.

Class XXI.
MONŒCIA.

1.	Monandria	1.
2.	Diandria	2.
3.	Triandria	3.
4.	Tetrandria	4.
5.	Pentandria	5.
6.	Hexandria	6.
7.	Polyandria	13.
8.	Monadelphia	16.

Class XXII.
DIŒCIA.

1.	Monandria	1.
2.	Diandria	2.
3.	Triandria	3.
4.	Tetrandria	4.
5.	Pentandria	5.
6.	Hexandria	6.
7.	Polyandria	13.
8.	Monadelphia	16.

Class XXIII.
POLYGAMIA.

1.	Monœcia	1.
2.	Diœcia	2.
3.	Triœcia	3.

Class XXIV.
CRYPTOGAMIA.

1.	Filices	1.
2.	Musci	2.
3.	Algæ	3.
4.	Fungi	4.

THE END.